IMPROVING
MORAL DECISION-MAKING

Michael Shute
Memorial University of Newfoundland

William Zanardi
St. Edwards University

 **Learning Solutions**

Boston   Burr Ridge, IL   Dubuque, IA   New York   San Francisco   St. Louis
Bangkok   Bogotá   Caracas   Lisbon   London   Madrid
Mexico City   Milan   New Delhi   Seoul   Singapore   Sydney   Taipei   Toronto

The **McGraw·Hill** Companies

IMPROVING MORAL DECISION-MAKING

1 2 3 4 5 6 7 8 9 0 BLA BLA 0 9 8 7 6

ISBN-13: 978-0-07-353769-6
ISBN-10: 0-07-353769-1

Editor: Sandra Hockenberry
Production Editor: Jessica Portz
Cover Design: Maggie Lytle
Printer/Binder: Blaze Digital Printing

TABLE OF CONTENTS

PREFACE

Years of teaching a variety of ethics classes have left the two authors dissatisfied with the standard college textbooks in ethics. The challenge was to write our own text and to avoid the problems we found in previous approaches. This Preface diagnoses a few of those problems, and the Introduction indicates what remedies we are recommending and pursuing.

So what are some of the problems? Imagine a ballet class for beginners in which the students never dance; instead, they read about the history of dance, learn what famous choreographers argued about, and watch others dance in various styles. Suppose the final exam for the class requires each student to choose one of those styles and to give a solo performance. Would you expect any improved performance because of the class?

Now imagine an introductory-level class in ethics. If you are familiar with the usual format, you can find parallels to what did and did not happen in the ballet class. The students will read works by famous thinkers, learn about their ethical theories and analyze the arguments supporting them. For the final assignment each student applies two of the theories to a selected controversy and indicates which resolutions are consistent with which theories. Would you expect any improved performance because of the class? If the goal of the class is to understand what some thinkers thought about morality, the final assignment could test skills in historical interpretation. If learning to recognize and to evaluate arguments was the goal, the final assignment could test skills in argumentation.

If you have read Plato's *Gorgias,* you can find similarities between the latter goal and the art of persuasion which Gorgias promised to teach his students. After reading Socrates' questioning of that master teacher, you might wonder whether some of his questions apply to today's teaching of ethics. In Socrates' day there was no shortage of arguments and skilled debaters. The same is true today as his successors produce an endless stream of skillful arguments about the naturalistic fallacy, freedom and determinism, deontological and consequentialist theories and so on. Is this the art ethics teachers pass on to their students – at least to those who show sufficient interest? Socrates, however, had his doubts about what Gorgias' art could achieve. He wondered what these skills would contribute to the lives of students and their communities. Did this education help them develop their capacity for excellence in thinking, speaking and acting or did it show them how to succeed in the "power games" of their time and tribe? Few teachers today would side with Callicles in choosing the latter goal as the purpose of education. But what persons might never endorse in word, they may yet support by unexamined practice.

Imagine another scenario. Persons suddenly appear at a backstage door; they walk through it and have a script thrust into their hands. With little time to prepare and no idea what play is being performed (only that it has been running for a very long time), they are pushed out onto the stage and asked to recite their lines. They are allowed some adlibbing. They play their parts as best they can still largely in the dark about what happened before they walked on stage and about what comes next. Then, the parts played, they exit stage left.

Is it worth puzzling over the play, over the drama of human history? Socrates said the unexamined part is not worth playing. But can the part be understood apart from the play? Years of thinking and puzzling may give us some insights, but further questions will turn up; so learning about ourselves, our times, our tribes and their place in an even broader context of history can continue for a lifetime.

What has this to do with the study of ethics? Presumably students and their teachers are playing roles in a drama larger than their individual lives. Perhaps the scripts they were handed contain lines of nonsense and superficiality. How would they detect the problems in the script? If you are willing to entertain another metaphor, think of the difference between map reading and mountain climbing. Reading a map can give you a sense of direction, but it is no substitute for actual climbing. In route to a summit, you may discover flaws in the map. Apply this metaphor to the study of ethics. Understanding what great thinkers have said about morality and acquiring skills in argumentation can give you a sense of direction, but ethics is about your deliberating, deciding and acting. The mapping exists for the climb and is not an end in itself.

The last sentence may seem uncontroversial, but the "script" followed in most ethics texts denies or evades it. A long history of conceptualism in philosophy has focused attention on ethical principles and reasoning deductively from them to defensible courses of action. The study of ethics becomes an estimating of consistency between generalities "mapping" the moral landscape and particular acts. You may already know the drill: first "clarify" the concept of justice or the concept of liberty; then work out its implications for different courses of action. What is missing here?

More recent cultural changes have encouraged evasion of the question of actually improving "excellence in acting." When audiences are so diverse and suspicions of moral authority so prevalent, it is much easier to focus on either historical texts or skill-building than to risk writing about moral development and conversion. Those who pursue the last option cannot evade taking a position on "progress," i.e. on less adequate and more adequate ways of thinking and deciding. The two authors of this text believe the third option is worth trying.

The proof lies in the doing, and so this text invites students of ethics, whether they be professors or undergraduates, to try something different. Perhaps the invitation should be issued to students instead of to professors. Inertia accumulates in human molecules and minds, so changing habits and reversing direction become more difficult with time. Still, we can begin with slow steps, perhaps encouraged by the slogan: "To be slow in understanding is not to be stupid; it's to be human." Socrates comes to mind as a self-confessed slow climber. The authors claim to be no better.

We do wish to follow some of the conventions, and so acknowledgements of debts and disclaimers take their place in the Preface. Two specific persons have left innumerable footsteps for us to follow: Bernard Lonergan and Philip McShane. Their climbing and pointing ahead toward the next mountain range offered encouragement and a sense of both the difficulty and the worthwhileness of the climb. Our faculty colleagues and the thousands of students who have endured our questions and puzzles have contributed to improvements in our own understanding and practice of ethics. If this text is "so very lucid but so very wingless," none of them is to blame. On the other hand, if it is found to be both lucid and able to inspire flight, then credit those who showed us the way.

Michael Shute
Memorial University of Newfoundland
St. John's, Newfoundland

William J. Zanardi
St. Edward's University
Austin, Texas

INTRODUCTION

A NOVEL FOCUS

This text offers an introduction to a field of inquiry commonly called "ethics." It departs from what commonly is done in such texts by inviting you, the reader, to become the primary text for the course. Instead of a survey of what others have written about moral deciding and acting, the focus is on what you are doing in your own decision-making and acting.

Why this shift in focus? Your experience in education has probably been one of "multiplicity." That is, your instructors have exposed you to any number of different theories, viewpoints and interpretations. Perhaps you have wondered on occasion how you were supposed to sort out or to evaluate the resulting babble of contending voices. If you have waited for your professors to point out "right answers" or to drop hints as to preferred views, they probably have disappointed you – at least once you got beyond introductory-level classes. If this text were to offer you a list or smorgasbord of rival viewpoints or to advance one theory as superior to all the rest, you would be in the same state of confusion. Either the list of multiple theories would be unsorted (the smorgasbord approach) or the recommended theory would be one more addition to the list. You could sort through the list by following the professor's advice and arguments – and so receive a favorable grade. But will you later have new doubts after encountering further additions to the list? Has your experience in college been one of "being convinced by the latest book read"?

What is an intelligent alternative to listening passively to contending views and voices? If you are listening to talk about moral choices and acts, then, much like an audience listening to a group of zoologists talking about animals, you might expect the talkers to present specimens as evidence of what they are saying. But this is the point of the uncommon focus of this text – take yourself as a specimen of what rival ethical theories are proposing. Check what they are claiming against your own experience of deciding and acting. What better source of evidence could you find?

But this bit of advice may leave you puzzled. Has your prior education included any exercises in self-attention? If not, how do you begin to pay attention to your own performance? This neglect of self may have continued during years of schooling when the emphasis was on learning information, techniques and other people's conclusions without any effort to understand the processes that preceded and produced them. You can easily check for this gap in your own education. Did you learn the Pythagorean theorem? Did your learning include more than memorization of the formula "a squared plus b squared equals c squared"? Did a teacher encourage you to understand "why it works"? Try another example. Did you learn that, whenever you multiply a positive number by a negative number, the result is negative? Do you know why or have you simply taken for granted that two times minus two equals minus four?

Years of education focused on memorizing conclusions and ignoring how they were reached may have left you indifferent to the further question about why something is true. Perhaps schooling has become not a question of understanding but a question of surviving, i.e. just passing the next exam. In the process the budding detective you were at age five with your insistent and incessant why questions may have vanished.[1] A tragedy may lurk ahead: first one needs to pass courses; when times are tough, one looks for ways to pass out; in the end one passes away; and maybe, just before the final scene in the little drama of a life, one returns to the earlier why questions.

How can you avoid this sorry finale? A minimal suggestion is to revive the five-year old's curiosity despite whatever harm your years of education may have done. Of course, the harm may not be apparent. Detecting whether any harm has occurred is the purpose of the section on "nominal understanding" in Chapter Two. For now it may be enough to suggest the following exercise.

Suppose you have to write a 250-word essay over the weekend. You can choose between two topics: (1) What goes on in a game of baseball? or (2) What goes on in understanding? Which topic do you choose? Most students report a preference for the first topic. But then the question is, Which are you closer to: baseball or your own mind? The indictment of educational practice follows: what is closest to us remains remote.

So how do you lessen this remoteness from yourself? A first step is to accept the invitation of this text to continue reading about yourself. The "subject matter" of ethics is fundamentally persons, you among many others, who raise questions about what is good to do. The questions may be quite personal and private, but they may also be about institutional policies affecting anonymous individuals, not just across town but across political borders.

You presumably already identify with friends and family; perhaps strangers evoke less sympathy. But your choices and actions may help or harm both friends and strangers, so you might ask how much you really care about others, those near and those far. But why should you care at all?

WHY BE MORAL?

The question "Why be moral?" would seem to be a fairly obvious issue to raise at the beginning of a discussion of ethics. Still, a well-known ethics professor once publicly admitted that, even after years of teaching ethics, he was taken aback when a puzzled undergraduate asked why she should be interested in being moral. Is this your question? Should you wait for someone else to provide an answer? If your education has been "normal," then you probably read on, eyeballs scanning the ink marks, waiting for an answer to be provided. What would reading be like if one paused over a question, lifted eyeballs from the page and puzzled out a response of one's own?[2]

It is possible your years of education have encouraged habits of self-attention and self-reflection. Perhaps you noticed in yourself or in others a fairly spontaneous response to other people's problems. The specific experiences will vary. One example that may evoke memories is of a parent taking a young child shopping at a mall. After a momentary distraction the parent suddenly realizes the child is no longer in sight. Where did she go? Is she lost and afraid? Has she been abducted? The parent is alert and focused on the child's well being; nothing else matters.

Why this response? Rather than speculate about some sort of innate parenting instinct that programs the adult to protect its offspring (and so prolong its genetic line?), let's suppose that persons commonly take an interest in the well being of others. Just who these others are may vary widely. Parents will care primarily about their children; children will delight in pleasing both the parents and the doting grandparents – witness their excitement in posing for photos. The range of caring about others may at first be confined to immediate family and friends. Later it may expand to wider populations. The basic insight is that caring about others is not initially a matter of choice or decision but a spontaneous part of our living. Attention to your own experience will likely turn up examples of your caring for others, responding to their problems, reacting sympathetically to their pain – not after a process of deliberation but spontaneously.[3] Of course the evidence lies not on a printed page but in you. For example, do you remember seeing a child about to fall and immediately lunging forward to catch her? Why did you do that?

Back to the opening question: Why be moral? Perhaps you never asked the question because it was never a puzzle for you. Caring about others was not in the first place the result of a decision. It was "behind the scenes," a basic dynamism of your living, perhaps evident in a parent's rushing to your rescue or in your less dramatic reaching for the falling child.

The Romans had a maxim: "Care is the mother of all things." What might this mean in your life? Absent care, how do you tend to behave? For example, if class assignments are matters of some indifference, how much energy do you spend in finishing them? If news reports tell of earthquakes or famines in distant lands, do you worry much about the victims? In contrast, if the problem at hand is how to get a date for Saturday night, how much thought do you put into finding an answer? If the emergency is finding the words to console a friend whose parents are divorcing, how much time do you spend choosing the words?

The basic insights into your own performance may be obvious: unless care is present, not much happens in your own thinking and deciding; but when care is present, then your questioning, understanding, reflecting, planning and deciding are far more serious and concentrated activities. Is there any difference in the outcomes between the careless operations and those that are careful, i.e. filled with care? Consult your own experiences here. Have there been times when you have been careless in planning how to finish class assignments on schedule? Have there been times when words thoughtlessly spoken have offended friends? In contrast, have you had experiences of personal crises when your attention was focused exclusively on solving a friend's problem or on preventing some harm from befalling a family member? How much different was the quality of your thinking and reflecting when "care" was present?

If you have taken the time to reflect on your own experiences, i.e. to lift your eyes from the page, then the old Roman maxim may now be your "truth" – not because someone else said it, but because it reflects your own experience. Notice how this approach shifts your learning away from memorizing other people's conclusions and toward understanding your own living. This new orientation in how you read and learn can help you handle the problem of multiplicity.

OVERVIEW OF THE CHAPTERS

The recurrent question in this text is, What are you doing in making moral decisions? The twelve chapters invite you to pay attention to what you are doing and, through a variety of puzzles and thought experiments, to discover some of the complexities in your own performance. Suggested exercises at the end of each chapter are further opportunities for expanding your self-understanding.

The first five chapters focus on some of the ways you go about making sense of your experiences. Chapter One suggests why you should care about understanding this process, and the next chapter challenges any claim that either the process or you are obvious. Chapters Three through Five introduce different "mappings" of how your mind presumably works in inquiry and decision-making. As part of this inquiry into you-as-inquiring, you will encounter some questions about patterns of moral development and about the functions of moral rules and methods in moral choices. Various answers turn up, but the repeated invitation is to check them against yourself as a specimen of moral decision-making.

Chapters Six and Seven continue with the question of moral development, but now it arises as one of the ways of investigating diversity in moral beliefs and practices. The opening puzzle about "multiplicity" motivates a review of five generic sources of moral diversity: developmental differences, limits on effective freedom and forms of bias (Chapter Six); the presence or absence of various differentiations of consciousness and forms of conversion (Chapter Seven). Some people respond to moral diversity by concluding that moral living is a realm of customary practices and private beliefs that fall short of any standard of knowledge. For them ethics is a field of study limited to describing what people happen to believe, but it is a mistake, they think, to ask whether any of these beliefs are objectively true. In response to this position, Chapter Eight takes up the question of objectivity in moral judgments and links it to the previous claims about how intentional operations are related to intended objects. The chapter concludes by pointing out the ambiguity of a popular view of objectivity as the publicness of knowledge.

Chapter Nine provides case studies for demonstrating the benefits of self-attentive inquiry. From there to the end of the book, the focus shifts from mental operations to the products or instruments they produce. In these final chapters, decisions (formulated as proposals for action) become objects for analysis and evaluation. What gradually takes shape is a procedure for understanding and criticizing proposals. The procedure takes the form of an ordered series of leading questions. Case studies with varying degrees of detailed analysis appear in the last two chapters. Practice exercises are found at the end of each chapter and in two appendices following the Epilogue. Ideally, with sufficient practice, some of these ordered questions will become "second nature." But then you will have acquired the habit of being careful in understanding and so have achieved at least one of the purposes of this text.

CARING ABOUT WHAT YOU DO $\qquad$ 1

WHY CARE ABOUT ETHICS?

Ideally the Introduction helped you reach two insights. First, ethics has far more to do with your own living than with the ink marks on pages left by writers of textbooks about ethics. Second, the study of ethics should begin with the study of concrete specimens, i.e. persons like you who exhibit varying degrees of caring about others.

So what does the term "ethics" mean? If this is your first exposure to ethics, you may not know that multiple answers are available.[1] Various theories provide different answers to or "competing voices" about this question. The theories and their responses are answers to questions; they are conclusions. But questions precede answers and conclusions, so what comes first is caring about understanding or the curiosity that generates questions. Take away caring about understanding and what happens? Do you ask any questions when you are indifferent to an issue? Does anyone develop theories when questioning is not heartfelt?

To repeat the remarks of the Introduction, if your prior education has stressed learning information about others' answers and has encouraged little attention to how they reached their conclusions, then perhaps you have few questions left besides the pragmatic concern of how to pass courses. Caring about understanding may have shrunk to memorization of facts and formulae for the next exam. Why pay attention to or care about anything more?

If you have at least a slight suspicion that your previous education has been a swindle, then there is hope. Hope for what? This text suggests that your learning can be more than internalizing information of use in playing "Trivial Pursuits" or in winning money on "Jeopardy." But what does it offer besides more information? If this were a conventional ethics text, then after reading it you would have learned all sorts of things about what Aristotle,

1

Kant, Mill and Rawls thought. Still, some questions would not have turned up. For example, even though you are a specimen of moral deciding, you would not ask what you are doing when you make moral choices. In fact, you would not ask what you are doing when you are reading and trying to make sense of these famous authors. The focus would remain on the theories, their supporting arguments and assumptions. But what if the focus shifted and the questioning was about you? What are you doing when you read, ask questions, puzzle over options, make choices?

Why even try to refocus learning away from the conventional patterns? Why delay studying what Aristotle or Kant wrote and begin instead with self-attention? Perhaps the earlier Roman maxim suggests one reason. If caring about understanding is missing, serious questioning is unlikely to occur. If no one is asking questions, no answers turn up, so no theories appear, no sciences develop, no ethics texts are available. Again, prior to the formulated theories of any writer, there are the questions of that writer. Perhaps you find it obvious that trying to understand answers without understanding the questions that preceded them is a faulty way of learning what was on someone's mind. In other words, it helps in understanding Aristotle or Kant to know what questions they were asking, what cares they had.

But then take another step. Do you understand and share their questions? Do you care about the same puzzles they felt? If not, then learning about their answers amounts to piling up information. But if their questions are your puzzles, then you can become a partner in their reaching for understanding. But what are you, the searcher, doing when you raise questions? Suppose you are doing something basic, something "foundational." That is, you are engaging in the very operations that once gave rise to the multiple viewpoints and voices earlier labeled "multiplicity." Operations of puzzling, imagining, judging, deliberating and deciding preceded Aristotle's and Kant's conclusions about ethics. If you pay attention to how you operate, might this not lead to some insights into how they operated in producing their theories?

We are back then to the earlier puzzle: How do you pay attention to your own mind-in-act? How do you "track" your own efforts to make sense of a situation and to decide what should be done? The next chapter will offer some suggestions and hints; some exercises will invite you to attempt this exploration of an "inner space." Why make the effort, especially if most classes do not require it? Two reasons may occur to you, the one "personal" and the other "pragmatic."

The personal reason is as old as the Socratic maxim that "the unexamined life is not worth living." Should you pause and puzzle over this claim?

Does it strike you as at all strange? Can it really be the case that a life is wasted if no self-reflection occurs? Is this an interesting question or a missed thought?

Perhaps you rushed on without pause to this next paragraph. If so, why should neglect of self-understanding leave you in any way impoverished? Perhaps the poverty appears in a liability to accept talk about yourself and others as complex machines or computers, or as products of social conditioning, or as the sum total of biological drives interacting with varying social environments. Does it sound realistic to talk of persons as "economic resources" which, if efficiently organized, will maximize the satisfaction of human needs? We now have offices of Human Resources in place of Personnel Offices, and no one seems to have objected to the change in labels.[2] But do you detect signs of barbarism? Why should anyone have qualms about mere changes in titles?

Perhaps the qualms and reservations arise from a sense of how complex persons are and of how superficial our talk about ourselves often is. If you need some evidence of this, pay attention to the strangeness of your own mind. Either in reading the ink marks on these pages or in listening to some professor in class, you have been experiencing light or sound waves having an impact on your eyes or ears. Have you made any sense of the fragmentary input? Have you understood any of the ink marks or sound waves?

The puzzle is how it is possible for light waves affecting your retinas or sound waves impinging on and vibrating parts of your ears to become meaningful or understood images and words. A simpler test is to ask whether there are any words on the chalk board after the mid-point of a college class. You may have learned that such chalk marks appear inverted on the human retina and then puzzled how they get turned right side up. How do they become familiar and meaningful words or symbols? If that question has not occurred to you, you might remember your last trip to an ATM. Do you remember seeing the braille pad supposedly offering instructions to blind customers? Were those "bumps" meaningful to you? You can see them and feel them, but are they words?

Such questions may lead you to reflect on how strange your everyday experience is. There is a chasm between hearing sounds and understanding them, between seeing ink or chalk marks and reading words. Somehow you routinely cross this gap between sensing and making meaning. But how do you do this?

Helen Keller's *The Story of My Life* may suggest how you initially experienced this gap. Struck deaf and blind at the age of eighteen months, she was incapable of communicating with words and so understanding what others were saying or writing. To indicate what she wanted, she used simple gestures. For six years she lived in growing frustration as her spontaneous curiosity and desire to communicate were blocked. She wrote:

> I do not remember when I first realized that I was different from other people; but I knew it before my teacher came to me. I had noticed that my mother and my friends did not use the signs as I did when they wanted anything done, but talked with their mouths. Sometimes I stood between two persons who were conversing and touched their lips. I could not understand, and was vexed. I moved my lips and gesticulated frantically without result. This made me so angry at times that I kicked and screamed until I was exhausted.[3]

Clearly the limited signs and gestures she used were failing to express all that she wanted to communicate. In what follows you can detect the intense curiosity which fuelled her anger and frustration.

> The desire to express myself grew. The few signs I used became less and less adequate, and my failures to make myself understood were invariably followed by outbursts of passion. I felt as if an invisible hand were holding me and I made frantic efforts to free myself. I struggled – not that struggling helped matters, but the spirit of resistance was strong within me; I generally broke down in tears and physical exhaustion. If my mother happened to be near I crept into her arms, too miserable even to remember the cause of the tempest. After awhile the need of some means of communication became so urgent that these outbursts occurred daily, sometimes hourly.[4]

Your own experience in crossing the gap between sensing and meaning was probably less troubled. What Helen Keller had to fight for was spontaneously acquired by you. Perhaps you know more of her story, for example, about how she discovered language with the help of a teacher and how that discovery launched her on the remarkable journey of her life. She wrote of that discovery:

> We walked down the path to the well-house, attracted by the fragrance of the honeysuckle with which it was covered. Someone was

drawing water and my teacher placed my hand under the spout. As the cool stream gushed over one hand she spelled in the other water, first slowly, then rapidly. I stood still, my whole attention fixed upon the motions of her fingers. Suddenly I felt a misty consciousness as of something forgotten - a thrill of returning thought; and somehow the mystery of language was revealed to me. I knew then that "w-a-t-e-r" meant the wonderful cool something that was flowing over my hand. That living word awakened my soul, gave it life, hope, joy, set it free![5]

Your own childhood leap across the chasm is presumably not a personal memory. When it happened a much wider reality opened up for you. Language allowed you to learn about worlds that had passed away (e.g. by reading history) and worlds that had never been (e.g. by reading science fiction). Perhaps you have a memory of the first book you were able to read on your own. Is there any happy memory of how fascinating you found it?

Helen Keller's breakthrough was to linguistic meaning.[6] By learning the meaning of the marks made on her hand, she was able to make sense of her world in a new way. This making sense, by way of understanding and using words, greatly expanded her ability to communicate with her teacher and her family. Later, when she learned to read, she had access to the written records of human meanings, and her world expanded beyond the confines of everyday living. Clearly the discovery of linguistic meaning – that marks on paper or the signs on Helen's hand make sense – is of great significance in human development.

What happened late for Helen Keller occurred much earlier for you. Still, the wonder of that moment of crossing is not totally irretrievable. The earlier puzzle about reading pages or chalkboards may set you to wondering about how you are able to make sense of ink marks or sound waves. Is this "obvious" experience becoming at all strange?

Perhaps this is all too obscure. In that case a "pragmatic appeal" may sell you on continuing to read this text. For years you have been thinking, questioning, problem-solving. Despite these years of practice, you may still find you operate largely by trial and error. You may at first have a hunch as to how to solve a problem, but, if that does not work, you may be at a loss about what to do next. Your search for understanding may seem haphazard, much like playing a new sport without any prior coaching or assembling Christmas toys without first reading directions. You care about solving a puzzle, but there is no plan on how to proceed.

Sometimes the best anyone can do is to rely on trial and error. But the problem is that haphazard efforts tend to make an inefficient use of time and energy, with success often proving elusive. Suppose you have to write an analytical paper on a moral controversy before the second week of a semester. You might experience some confusion and floundering about in unfamiliar territory. What you can expect in later chapters is an introduction to a procedure for finding your way around in moral controversies. By the end of the semester, you should be familiar with and practiced in applying a "road map" to moral decision-making, one that guides you in asking relevant questions about moral controversies. While the mapping will be far from complete and no more than a checklist for guiding your thinking, it will be superior to a hit-or-miss series of guesses.[7] Proof of the advantage lies not in the saying but in the doing, and the latter must come later. Still, you might think back to the advantage gained when you first learned to compose an outline before writing a research paper. Did the outline save you time and energy? Did it give you a general framework for ordering your thoughts more carefully?

So there is a personal reason for paying attention to your own mind and its puzzling strangeness. There is also a pragmatic motive for learning more about your own mind. You are using it all the time. Why not take more deliberate control over how you are thinking? In time, with practice, performance may shift from trial and error toward more careful and deliberate ways of operating. After all, why should improving your performance in playing sports be all that different from improving your performance in thinking? Practice builds habits whether in sports or in moral decision-making.

A caution concludes this opening section of the chapter. College textbooks should come with a standard warning that they are only scratching the surface of complex matters. Too often writers and readers assume they are doing much more. To counter this illusion, consider these climbing metaphors. At the end of college, you will arrive at the foothills of a mountain range, and, if you have been lucky, you will have some surviving interest in climbing higher. This text is analogous to setting up a base camp, that is, a starting point for further serious climbing. The tragedy for too many novice climbers (as well as for many with a Ph.D. after their names) is that they stop climbing prematurely. Many may believe they already know everything worth knowing or that what remains to be known will require only a little more effort on their part. In either case, with the exception of job-related learning, they may give up on further inquiry. But will they then miss Helen Keller's experience of a "living word [that] awakened my soul, gave it life, hope, joy, set it free"?

WHAT IS ETHICS?

What is the right way to live? While an important question, it still may not be one you have explicitly asked. It is quite possible to go about your normal routines without raising the question and all the while be acting in morally responsible ways. Most of the time you have been able to figure out what you should do without having to wonder how you were able to tell the difference between right and wrong. Your ease in responsible living was largely made possible by the instruction and example of parents and teachers. By word and gesture they shared their understanding of moral living, and gradually you caught their meaning, their "values," and made them your own.

The question about the right way to live usually emerges when persons find themselves in new or difficult situations where it is not clear what they should do. It may not take a moral crisis for the question to turn up. If you ever find yourself in a dead-end job but dependent on it to pay the bills until something better turns up, you will be puzzling about alternatives. If you struggled to choose between a college close to family and friends and one halfway across the country, you found yourself in a state of not knowing what to do. The questions then were: How do you make a decision? How will you know which option to choose? But these are versions of the earlier question about the right way to live, and you asked the questions because you did not know the answers. Still raising such questions does offer a clue as to how ethics is part of your own living.

Consider other situations that evoke similar questioning. You may some-day have to decide whether or not to continue treatment of a loved one who has Alzheimer's disease. You may find yourself, on the one hand, wanting to ease the suffering of the loved one but, on the other hand, not wanting to let go of the person you love. You may believe strongly that life should be preserved but also that avoidable suffering should be prevented. Suppose the doctors advise no further treatment. Will this decide the issue for you or will you still have to struggle with not knowing what to do?

What if a college friend confides in you that she is thinking of having an abortion? She asks your advice. What do you say? What do you do if she chooses to have an abortion after you have advised against it? How do you behave around her in the future? In such cases the stakes are higher than finding right answers. The lives and well-being of others are involved. In addition, your decisions say something about who you are, what you stand for and who you are trying to become. Situations of this sort test you as a person.

Personal relationships will give rise to ethical questions but so will political relationships. Events such as wars and economic embargoes can cause you to wonder about the rights and wrongs of collective actions. Should you support your government's policy or protest against it? If you feel betrayed by institutions or authorities you trusted, new questions may arise about your continued loyalty. You may even begin to wonder why you were loyal in the first place. If your outrage is strong enough, you may become suspicious of all authorities and legitimately wonder if you should ever trust anyone in the future.

Such negative experiences can be opportunities to reflect on what you really believe is worthwhile. Out of disillusionment can come a new round of questioning about how you can know what is worth believing and doing. Of course, the pain of disillusionment can have other outcomes. For awhile one may "retreat" from all loyalties and commitments and with a cynical voice deride earlier beliefs as naive and foolish. This strategy may work to prevent future pain, but it is unlikely to be more than a temporary stance. Sooner or later new situations will arise that require positive decisions and actions. The earlier cynicism will then appear unhelpful since it delays deciding, but the pressing situations call for action.

The question returns: How do I determine the right way to act or what course of action is really worthwhile? So far these pages have tried to convey an invitation to you to discover in yourself a spontaneous caring about understanding and about others. This offers a first clue as to how to answer the question. But you are not the first person to ask the question about the right way of living or to notice the clue. This question has a history, so a few words on the history of ethical reflection may help place your inquiry in a broader context.

Persons have been concerned about right and wrong as long as there have been human communities. Every society has customs and laws that are the products of prior inquiries into what should and should not be done in various types of situations. Every society confronts the "generational problem;" namely, its survival depends on successfully transmitting the society's customs and laws to the next generation. Early education in the home began your induction into a particular society's traditional beliefs and practices. Parents offered advice, set an example and bestowed praise and blame as ways of passing on what they themselves had inherited. Perhaps you remember some of the old platitudes: "If all the other kids were jumping off a cliff, would you do the same?" "How would you like it if someone did that to you?" "It doesn't matter if he hit you first; two wrongs don't make a right."

From such maxims you gradually learned some of the common-sense moral wisdom of a larger community. For some people knowing right from wrong appears to be a matter of having common sense. The word "morality" comes from the Latin *mores*, which means "custom." Customs are the habitual ways communities get things done. Of course you have heard it said, "When in Rome do as the Romans do." Another simple maxim with a practical purpose, it warns against assuming that your common sense is common sense everywhere. Failure to heed this warning has landed some travelers in jail.

While variable, customs serve a common function. They provide a predictable way for people to live with one another. Consider how various rituals and habits order much of your day and ensure you and others can cooperate and avoid conflict. Why do you use an alarm clock, a turn signal, a handshake, a nod of the head to indicate agreement? Imagine if you had to start each day unfamiliar with any of these routine ways of living. Expand this fantasy to include the "generational problem" and you can recognize how important it is to teach children both the customary practices and the moral wisdom of their society.

Morality, then, refers to a shared or common understanding of right and wrong reflected in the customary practices of a society. But then morality will vary from culture to culture and from one age to another in the same culture. In those different places and times, persons had practical goals and knew they needed to cooperate to reach those goals. As conditions changed, the practical insights embodied in morality may have changed. All this variability suggests one way of introducing a conventional distinction between morality and ethics. It is a distinction between practice and theory.

If morality is a localized common sense concerned with getting things done here and now, ethics aims at being a theoretical discipline. What's the difference? Suppose you are at home preparing supper. One of the practical tasks is to boil some water. You can do this without knowing any physics, but, if your question is why water boils, then you will need to learn some theory. This analogy may help you understand why the questions in ethics tend to be of a generality that is usually absent from everyday routines.[8] If the ethicist asks whether there are common features to moral decision-making, this is not the sort of question that usually turns up in practical living. If the question is why one should be moral, persons preoccupied with their daily tasks are likely to look puzzled or to think the answer all too obvious and the question a waste of time. At the practical level of common-sense living, such a reaction is defensible. You can be a good person without studying ethics, but the ethicist wants to know why.

This asking of why-questions has a history. Morality has been around as long as there have been communities, but ethics originated as a distinct inquiry with the Greeks, approximately 2,500 years ago. Greek philosophers puzzled about moral customs that varied from place to place. Socrates noticed that, while people claimed to know the meaning of words such as "justice" and "courage," they had trouble defining the terms in ways that embraced all the varied meanings. The citizens of Athens could describe their own customary beliefs about virtues, but they could not explain why their views were better than those of some other culture. Socrates was, in effect, questioning whether believing in one's own customs was the same as knowing what was right.

Socrates' questioning got him in trouble in his day. Today the risk lies in questioning the view that morals are just personal or conventional opinions and values. How is that different from an appeal to custom as justifying how you act? Have you ever questioned or criticized what others taught you? If so, then maybe inheritance is not the final word on what is right. Or perhaps you have changed your mind over time as to what is good to do. If so, then would you say that at every moment of your life you have been equally adept at deciding what was right? If not, then why should you assume that every person's opinion is equally valid?

But how do you sort out the multiple opinions that people do advance? Will it just be a matter of personal likes and dislikes or of private intuitions? Since the time of Socrates, philosophers have tried to find a less variable basis for judging among multiple opinions. They have asked questions about the foundations for human choices and have formulated principles and theories to distinguish between justifiable and unjustifiable choices. Despite a long history of caring about these issues, philosophers have not reached consensus. Indeed, some philosophers doubt whether consensus is a worthwhile aim. In later chapters, you will be exposed to differing ethical theories. But for now the point has been to suggest that, prior to such debates among ethicists, are the questions that arise from your own experience. And this experience is one of caring about understanding and about others.

WHY ASK WHY?

Perhaps you are now convinced that you should take yourself as a specimen of what ethicists are talking about when studying moral decision-making. Are you equally persuaded that your past learning has been defective in so far as it occurred without referring to yourself as an inquirer? Do you begin to recognize the implied criticism of ethicists who construct their theories without any reference to their own experience in making moral choices?

But where should such self-study begin? Consider some ways of answering this question. Some may say that, since persons are "social animals," the place to begin is with mores, with the social inheritance of common beliefs and practices. Others object to this highly variable starting point and search instead for some basic fact or "given" reality as the common foundation for moral choices and acts. The search for a bedrock position or primitive "given" has provoked any number of controversies. An opening chapter is not the place to review those debates, but it does help to be aware that they exist and show no sign of abating. Faced with this further instance of theoretical "multiplicity," you may begin to appreciate the alternative route of this text.

Suppose what is "given" is the debating, the puzzling, the questioning by all sorts of members of the human species. While they take different positions in their debates, what preceded their answers (inherited or otherwise) was their puzzling and questioning. This much seems uncontroversial, but it also indicates how to avoid the endless debates about the "given." If your understanding is testable and corrigible, if what you begin with is subject to further questioning and open to correction, then it matters less what initial position you hold. What matters more is whether you are "on the move," asking further questions and intent on developing in understanding.

Aristotle emphasized the same point with his opening words to the *Metaphysics:* "All persons by nature desire to know." You may wonder whether this is true. The proverbial couch potato may come to mind as one possible exception. Despite any number of exceptions, could Aristotle have been taking himself as a representative specimen of what he found distinctive and best in the human species? Was he reflecting on his own living and generalizing to the entire species? Do you think this is a legitimate maneuver?

Well, what is distinctive and best about you and all of us who are specimens of the human species? What sets our type apart from other species? A traditional claim was that the range of human curiosity distinguished persons from other types of living things. While animals have needs, the human fascination with knowing and the practices it evokes supposedly move us beyond the level of instinct to a higher level of living that is both instinctual and intelligent. The latter we exhibit in raising and answering questions; the former we experience in reflex responses to different stimuli. If you have shuddered or sneezed, you have experienced reflex responses. If you have paused and reflected before reacting, you have experienced the difference between instinct and intelligence. But surely animals manifest curiosity and find intelligent solutions to the problems of living in changing environments, so is there really a difference?

The traditional claim was that the range of our questioning sets us apart. We can and do ask questions about all manner of things. In principle our questioning is unrestricted since we can ask about anything and everything. You may have noticed that most adults tend to restrict their questioning to practical matters about earning a living, raising a family and getting along with other people. In spare moments they may wonder about what is happening in a broader world or about what the future may bring. For some there will be time and talent for deeper questions about the sweep of human history, the meaning of our lives in time, the roles of individuals in the vast impersonal processes of modern societies. But this range of possible questions is present in young children who ask questions about everything they encounter. They apparently want to know everything about everything; they constantly ask why. In doing so they strain the adult's capacity to provide answers. How many parents eventually are driven to say, "That's just the way it is"? But the children may be exhibiting what Aristotle thought was part of the nature of the species – they are wondering.

But why do we ask why? Here we are back to the question of the "given." As a matter of fact we ask questions – that's just the way it is. Is there any purpose to this incessant puzzling and questioning? The Epilogue will offer a few hints, but the broader implications of human wondering are beyond the limits of an introductory text in ethics. Still, you may wonder why there are such limits.

EXERCISES:

1. Describe how you have experienced "multiplicity" in education.

2. Describe an instance when you were careless in choosing.

3. Describe an instance when you were careful in decision-making.

MAKING THE OBVIOUS STRANGE

2

HORIZONS OF CARING

What example did you use for the third exercise in the preceding chapter? Was it personally significant but publicly undramatic? Standard ethics textbooks usually provide dramatic examples of moral choices for readers to analyze. The problem is that the cases (frequently mislabeled "moral dilemmas") are often very difficult situations that discourage readers from attempting careful analysis.

The approach here is to begin with what is simple (perhaps only apparently so?) and gradually to invite you to discover in your own experience what these ink marks really mean. So far there have been a number of claims with which you may agree or disagree. The point is to test them against your experience. Is it plausible to suggest that persons have priority over textbooks in being the subject matter of ethics? If the goal is to understand what happens in moral decision-making, is it credible that persons who care about others to varying degrees are the fundamental data? Or is it more believable that the place to begin is with a survey of already produced theories about moral choices? The latter is easier because most persons are unpracticed in paying attention to their own performance. Still, the easier way may be illusory. Can you recall the personal and pragmatic reasons for trying the harder way?

Both types of reasons cited the need to pay attention to your own performance in evaluating and deciding. Where do you begin? The earlier exercises may have offered you a start. Perhaps a few anecdotes will nudge your memory of earlier ways of evaluating actions that now seem at odds with your current performance. The contrast may shed some light on both your past and your present performance and, in doing so, make what was once "obvious" seem strange.

Imagine two children being told to help clean up the dishes after dinner. The first child helps willingly; she collects five glasses on a tray and heads for the kitchen. Halfway there she accidentally drops the tray and all five glasses are broken. Her brother helps reluctantly; he picks up only one glass and then deliberately drops it and it breaks. Which child's action is more reprehensible? Presumably you now answer, "The brother's." However, if you are to believe the developmental psychologists, there was a time in your life when you would have answered, "The sister's." Why? It seems that young children tend to evaluate such actions in terms of the amount of harm done. Deliberately or intentionally doing some harm was not always a relevant issue for the very young child. So how have you changed? Has intention (an instance of the lawyer's *mens rea*) somehow become relevant?

For a second example, imagine a child tells a lie to her mother and then later in the day falls on the sidewalk and injures her knee. Again, if you are to believe the developmental psychologists, the child is likely to understand her injury as punishment for telling a lie. How do you evaluate her accident? Does the last word in the preceding sentence seem appropriate?

The point of both anecdotes is twofold: to ask if you have changed in how you understand and evaluate actions and to ask if further development can occur. Both questions ask you to attend to your own experience, both past and present. So have you changed? To make answering easier, think of the old sing-song rhyme "Step on a crack and you'll break your mother's back." The question of future development may prove harder to answer. The notion of "horizon" may help identify some of the difficulties.

Literally a horizon is as far as a person can see. Shift your thinking slightly so that the term means the range of questions you can raise and find significant even if you cannot answer them.[1] Notice the word "significant." What lies beyond your horizon is not something you care about, ask questions about or take into consideration when acting. It simply doesn't register on you as being important.

Some examples of what lies beyond many people's horizons may help. Most people who go shopping for groceries and buy strawberries give no thought to who picked them, what they were paid or what health hazards they faced in the fields. Similarly consumers purchase items of clothing with no questions about where they were made, by whom and under what conditions. Notice, if you had to provide your own examples of what was "beyond your horizon," you might find it an impossible assignment. At best you discover the further relevant questions in retrospect. Why? If they were beyond your range of caring, then they were initially unnoticed.

But can horizons expand? Test the following claim against your own experience: "Caring about understanding is a dynamic and expansive part of human living." You may recall as a child being curious about all sorts of things. Why do trees have leaves? Why does it snow? Where does money come from? Your incessant questioning may have exhausted your parents. What if they had tried to answer your questions in terms of photosynthesis, the hydrological cycle and economic flows based on invisible acts of promising and trusting? Would the answers have made any sense at the time? Why not? The easy answer is that a child lacks the needed background understanding, e.g., prior studies in the natural sciences or economics.

A further answer is that the child's horizon (and that of most adults?) is one of emerging common sense. For common sense, what is real is assumed to be what one can see, touch, imagine. What is really significant is how one is affected by something. But the why-questions of a child call for answers not available in these terms. Only the slow historical emergence of the horizon of theory provides some of the demanded answers. Within that horizon the focus is not on things in relation to us but on things in their relations among themselves. Think of the difference between observing that "things go faster" and working out a law of acceleration, or think of the effort required to understand money not as imaginable coins or scraps of paper but as an electronic entry in a bank's records of a loan created by acts of promising and trusting. This shift in orientation in how you understand things comes neither easily nor quickly.[2]

What is true of caring about understanding may be true of your caring about others. Have you experienced changes in this horizon of care? To detect a possible line of expansion, consider three meanings or uses of the word "good." The first use is seen in a child's estimate of what is good: whatever benefits "me and mine" (e.g., family and friends) is good. "Bad" is whatever brings harm to me or mine. For example, actions that parents approve of are good; ones for which they punish me are bad. Being good, then, is matter of avoiding punishment and winning approval, i.e. being called a nice girl or boy. In this common-sense horizon of understanding, you evaluate something in terms of its relation to you, how it affects you and those around you for whom you care.

There is a second use of "good" that assumes an expansion of the range of concern beyond immediate friends and family to larger groups. "Good" may then mean whatever benefits your tribe, profession, class, fellow citizens, country, and so on. "Bad" means anything that harms the interests of the group you identify with, are loyal to and want to protect. For example, in political struggles between rival parties, "good" may mean whatever advances the legislation your party favors. During high school, you may have belonged to an in-group or you may have been one of the outsiders. Did estimates of what was "good to do" vary depending on which group you were in? Further examples of the "good of the group" show up in the benefits available to citizens that are withheld from non-citizens, and in the policies of nations and trading blocs pursuing their own interests.

Are there limits to this pursuit of group interests? Can you imagine situations in which persons seem to have cared for and tried to protect goods besides those of some group? At least in word, if not in action, you have heard people talking about a third use of "good."[3] Is there a broader horizon of significant questions behind this talk? What sense does it make to you to talk about what is "good for any and all persons"?

This third use of "good" may be familiar to you if you have heard persons criticize laws or policies as violations of human rights or denials of human dignity. If you are to make sense of such criticisms, do you have to presuppose that these critics are measuring the laws of some group against a standard higher than the good of that group? Perhaps the example of Martin Luther King, Jr. or of Gandhi comes to mind. Each man broke the laws of his society and so seemingly acted against the interests of groups in power. Were they just partisans for groups out of power who were trying to substitute one set of interests for another?

At least they claimed to be doing something else, e.g. fighting for the rights of all persons, for what would be good for any and all persons. They appealed to ideals of freedom and moral equality and called for all persons to have a political voice and opportunities to pursue a decent life. Practices of their times and tribes denied these goods to some, and so they were challenging those practices within given social orders and calling for an end to injustices that denied the worth that every person presumably possessed. But what is this inherent worth or dignity? How is it a measure of relations among persons? These are tough questions, but for now a few clues may help you begin thinking about this third meaning of "good." An old maxim provides a first clue: "Good is what good persons do." What did so many find admirable in the lives of Martin Luther King, Jr. and Gandhi? Closer to home you have undoubtedly admired some persons for how they lived their lives. Can you identify what they embodied that evoked your approval? As a second clue, try thinking of "goodness" not as a property of some object, i.e. something it possesses, but as a feature of a relationship between the object and someone who affirms it as worthwhile. Is something good, then, inasmuch as it is known to be worthy of approval and even love?[4]

This simple map of three uses of "good" may help you identify various expansions of your own horizon of caring. But is there any evidence that these three uses reflect a developing understanding of what it means to be moral? Do they represent a hierarchy of views? In short, is the third understanding of what is worthy of care superior to the preceding viewpoints?

Again, checking your own experience may be a better test of these suggestions than a survey of various arguments or theories. But how do you go about such self-reflection? Some help is available by considering three basic insights you have had for some years:

(1) What seems good is not always the same as what is good. (Are a child's likes and dislikes the measure of what is good?)

(2) What is good for me is not necessarily what is good for others. (Think of children learning to play with others and slowly learning that demanding their own way all the time quickly puts an end to playing in groups.)

(3) A minimal step in expanding one's moral horizon occurs when one learns to stop before acting to consider the effects of one's actions on others. (Did your parents ever ask you: "How would you like it if someone did that to you?")

A further suggestion is that these three insights give a minimal content to what it means "to be careful" in moral decision-making. Can you think of people who need to be more careful in exercising some self-control over their likes and dislikes? Does "acting on impulse" sometimes lead to later regrets? Are you familiar with persons who do not seem to care about the effects of their actions on others? If you have ever been on the receiving end of such thoughtless actions, have you wished for a little more consideration? If you have answered "Yes" to these questions, what have you been assuming about moral growth?[5]

NOMINAL UNDERSTANDING

You have your own history of personal growth and development in being careful in inquiry. You may be able to cite examples over time of your own improving performance. It is not a huge reach to detect broader cultural developments in caring about understanding. The emergence of methods and procedures in numerous disciplines has over time replaced trial and error with deliberately designed ways of being more careful in inquiry. Some familiarity with the history of chemistry emerging out of alchemy may suggest examples belonging to a broader cultural history. If you have read something about double-blind experiments in medical research or about the use of control groups in medical and social research, you will recognize how designed procedures have become commonplace ways of being careful in inquiry.

How is it that human beings are able to improve their own performance in thinking? Does this strike you as a question having an obvious answer? If it does, then the following paragraphs may be unsettling. One purpose of these early chapters is to introduce you to the strangeness (weirdness?) of your own mind. This purpose challenges an assumption that there is nothing very amazing about persons. It is not uncommon to hear that physics courses are more difficult than psychology classes. Does this mean that persons are easier to understand than subatomic particles? Did you expect that this ethics course would require less work than a class in chemistry?

One way of challenging such expectations is to present puzzles that turn what you take to be obvious into something strange.[6] Before turning to puzzles from psychology of perception, you may discover in the following comments on nominal understanding something surprising about your years of schooling. A clue to the surprise was given in the Introduction with its remarks on the Pythagorean Theorem and a simple mathematical rule. Try a new example. Imagine a parent and five-year old visiting a zoo for the first time.

'What is that, Mommy?' asks the child visiting the zoo.
'A wallaby, dear,' answers the mother, after a quick glance at the notice under the cage.
'What is a wallaby, Mommy?'
'That is, dear.'
'Why, Mommy?'[7]

You can guess how the next few moments go. Perhaps the parent points out the visible features of the wallaby emphasizing its large hind legs, tail and capacity to hop. You might also guess that the child still asks more why-questions. What repertoire of responses does the usual parent then draw upon? "That's just what they're called" or "Ask your father when we get home" may occur to you. Of course, there is always the strategy of distraction: "Oh, let's go look at the tigers."

The question is, What has the child learned about a wallaby? Is it more than a new word or name? Perhaps the child will be able to describe to class-mates what a wallaby looks like. So the child's questions have produced a label and a description. But have the child's questions really been answered? Does the child know why a wallaby is the way it is? Is it possible that the child can in time learn to settle for names and descriptions and not even notice that the why-questions are not being answered?

Perhaps you have already guessed where all this is leading. Is it possible for years of schooling to produce a habit of taking an expanding vocabulary and familiar descriptions of what things look like for serious explanations of those things? Is it obvious that, when you can name and describe something, then you know what it is?

What more is there to learning? Has anything been missed? Compare the years of study by a zoologist interested in wallabies. In reaching for a seri-ous understanding of them, the scientist has spent years studying the com-plex interacting systems of a wallaby. Study of its genetic make-up, muscu-lar-skeletal structure, circulatory system, digestive processes, mating and feeding cycles are just part of the years of inquiry. This "climb" has taken time and energy, but intense curiosity was what moved the zoologist higher.

Contrast this to your own years of education. If they have contained the usual fare, then your vocabulary has expanded; you can repeat names, dates and formulas, but you may be at a loss to explain why any one of those for-mulas is true. Recall the earlier example of multiplying positive and nega-tive numbers. The surprising discovery may be that, despite years spent in classrooms, you are not able to cite a single example of your own serious understanding of something. Is this a troubling discovery?

Let "nominal understanding" (*nomen* in Latin means "name") be the label for this usual type of learning. Even if there is a Ph.D. after your name, it may be all the learning you have. Years of education may have been little more than a search for synonyms resulting in mastery of verbal formulas. Think of how you would respond to questions about what an instinct is or what money is. Synonyms come readily to mind, but are you going around in a circle? Of course, a lack of serious understanding can hide behind an inflated vocabulary. If a speaker announces a lecture on "dyadic encounters" or "multi-personal interfaces," an audience may think they are moving into deep waters, but the talk may be no more than chatting about chatting. Will anyone ask, "What makes 'talk' talk?" Will the audience be any the wiser if they are unacquainted with the missed-understanding of the child visiting the zoo?

This is a good place to pause, lift your eyes from the page and ask yourself if you really understand anything.

Most readers will skip the invitation and quickly read on to this new paragraph. Old habits were a long time in the making and are not easily left behind. Maybe there is still an intact and unchallenged sense of the obvious. After all, you know how to use language to talk about all sorts of familiar objects and events. You know how to carry out practical tasks like driving a car, using a computer or getting money from an ATM. What more proof does anyone need that you know plenty? But do you have further questions about how and why these instruments work? You know how to speak, but try explaining the common event of talking. In a moment of honesty, there may be a feeling of embarrassment. What is there to show after so much education? Perhaps you have a dog; do you understand what it is? You can recognize it, call to it, play with it, but is that anymore than what it can do? If understanding your dog in a serious way is now in doubt, think of the difficulty if the question had been, What is God?

Personal embarrassment need not be the only result of a discovery of the prevalence of nominal understanding. A positive outcome can be the recognition that, like the child at the zoo, you once had further questions and did not settle for names and synonyms. Perhaps the memory of the budding detective you once were can reawaken some of that earlier curiosity and intense caring about understanding. The outcome may depend on whether you are sufficiently curious about something so that it absorbs your attention. Some young zoologist began with a fascination with wallabies and allowed it to direct years of inquiry. Maybe wallabies are not your passion, but what is?

PUZZLES FROM PSYCHOLOGY OF PERCEPTION

A second way of making the obvious strange is to sketch some puzzles from the field of psychology of perception. A famous example is the prism-goggles experiment.[8] Imagine volunteers putting on prism goggles that reverse images so that what seems up is actually down and what appears to the right is in fact to the left. Initially the volunteers are disoriented since the visual data provide confusing clues as to where things are. Simple tasks such as reaching for a door handle or a drinking glass become difficult. The goggles-wearers reach for items and grasp thin air. However, in a few days the old tasks become familiar routines once again. The volunteers are able to identify objects without hesitation and can reach for an item without missing their target. What has happened? Their eyesight has not improved, so what has changed?

You might guess that eye-hand coordination has returned because the test subjects have adjusted to the strange clues; they have learned from their mistakes and have adopted new ways of reading the visual clues. If so, where's the puzzle? So far this is no big surprise. You would expect that persons could learn from their mistakes and adapt to puzzling sensations just as you once learned to walk around in a darkened room during a power outage. Human understanding is corrigible and improvable, but that was obvious from the start, or was it?

The real surprise comes when the goggles are removed. The test subjects have unimpaired vision, yet their disorientation returns. The visual data again are confusing, and it takes several days of "normal" sight before routine tasks are deftly handled. But the question is, Why is there this second period of confusion? If seeing what's "out there" is just a matter of opening your eyes and looking around, why do the volunteers, freed of the goggles, have so much trouble recognizing things? Their eyesight is unhindered, so why the delay in seeing clearly? These are fine questions to ponder for a day or a week depending on your interest in such a puzzle. The difficulty may arise from what you take to be obvious. Suppose you are asked during a class, "Are the lights on in the room?" Your first reaction might be to look up at the light fixtures in the ceiling. Why this response? Presumably you assume this is the way to settle the question since light sources are real objects outside yourself and you can know whether they are on or off by taking a quick look. Could anything be more obvious? But what if your pet dog is asked whether the lights are on? Does it look up or just wag its tail?

Recall the point to these puzzles is to challenge your understanding of the obvious. If you need some further clues, consider the following thought experiment – one that requires no expensive apparatus and can be "cheaply" performed.[9]

Suppose you have 20/20 vision, but a friend requires thick-lensed glasses to see clearly. Now imagine that you borrow your friend's glasses and put them on. What happens? Everything you look at grows blurry or hazy. Where has the change occurred – behind the lenses or on the far side of the lenses? Your common sense pushes you to conclude that nothing has changed beyond the lenses. Real objects around you do not lose their sharp contours just because you happen to be wearing the glasses. But what has changed? To avoid talking of specific objects, let's say everything in your "visual environment" (everything as seen by you) has changed. So what is this visual environment? Where is it? How do you know that it is what has changed and not the real objects?

If you are still at a loss for the significance of these puzzles, try an even simpler case. Suppose you have been in an auto accident and for several days you suffer from double vision. You still manage to attend class, but the enrollment in the class suddenly doubles. Do you surmise that there has been a mid-term surge in enrollment or do you conclude that all the doubles are "behind your eyeballs"? If the answer is obvious, take a step back and ask, "Before the double vision episode, where were my fellow students as seen by me?" There's no problem admitting the doubles are "inside," but what do you say about the singles?

A pause of a day or a week is recommended here. Habit and the press of academic deadlines may rush you on in your scanning of ink marks and coverage of assigned pages. The price you pay may be to leave old habits intact and a sense of the obvious unchallenged. Just what deserves challenging here? Some would say our "oldest prejudice;" namely, that what is real is what is already out there waiting to be observed and that knowing what is real is a matter of close observation or looking.

The preceding puzzles are one way of disrupting these "obvious" views. Another source of disruption is the study of clinical cases from psychology of perception. A basic claim in the field is that the visual environment is part of the central nervous system. Numerous experimental results support the claim. Fortunately some of the evidence is popularly available in the works of Oliver Sacks. You may be familiar with movies based on his clinical work, e.g., "Awakenings," "Rain Man," "Love at First Sight."

One of Sack's clinical cases offers repeated instances of how visual environments are "constructed" inside though they appear to be outside.[10] The patient's name is Virgil. A childhood illness deprived him of his sight. In his forties he underwent a new surgical technique that promised to restore adequate vision. Sacks describes the episode when Virgil's bandages are coming off after the initial surgery on one eye. In the doctor's office are several people interested in whether the surgery has been successful. After the bandages are removed, Virgil slowly turns around and appears to be scanning the room. Finally, the doctor impatiently asks, "Virgil, tell us what you see." He replies, "Oh, I see a face." In retrospect Virgil told how he was looking around the room and seeing blobs of colors that he did not recognize, but suddenly there was a voice coming from one of those color blobs asking what he saw. In language Virgil would not use, a specialist might say that Virgil inferred that such sounds come from mouths, mouths are parts of faces, so the color blob must be a face and the other similar blobs of colors must also be faces. Once again, then, where are the faces of your fellow classmates as seen by you? Pushing you further in your puzzling – where are the words you are reading? Recall the earlier puzzle about the chasm between a teacher emitting sound waves or scribbling chalk marks and your understanding of the sounds and sights.

If the puzzles are wearing you down, endure one more. The television "couch potato" is said to be passive, just sitting there absorbing whatever is on the "idiot tube." But is this fair? What is on the television screen? A little research will uncover talk of pixels and further talk of sound waves emitted from speakers. But the so-called couch potato does follow the soap opera or sit-com, so there is some recognition of dialogue and images of action. How does the supposedly passive television viewer go from absorbing sound and light waves to understanding the show?

You might expect an answer, but the truth is that contemporary psychology of perception is embarrassed by this question. How the gap between sensing and understanding is crossed is not something experts can explain. As a matter of fact you cross this gap everyday, but you can also boil water without knowing why it boils. The further why-questions about perceiving and recognizing remain unanswered. All that anyone can surmise is that your mind is active in constructing some meaning out of fragmentary sensory input. Are you aware of this capacity in yourself to integrate and order your experiences? Is this awareness at odds with what previously was "obvious;" namely, looking reveals what is out there and what is real is what is out there awaiting your looking?

Perhaps you have had one puzzle too many, so it is time to end this chapter and shift the focus. Allow a summary of the purposes these remarks served. The limits of nominal understanding and of previous education may have been a surprising personal discovery. If so, this is one step toward undermining a sense of the obvious, awakening a sense of wonder and prompting further questions about all sorts of things you may have thought you already understood. At least there should be some expansion of horizon, a glimpse of how much more there is to understand. The puzzles from psychology of perception are clues to the strangeness of your own mind, and so a further erosion of the obvious may have occurred. If new questions abound, then you are on the move – evidence that further intellectual and moral development is possible. But then you may sense what an unfinished work of art you still are. This may be enough to begin creating a different pattern in living and learning, an alternative to passing courses, passing out and eventually passing away.

EXERCISES

1. Describe an instance of development in your own horizon of caring about others.

2. Describe how three persons, each operating with a different understanding of "good," would evaluate the same situation.

3. Describe several of your own experiences of nominal understanding.

MAKING SENSE OF THINGS

3

HOW DO YOU MAKE MEANING?

The puzzles at the end of the last chapter ideally led you to pause and to think about how you might make sense of them. Making sense of things is something you have been doing for years, but just what you were doing, how you were operating, probably remains a mystery. At least the thick glasses experiment should have cast some doubt on the "obvious" answer that taking a close look is all you need to do to find the meaning of something. Have you sat in a math class, stared intently at the equations "on the board" and still been lost? (By the way, were there equations on the board?)

If further examples are needed, recall the case of Virgil. Oliver Sacks tells how, after two eye operations, Virgil returned home with adequate eyesight, but he still encountered problems that sighted persons do not experience. An especially interesting puzzle was the trouble he had in "correlating his cat." For years Virgil had had a cat and a dog. However, after his operations, Virgil was unsure which was which just by looking at them. Until one of the pets came close enough for him to reach out and touch it, he remained unsure. Why did his touching, and not his seeing, settle the issue? What does it mean to "correlate" a cat, a dog or any object?

Recall the earlier example of the parent at the mall suddenly noticing that the child is missing. Where did she go? Is she lost and afraid? Has she been abducted? Without voicing these questions explicitly, the anxious parent is asking them. They are the invisible mental acts of the now alert parent. Why does the parent quickly scan the area? What is she looking for? Perhaps you know what detectives listen and look for – more clues. So the parent is searching for more clues. Of what use are they? If the unvoiced questions are to be answered, more clues will be needed. As more clues are quickly found, they allow the anxious parent to begin answering the unvoiced questions of whether or not the child is in danger.

Return to the earlier question about "correlating" any object. If your questions are a reaching for the meaning of some sound or sight and if auditory and visual clues help you settle on the answers, might "correlating" be a process of linking the clues to something? But what is this "something" to which you link clues? Here you might pause – again? This question points toward a new complexity in how you make meaning.[1]

Years of self-attention may lead to greater understanding of the complexities in even simple experiences of puzzle-solving. You might expect an introductory text to offer some mapping of what lies ahead on such a journey of self-discovery. The problem is that the mapping may become an exercise in nominal understanding and memorization; then repetition of formulas may take the place of serious self-inquiry. Still, from the examples already presented, you can follow the mapping and test it against your own experience with puzzle-solving. Perhaps the hint that the mapping is quite incomplete will lead you to investigate where the omissions occur. Detecting them will involve you in the very exercise of self-attention this text invites you to undertake.

Where begin the mapping? Where do you begin the process of making sense of your experiences? Keeping in mind the previous hint, you might guess that the process begins with some sort of sensible event. A noise will do; for example, a noise in the middle of the night awakens you. In this case a question follows: What was that? The sensible event is what evokes the what-question, and the question is how you respond to the event. Just as the parent may quickly anticipate the worst ("Has my child been abducted?"), so you may guess that the noise in the middle of the night might be the sound of an intruder. But other guesses are possible, e.g. maybe it is the neighbor's cat on the roof.

If the situation is serious, you probably will not settle for your first guess. If your answer is, "Maybe it's an intruder," do you just roll over and go back to sleep? More likely you listen for more clues; perhaps you get out of bed and do some checking around the apartment or house. Why are you doing this? "Better safe than sorry" might be an answer that comes to mind. A more basic answer is that a guess is not enough; you want something more. You want to answer a further question, "Is it an intruder or just the cat?"

Notice that this further question is different from the first what-question. Now you are trying to establish what is the case, to settle a matter of fact. A guess amounts to an idea about "what may be the case;" the new questioning seeks to know "what is the case." Let this is-question be a second type of searching. To pin down the difference between the two types, think about possible responses to each and how they differ. Is-questions seek responses in terms of "Yes," "No" or "I don't know." In contrast, what-questions seek responses that supply further information, e.g., if someone asks you your name and you reply, "Yes," expect a puzzled look from the person.

So far in the mapping of the process of making meaning, you may have noted four operations: attending to something puzzling, questioning about what to make of it, answering that question and questioning whether your answer or guess is correct. You can check these early details of the map against the earlier puzzle about Virgil's cat. The visual clues of either the dog or the cat were not enough for Virgil to answer which pet it was. He might guess, but what did he need before he could confidently say which it was?

You might pause here and ask what is at stake in distinguishing what-questions from is-questions. One of the earlier puzzles from psychology of perception may still intrigue you. What of the claim that the visual environment that appears "outside" is really "inside"? Your friends, as seen by you, (as well as their doubles if you have double vision?) are part of your visual environment. Is that a strange but inescapable claim? Does it bother you at all to think that maybe you are really quite alone?[2]

To return to the mapping of your mental operations, suppose you answer, "Yes, it is an intruder." What do you do next? If you enjoy word play, you might appreciate that the answer is "Yes." Come again? When the situation calls for more than determining what is the case, e.g. when what is the case is in fact threatening, you spontaneously focus on changing the situation. Now the question is, What can I do? Think of your possible responses to discovering an intruder at home. Do you scream, hide, run to the phone, try to leave the house, search for a weapon? All may be options that race through your mind. They occur to you because your attention is focused on meeting the danger, and how to do this is what is in question. Let this be a third type of question, though quite similar to the first type, the what-question. As a label convenient for mapping different operations, use the name "question for deliberation." Now the issue is not what is the case but what is possible, what can be done.

What you are deliberating over are possible courses of action. The earlier hint about the incompleteness of the mapping applies even here. What options occur to you? Depending on your material resources, intellectual habits and present state-of-mind, some alternatives may seem more realistic possibilities than others. Do you have a black belt in karate? Are you calm and decisive amid crises or does fear unnerve and paralyze you? Answers to such questions determine when and by what means you can act.

The danger of the moment speeds up your thinking about options. Possible scenarios race through your mind. Your deliberating may be far from calm and collected, but it is a distinct moment leading to action. What follows is a fourth type of questioning: Which option should you choose? What should you do? Deliberating is at an end, and it is time to make a decision. Let the label for this fourth type of searching be the "question for decision." How is it distinct from the preceding?

The issue previously was what courses of action were available to you. Now the issue is choosing among them. But which do you choose? How do you know it is the right choice? Recall how these questions turned up earlier. The central questions in ethics were: What is the right way to live and how do you know which it is? These questions are very general. In the middle of the night, confronted by the threat of an intruder, you will ask far more specific questions. All the same, thinking of options is distinct from deciding which of them to pursue. No matter how fast you leap to a choice, are there options from which to choose?

The whole momentum of the decision-making process brings you to the moment when you must decide which option to choose from among those that are available. Once you have decided, the entire movement comes, at least temporarily, to a rest. Your course of action is settled. Have you noticed the great sense of relief that comes when you finally resolve what to do? As events unfold, further questions may arise which require adjustments and, in some cases, a disconcerting rethinking of your original plans. Still, the important thing to note here is that there is a pattern to the process that begins in your caring about the situation you face and ends with the judgment of what is worth doing. The human desire to do good, when followed up, results in the occurrence of a set of internal acts that ends with a decision to act responsibly. This is how you put your caring into action.

Still it may seem something has been overlooked. Do we always do what we know we should do? Do we always avoid doing what we know is the wrong thing to do? Personal examples may be embarrassing but not difficult to find. So is there a further question about being willing to carry through with what you have decided you should do? In other words, are deciding to do something and willing to do it two separate questions? There is a subtle issue here about free will. For example, it seems obvious that persons can know what they should do and still choose to do the opposite. What they intelligently grasp and reasonably affirm as good to do need not be what they freely choose to do. Still, this separation of the two questions and of deciding and willing may not be so obvious.

In paying attention to your own decision-making, you may notice that, when you really care about some issue, your willing is cooperating with your intelligence throughout the process.[3] The cooperation shows up when you willingly choose to do something about a situation that puzzles you. Absent a willingness to investigate, your inquiry would go nowhere. Furthermore, if the situation is one calling for action, cooperative willing shows up in the effort to devise plans to change the situation. To put it simply: a responsible decision is the product of an enduring desire to do the right thing. So what is the "subtle issue" here? If intelligence and desire (or willingness) have been cooperating all along in the process, then, when you reach a judgment about what you should do, included in the judgment is the willingness to act accordingly. In other words, once you have decided on the right option, there is no need of a further question to determine if you are willing to do what you have decided. Why would you need such an additional inquiry? You have already thought about the options and reached your decision. There is nothing more to learn and so no need for a further question.

Nevertheless, we can refuse to cooperate with our best judgments.[4] There are many ways of resisting or distracting our desire to know and to do the right thing. Is there ample evidence of the results of careless, unintelligent and irresponsible decision-making? Evidence of unreasonable and poorly planned responses to public crises is not in short supply. The lingering consequences of intellectual and moral failures are part of the context for current efforts to do the right thing. In trying to make sense of events and of human actions, you will often encounter the accumulated nonsense of prior bad decisions. Later, when the topic of "bias" is introduced, you will find more discussion of the origins and consequences of bad decision-making.

To summarize, this section has mapped a few basic operations in the making of meaning. Keeping in mind the previous warning about nominal understanding, you might string together a series of labels that reflect your emerging understanding of what you do in making choices. The chart that follows suggests what such a string or pattern of labels would include.

OPERATIONS	OBJECT
Question for Decision ("Which should I/we choose?")	What's Best to Do
Question for Deliberation ("What can I/we do?")	Possibilities/Options
Is-Question ("Is it the case?")	Fact/What's True
What-Question ("What? Who? Why? How often?)	Guess/Hypothesis
Sensibility	Clues/Data

Is familiarity with this map a sign of a serious understanding of how persons make meaning? It really is only a heuristic tool for making further discoveries, for detecting further complexities in you. Its usefulness, however, is testable. Recall the earlier puzzle about the visual environment growing hazy when the thick glasses were put on. Your common sense resisted any suggestion that reality grew blurry as a result. So you may have reached the conclusion that reality and your visual environment are not identical to one another. But then what do you mean by "reality"? Does the map help you locate which type of mental operation is key to settling the difference between sensing and knowing what is real? If looking is a form of sensibility, are you ready to look elsewhere on the map?

Another benefit of the map is that it suggests the role that care plays in your own thinking. What moves you along through the different but related types of operations? If you could not care less about some puzzle, then the questioning stops, and perhaps you settle for a first guess. However, if you care strongly about some problem, the questioning probably continues until you think you have answered all the relevant questions. With care and willingness present in your thinking (with the desire to know and to do the right thing in control?), your reaching for meaning tends to be much more thorough and deliberate. Notice that the map provides something of a checklist for tracking just how you may go about being careful in inquiry. Still, do not believe a word of this. You, again, are the specimen against which to test these claims about how persons make meaning.

SOCIAL DIALECTIC

You may be wondering how the preceding claims about mental operations are relevant to the study of ethics. Recall the earlier statement that without minds there would be no theories, no sciences, no economies. The same is true for ethics as a field of inquiry. Ink marks appear in textbooks, but, for both the authors and for the readers, the meanings of those marks are "in heads." Moral decisions and theories about them are products of invisible acts of meaning. Once that is granted, the next steps are fairly apparent. If you want to improve your chances of making good choices, it will help to understand what goes on when you make choices. The next step will be to take some deliberate control over how you proceed in the varied but related operations leading to a choice.

Neither step is taken quickly and without sustained effort. Obstacles abound, but the previous mapping may offer some help. For instance, besides answers to what-questions that are more or less bright ideas, there is the further operation of judging or trying to answer the is-question about such ideas: Are they correct? Perhaps you have noticed that many times people pass around the latest news and novel opinions that they have recently heard. Maybe they preface their remarks with the commonplace: "They say…" All the same, you may be more aware now that there may be a missing question: "But is it true?" Of course, the habits of nominal understanding may discourage this further questioning and confuse eloquence and simple repetition of what "they say" with truth.

None of us likes to admit that favored views are just a repeating of what we have heard from others. Still, with a little insight into the prevalence of nominal understanding in your life, it is not a stretch to suggest that most of what you claim to know is in fact borrowed. A distinction between "believing" and "knowing" may underscore this common indebtedness to others.

Let "believing" mean affirming what others may know but what you possess on the basis of trust in their word, competence or reputation.[5] Your experience in geography class probably supplies easy examples of such trusting, e.g. how do you know that Spain is on a peninsula? Do you have any reason to suspect a conspiracy among cartographers, textbook publishers and teachers? In contrast, let "knowing" mean affirming what you have discovered through the different but related operations outlined in the previous map.

Try applying this simple distinction to your own moral convictions. Why do you think persons are deserving of respect as persons? Why do you think freedom of the press is important or private property should be respected or religious tolerance practiced? In one or maybe in all of these cases, you may have answered: "That's what I've always been taught" or "That's what everyone around me says." In other words, your strongest convictions may be borrowings or beliefs that you have taken for granted for years. So what? The problem is that borrowed beliefs may be a mix of good sense and nonsense, of what is true and of what is false. If you have ever read about how parents tend to pass along their own prejudices to their children, you may already be aware of the problem. So how do you learn the difference? How do you sort out the good sense from the nonsense?

Whatever mixture of the two you may have assimilated will be due to a series of accidents. When and where you were born, the times and tribe you showed up among, were the initial context for your borrowing what others already knew or believed. Through what writers call the "socialization process," you were inducted into the shared meanings of various groups. If by now you have rejected some of what you were earlier taught and have affirmed a different group's understanding, the old problem may still be present. How do you know that the new beliefs do not contain just a different mix of good sense and nonsense? Is all of your life just to be one borrowing after another, each time running the risk of buying into the nonsense of some new group?

If you paused over the earlier question about what moved you through the various levels of operations in making meaning, you may have a clue as to how to lessen the risk. The dynamism of caring about understanding takes the form of questioning. Your own spontaneous curiosity offers the possibility of resisting group opinion, peer pressure and tribal mentality. How so? Is your questioning conditioned by your upbringing? Undoubtedly what others say and believe affects your thinking, but are you limited to repeating what others say or permit you to say in public? Is it at least possible that you can question anything you have been taught? Habits of trust in early education and a heavy emphasis on repeating answers given by authority figures may have discouraged you from asking questions in class or at home. What has your experience been? Have teachers and parents invited questions or have they been busy supplying "all you need to know"?

The puzzle may be how you are to break habits acquired through years of education and socialization. What allows you to challenge habits and received opinions? Playing with language returns: the answer is "yes." Forgive the neologism, but "whatting" is you at five years of age at a zoo, not yet indoctrinated into settling for nominal understanding. You still have this capacity to question, and this by itself offers the possibility of challenging received answers.

Put in more scholarly terms, you may recognize a type of dialectic between public words and your own spontaneous curiosity. A group may tell you what to believe, but the game need not be over. As a player you can send the ball back as a question: Why should I believe this? For example, through media advertizing you may have been led to believe that dating and true love were matters of good hygiene, the "cool" car and finding the right words. In time, if your special someone has the flu or a family crisis, you may discover that true love includes inconveniences, misunderstandings and fumbling efforts to repair them. What the ads failed to mention you may learn in the school of hard knocks. But then you will have detected the superficiality of the public words and the media ads. Here "dialectic" means your capacity to act back upon, to criticize and to revise public meanings. Instead of being the sum total of your social conditioning, you may be a source of criticism of and innovation in those prior conditions. Can you think of an example when you have made a departure from what "they say"? Are there any memories of you being a critic of what everyone else was saying and doing? How were you able to stand apart and dissent? What is it that can set you at odds with the prevailing opinions of your times and tribe? Again, the answer is "yes."

WHY HAVE MORAL RULES?

As part of the socialization process, a society passes on to the new generation its shared understanding (and possibly misunderstanding?) of right and wrong. The group may formulate its understanding in proverbs, maxims, stories about heroes and villains; but it will also share its meanings through rules and laws. In the past various writers have even identified morality with such laws. That is, to be moral was to be obedient to laws. A further assumption was that knowing the laws was the same as knowing what the right thing to do was. All you had to do was to learn the laws and that would settle any doubts about right and wrong.

Are you already familiar with some of these laws and rules? What is the Golden Rule? Can you recall the Ten Commandments? Have you ever heard that persons should never be treated merely as means but always as ends in themselves? Perhaps you can think of others. For example: "For favors received, favors are due;" "Treat equals equally and unequals unequally in proportion to their differences;" "Persons should enjoy the maximum liberty compatible with the same for all others."

Now the question is whether knowing these rules and laws is the same as knowing what you should do. Two problems may occur to you. First, the rules you have learned are quite general. They formulate what persons have previously learned about doing good and avoiding evil. But the advice they capture is not tied to single instances of decision-making; rather, the rules are meant to be guides to a variety of instances, the details of which may vary. The fact that rules are multiple is one indication that not every instance of decision-making is the same. As an analogy you might think of Galileo's law of acceleration as a general rule, but do you recall that his rule ignored the variable of resistance or friction? You might also puzzle why the rule does not mention differences in gravity.

So rules are general guides to your decision-making. They pass along to a new generation what predecessors have learned and thereby save successors the need to "re-invent the wheel." All the same, knowing the rules is not the same as knowing what you should do. There is still "the diagnosis problem." To make a decision you may need to understand a variety of rules, but then you will need to know which of the rules is relevant to the situation you are facing (the question of relevance), and to know that requires that you understand the situation at hand. By themselves the rules do not provide answers to the question of relevance and to questions about what the situation is like. Another analogy may help here. Go to medical school and you can learn all sorts of reliable theories for understanding and treating various diseases. Such medical lore is invaluable; however, if a doctor misdiagnoses a patient and applies the wrong therapy, the condition of the patient may worsen. So the generalized medical knowledge is one thing, but the diagnostician identifies the relevant therapy only after close study of the particular patient. (Is this another instance of the approach to ethics in this text? The field of ethics contains all sorts of generalized understanding, but the study of specimens occurred first and must occur again if the generalized insights are to guide action.)

The diagnosis problem may help you detect the main oversight in the claim that knowing the rules is enough to settle the question of what you should do. What this claim overlooks is you, the moral inquirer. You are the one who acquires or misses the insights needed to diagnose the specific situation. You are the one who must link relevant rules to your understanding of the situation. Most important of all, you are the one who must be willing to discover and to do the right thing.

So knowing the moral rules is one thing; knowing how and when to apply them is another; being willing to follow them is yet a further challenge to anyone who cares about the right way to live. All this may seem plausible, but then why was it once so easy to identify morality with laws and their observance? You might think back to earlier comments about nominal understanding and habits in education. Is it possible to convince yourself that questions are unimportant and that repeating answers given by others is what education is all about? Transfer those views to moral decision-making and what you may find is a similar mindset: "It is enough to know the rules; you do not need to ask any further questions in making decisions."

To challenge this mindset in one more way, consider this unconventional understanding of being moral: "Morality is being careful in providing someone with a better time." If you have ever read standard ethics texts, this view of morality will come as a surprise.[6] But should it? Do you recall what the "foundations" of morality are? Did you pin down in your own life the meaning of "horizon" and identify from memory experiences of developments in your own moral understanding? Such personal experiences are clues for making sense of this unorthodox view of morality.

Who is the "someone" who should have a "better time"? You might find some clues in the earlier remarks on horizons of caring that can expand over time. Initially the "someone" may be "you and yours," i.e. what is good to do is identified with satisfying personal needs. Later the good of a wider social grouping may be your measure of what is right to do. Protecting and enhancing the well-being of some social order may be an objective of your caring, sometimes overriding personal interests. On occasion "someone" may include the outsider, the person whose claim on your attention and care is based on something more fundamental than personal attachment or group membership. So the "someone" can be narrowly identified with self and tribe, but also more expansively understood to include any and all persons.

If the populations whose "good times" are at issue can vary, then so can the relevant rules. For example, suppose one day at work your supervisor unexpectedly criticizes your recent job performance. You are taken by surprise and make no response, but later that night you grow angry at what seems a totally unjustified criticism. In mulling over what you can do, you imagine going into work the next day and defending yourself. Perhaps that will change the supervisor's mind. You also consider keeping quiet since the former option may risk an angry confrontation that could worsen relations between you and the supervisor. However, you know yourself well enough to foresee that silence will lead to a nagging sense of injustice that will produce bitterness and hostility potentially damaging relations at home and at work. What are you to do? A "better time" for you is the issue. Ideally you would prefer to speak up and clear the air rather than keep quiet and risk turning bitter. As a rule that seems to be the good course to take. However, you also want to keep your job (maybe you have a family and a mortgage?), so avoiding an angry confrontation is important. The diagnosis problem reappears here. Can you speak your mind without losing control and provoking a defensive response from the supervisor? Is the supervisor the kind of person who will listen and possibly admit an error in judgment? Depending on how you answer these questions, the choice of what to do the next day may become clearer.

You could formulate your reasoning as a general guideline: "Whenever you have been the victim of unjustified criticism, prefer speaking up and trying to clear the air over keeping quiet and turning bitter, unless doing so is likely to provoke an angry confrontation that endangers your job security." Such a guideline may not be something you ever bother to formulate as a rule, but something like it may come in handy if you have to give advice to someone else in the future.[7]

What if the issue is a "better time" for a larger group? Suppose you find yourself rushing around one morning trying to leave the house by ten o'clock in order to pick up some teammates whom you promised to drive to the game beginning at eleven? Why are you inconveniencing yourself by rushing to stay on schedule? You have known others who were always late in arriving, so that clearly is an option. Why not slow down and take it easy? If you reject that option, perhaps you operate according to a different understanding of what is good to do. Your reasoning could be formulated as a rule: "Prefer keeping your promises and avoiding inconvenience to others over breaking your promises just to serve your own convenience." Whose "time" do you care more about in this case?

A final example may suggest how third meanings of "good" and of "someone" are present in various rules. Perhaps you have heard about various "dumping" controversies. As a matter of law some pesticides manufactured in the USA cannot be sold in the USA because of environmental hazards. Similarly some types of children's clothing, deemed insufficiently flame retardant, can be made in the USA but not sold there. So why produce them? Other countries impose fewer restrictions, and so they are export goods. The question is whether they should be exported if they are known to pose a threat to human well being. One response is that such economic transactions are perfectly legitimate if both exporting and importing parties are in compliance with their respective legal codes. To ban such exports uni-laterally is to put one's country's economic interests at a competitive disad-vantage since its competitors are unlikely to restrain their exports out of con-sideration for the well being of non-citizens. The argument concludes: It is up to each country's government to safeguard the interests of its citizens; it is not the job of foreign governments to protect those same citizens.

What do you think? Is any country ever obligated to put its economic self-interest second to the well being of non-citizens? What would an affir-mative answer presuppose? Are there goods that are due your protection even if they cost your "tribe" some benefits? What rule would express this vantage point on what "someone" is due? Perhaps the generality of the Gold-en Rule comes to mind. With more precision, the rule might read: "Before acting in ways that affect the well-being of others, stop to consider whether you would think them justified in treating you the way you are about to treat them." Here there is no mention of who these others are; they could be fam-ily members, friends, complete strangers, foreigners. Does the rule make these distinctions? Are they perhaps not relevant differences? With this last question you have come full circle back to the diagnosis problem: What details in a case make one rule relevant and another irrelevant? This is not an easy question to answer since the response will often vary with the per-son who asks the question. "Relevance" or significance will vary depending on the person who asks the question. Why? You might recall the meaning of "horizon" discussed in Chapter Two. Later chapters will provide even more clues to this latest puzzle.[8]

WHY ARE THERE METHODS?

If you understand that moral rules are part of your inheritance but that you still need to raise and answer further questions before applying them, then talk of a "social dialectic" may not be so mystifying. What you inherit or bor-row from others is a starting point, but in time your questioning may erode your confidence in what you first learned. Can you think of an instance when you reflected on something you had always assumed to be true and wound up changing your mind? What do you think now about that experience? Did your understanding change for the better? Was this an experience of being more careful in moral inquiry?

If you are starting to develop the habit of pausing to answer such questions, you may be accumulating evidence against some popular beliefs and clichés. For instance, have you heard people say that morality is just a matter of personal opinion or preference? Have you heard some say that morality is just a matter of social conditioning? The first claim implies that morality is a private affair, more a matter of private intuitions than of shared meanings. The second view makes morality a social product individuals presumably adopt without questioning. Each of the two views ignores one or the other polarity in a social dialectic. Take the diagram S < – > I as suggesting the two terms in the dialectical relation between some social order (S) and some individual (I): "Society forms the individual, but the individual can act back on society." To deny either term in the relation is to ignore some part of reality.[9] Either one overlooks the prevalence of belief or shared meaning in moral understanding or one ignores the capacity individuals have for knowing the difference between the good sense and the nonsense they may have inherited.

Each oversight promotes the view that ethics cannot be a field of serious inquiry since what it studies is either private opinion or the undetectable prejudices of some group, neither of which is properly termed knowledge.[10] If this were the case, then why bother with a course on ethics? More personally, why should you ever try to change other people's minds by arguing with them about some moral issue? Indeed, why should you ever try to be careful in making decisions if choices are merely matters of personal intuitions or public indoctrination? If your own performance in deciding how to act is familiar to you, then you probably already recognize that personal intuitions are much like guesses. They lead up to but do not answer the further question about what is true. Similarly, you know that what "they say" is a starting point but not necessarily the final word about what you can claim to know. All of this will, of course, be more apparent if you have practiced self-attention and have taken the time to reflect on your own performance in decision-making. The self-study of you, the inquirer, will begin to provide evidence against clichés about morality and ethics.

Besides such personal evidence, there is historical evidence that moral inquiry and other forms of inquiry are neither wholly private nor wholly public. Much of what the preceding section on moral rules contained applies as well to methods. For instance, just as early socialization allows the next generation to share in the group's understanding (or misunderstanding) of right and wrong, so schooling introduces future scholars and scientists to the agreed upon procedures in different disciplines. Were you gradually taught the difference between right and wrong ways of doing things? You might easily think of examples starting with basic addition and subtraction exercises in elementary school. Did you learn how to operate with algebraic equations in high school? When did you first discover the benefits of composing an outline before beginning to write a lengthy paper? Perhaps in college you have learned something about random sampling techniques. Was this another case of acquiring nominal understanding or do you know why randomness requires more than stopping people on the street and asking their opinions?

In graduate school you may learn procedures in medical research or methods for dating fossils. In the work force you may learn quality control procedures on a manufacturing line or methods for tracking consumer spending patterns. When any of this is happening, you are not expected to discover on your own how things should be done; instead, you are being taught how others already think things should be done. In a variety of ways others will test your understanding of their understanding. They will expect you to become competent in their procedures and ways of evaluating the results of inquiry. In general, competence means thinking and acting according to the conventions of some group. Failure to conform to those conventions will sometimes provoke a judgment of incompetence.

So far these remarks on methods have stressed the social pole in the dialectic. Where does the other pole appear? Methods do not guarantee good results. They serve as intelligent ways of going about tasks, ways that shift the odds persons will successfully complete the tasks. Again, the easiest examples may be the earliest. Think of the advantage of doing an outline before beginning to write a long paper. What is the alternative? Putting ink to blank pages with no clear plan in mind is likely to produce unexpected dead ends and disorganized remarks. Without a plan the writer encountering a dead end may throw away what is already written and start off with a new blank page – hardly an exercise in efficiency.

But an outline does not guarantee that the paper will be worth reading. Following medical procedures does not guarantee that a diagnosis will be accurate or a treatment successful. You know as much already from an algebra class; following the step-by-step procedures did not always lead you to the correct solution. Why not? Again, as in the case of moral rules, knowing a procedure does not answer all the relevant questions. A procedure is analogous to a tool whether it be a hammer or a piano. Just having either instrument offers no assurance that a house will be well built or a musical composition well played. What more do you need? An easy answer is you need an intelligent and competent user of the instrument. Is that enough to give due credit to the individual pole in the dialectic between inherited procedures and the persons who employ them?

More credit than this is due to intelligent subjects; for how do methods originate? A simple example may suggest something about the origins of fairly sophisticated and possibly mysterious procedures in the sciences. Imagine a sixteen-year-old getting his first car. He goes out one morning and it will not start. Knowing next to nothing about auto mechanics and having no family member or friends who know more than he does and being strapped for cash, what is he to do? For lack of a better alternative, he opens the hood and begins tinkering. His approach is one of trial and error. Suppose he tries first this and then that, but still the car does not start. Finally, on his eighth try the engine turns over and off he drives. What new insights does he drive off with? You might guess he has a positive insight about what specific action seems to have solved his problem. Do you suspect he also has some negative insights? What has he learned from his first seven attempts?

Suppose the car refuses to start a week later. Where does the young owner begin this time? Unless he likes to waste time and energy or has a poor memory, he begins by rejecting the first seven trials and adopting the eighth.[11] Now let him spend a number of years tinkering with cars and he may acquire an extensive understanding of how they work and of what needs to be done when they break down. Through personal inquiry and testing of guesses, he may become something of a master mechanic.

Obviously other car owners encounter problems, but the master mechanic now offers them a shortcut – he publishes an auto repair manual. In effect, the slowly accumulated insights of the single individual can become a public possession, not as ink marks on the manual's pages but as shared meanings readers grasp with far less effort than the author expended originally. Such is the case with far more elaborate procedures in research and problem-solving. The understanding that creative persons first achieve through trial and error gradually accumulates in them as mastery of some area of inquiry, and they can share it with others.

What tends to happen is that later generations encounter the formulated results of such efforts and learn little about their genesis. Have your textbooks tended to repeat answers, conclusions and procedural guidelines without mentioning anything about the slow process that led up to them? Of course, Newton and Einstein get credit for various laws, but where are the records of their climbing toward those conclusions? How was either individual operating along the way? If your classes have ignored the performance that precedes the conclusions, you may have difficulty with this next puzzle: Did Sir Isaac Newton discover or invent the law of gravity? What have your textbooks said? Do you know why they are only half right?

Before concluding this section on methods, you might notice something strange about the original designers of such procedures. While later generations may copy what predecessors said were better ways of doing something, how did the latter ever discover that there could be improvements in how they did things? Presumably they were going along doing things in the old ways they had inherited; how then did they learn to try something new? Rather than talk of "genius" or "serendipity" or "creative inspiration," you might notice a feature of your own thinking (noticed already if you have been pausing at the recommended places in the text). You can ask questions about anything, and so you can make your own conscious operations the objects of your attention and questioning. A fancy word for this is "reflexivity." A useful image may be that of a loop that bends back on or returns to its starting point. In other words, some creative persons paid attention to how they were operating; they gained some insight into what they were doing, and by trial and error they thought of ways of doing things better. In deciding to do things differently, they were choosing to reorganize how they were operating in research or problem-solving. Such deliberate reordering of how a person operates may be an individual's contribution to the dialectic with its two polarities (S<–>I). Later generations may not make original discoveries about methods, but they will have the advantage of inheriting better ways of operating intelligently.[12]

Recall that one of the purposes of this text is to encourage you to reflect on how you operate in making moral decisions. As mentioned previously, you have been thinking and deciding for many years, but your efforts have largely been haphazard. A first step toward improving your own performance is to become more deliberately self-conscious of yourself as a detective, a correlator of clues. Has this chapter shed any light on you as a source of light?

EXERCISES

1. Describe one of your experiences in "playing detective," in trying to correlate clues and to answer is-questions about your guesses.

2. Describe an instance of the social dialectic in which you challenged an inherited belief.

3. Describe how the "diagnosis problem" showed up in your own moral decision-making. What was the moral rule that you judged relevant to the specific situation?

PATTERNS IN PERFORMANCE 4

WONDERING ABOUT WONDER

If any of the puzzles in the preceding chapters attracted your attention and you spent time puzzling over them, then you have a reference point for talk of human wonder. Likewise the earlier comments on caring about understanding will have a reference point in your experience of sticking with a puzzle and not letting it go until you solved it or were exhausted. But perhaps none of the puzzles delayed your reading. Is the old habit still in place: eyeballs scanning ink marks driven by the need to finish so many pages before the next class? If that is the case, then try to recall some instance when a different puzzle grabbed your attention and evoked the detective in you. The earlier quotations from Helen Keller's autobiography reflected her frustration and intense searching for a breakthrough regarding her puzzle. A reader can easily detect the intense curiosity which fueled both her anger and her frustration. Her curiosity (and her frustration) did not go away but steadily increased in intensity. However, the goal is not to learn about other people's minds but to discover yourself as a specimen of moral decision-making. A promising way of beginning is to focus on your experiences of puzzling.

If any of those experiences have been intense enough and if you have memories of their intensity, then some general remarks on human wonder will not seem all that strange. It is your spontaneous wondering that can set you on a new course in life. Intense caring about understanding begins a search for meaning that can occupy a lifetime. Unfavorable conditions (e.g. the press of daily work, poor schooling, noise from the street or from the tv screen) may delay and interfere with the searching, but the basic capacity is still present, much like an ember that with favorable conditions can reignite and flame forth.

As long as the capacity is present, there is hope for more light in living, for heightened self-awareness in your own search for meaning. However, obstacles are not rare. Schooling may have fostered the illusion of nominal understanding. Repeating what others have said and getting good grades for feats of memory may have given you a secure sense of knowing many things. Did the section on nominal understanding and the puzzles from psychology of perception erode your sense of security? Did the comments on moral rules leave you wondering what moral knowing is if it is not repeating what past generations have uniformly believed? Do you find yourself wishing for some relief from puzzles and questions, for a text that supplies answers and conveniently packages definitions?

Wonder is one of many desires, and you may be familiar with how they can compete for your time and attention. Do you want security and predictability? Yes, but sometimes you want adventure and novelty. Too much security and predictability and you probably feel bored; too much adventure and novelty and you grow exhausted. Has the work routine left you longing for the next vacation? But has a vacation ever left you exhausted? Where does wonder show up in this oscillation between rest and restlessness?

Suppose that any desire is a tending toward a desired objective, whether it be a means to an end or an end itself. When you are hungry you seek food; when thirsty you look for something to drink. When these desires are fulfilled, you are satisfied until desiring recurs. So there is both a tending towards and a resting. The tending is in the desiring and the rest is in the satisfaction. These recurring tendencies are part of human living. If people did not get hungry, they would soon starve. If they did not have sexual desires, the human race would eventually disappear for lack of offspring. But your wonder is a desire the primary end of which is more than the survival of the species. When Aristotle wrote that "all persons by nature desire to know," he was not talking about a desire for biological survival. To desire to know is to wonder about something as yet unknown. As unknown it may turn out to be an understanding of some practical use, but it also may not. The wondering, in general, is a reaching for an understanding which you do not yet have. If it is a restlessness similar to biological urges, it still is seeking more than an understanding of how to obtain food, shelter and sex. It can be a higher pull than the "laws of nature," and the evidence for this difference lies in what it leads to, e.g. human laws that redirect biological demands. Consider how, after the workday and supper, you can turn your mind to all sorts of fantasies, practical schemes, artistic musings and scholarly projects. In contrast, your pet dog, if left alone, will fall asleep and perhaps dream after eating. No grand projects or poetic reveries entice it into staying awake. So why are you different? Suppose this wondering is a source of human creativity, of the restless movement of human history. Why does the motion not cease? What would it be like if no one had any further questions?

If you paused over the last question, you may have noticed how much you have taken wonder for granted. Is it really possible that questioning would dry up, that no more bright ideas would occur? Would there be a loss if such were to happen? Imagine a new generation of children without any questions or a society of adults smugly confident in having all the answers. Would this be a society worth belonging to?

The possibility of such a situation need not worry you. The range of wonder is unrestricted. In principle you can raise questions about anything and everything. In practice you settle for far fewer questions, but can you anticipate what questions will occur to you tomorrow or the next day? If you cannot foresee what novel directions your curiosity will take, what dictator intent on mind-control can succeed in blocking all dissenting views? What set of inherited answers will anticipate every question from the next generation? Persons can and do ask questions about all manner of things. Of course, the press of daily occupations may often limit the range of questioning to practical concerns. Still, in moments of quiet reflection (while the dog is sleeping?), you may be drawn to deeper questions about life and death, about the past and the future. Are such questions worth cultivating? Are you worth cultivating? Just as caring about others emerges spontaneously and, absent serious trauma, develops to include broader populations, so caring about understanding emerges spontaneously and, absent serious head injury, develops to include broader ranges of inquiry. Can this development occur more deliberately? That is, can you give some direction to how this development goes forward? The last chapter indicated that methods are products of such deliberate direction of inquiry, so how you develop and expand your inquiries may be at least partially subject to your own conscious decisions. In ethical inquiry the strategy of self-attention is a first step toward such guided self-growth.

CULTIVATING SELF-KNOWLEDGE

Self-attention is a strategy for exploring how your mind works, for understanding what you are doing in puzzling, guessing, reflecting, deciding etc. It assumes the explorer is conscious, but what does it mean to be conscious? A contrast may help. If you are in dreamless sleep, there will be nothing to recall when you awake; but when you are awake, you at least are aware of

45

something and can recall this awareness later. You may be minimally aware in hearing sounds of passing traffic or you may be more fully aware in listening for the sound of an ambulance you have summoned.[1] But you may notice that you are conscious in two ways. First, you can be consciously attending to something, e.g. words that you recognize or ones that you are puzzling about. Are you conscious of these ink marks? Second, you can be conscious of your looking at ink marks or listening to sounds. In this second way consciousness is self-presence or awareness of yourself as looking and listening.

Paying attention to how you are conscious is not some sort of inward look by which you see or imagine what is happening in your mind. The conscious mental activity is not something visible or imaginable – like the bubbles used above the heads of cartoon characters. For example, you can look out the window and recognize the trees, the road, the neighbor's house. You are conscious of these objects, but you can also reflectively distinguish between what you see and the act of seeing. You can think to yourself: "Yes, I see the trees, but I am also seeing." The latter is a conscious act. You can stop it by closing your eyes or you can redirect its focus by turning your attention to a different object. But is the activity of seeing not also an "object" of which you are conscious? How can the visible trees and houses be objects of consciousness and the invisible activities of the mind also be objects of consciousness?

A convenient labeling may help you track the differences in these objects. Let the trees and houses as seen be called "data of sense." Let the acts of seeing or listening or imagining or puzzling be called "data of consciousness." Clearly they are related since without acts of seeing there are no objects seen.[2] Or if you prefer: If a tree falls in the forest and no one is around…?

The strategy of self-attention focuses on both the data of consciousness and the data of sense. The earlier invitation was for you to track how you are operating in moral decision-making, and the novel request was for you to track both the details of the situation you were trying to change and how you proceeded to understand and to evaluate the situation and your options. The elementary mapping of Chapter Three was to provide some help in this effort to attend to your own invisible mental performance. The hope is that you can "raise" your own level of consciousness so that you will begin to take more notice of the mental acts by which you come to know what a situation is and what you can and should do about it. The shift in focus from the objects seen and understood to activities by which you see and understand is not commonly made. But the climb to self-knowledge requires this shift. If you remain a stranger to your own mind, how much self-knowledge can you claim to have?

The climb to self-knowledge may begin with noticing the data of your own consciousness, exploring their differences and trying to relate them to each other. How do you begin to focus on these possible ways of learning about yourself? The puzzles and questions in previous chapters were one way of beginning. You might pause here just to daydream. Do you notice that various sights and sounds occur, that random images appear and disappear, that various thoughts, memories and expectations occur? Now imagine what happens when something or someone disrupts your daydreaming. The flow of feelings and thoughts is interrupted. If the disruption is startling, you may ask, "What was that?" You are surprised, and the response is one of at least mild curiosity. A trivial example of such surprise is what happens when your routine walking down stairs is disrupted by your expecting a final step where there is none. Suddenly the bottom of the stairs is not where you assumed it would be. The surprise shifts your conscious operating into a new gear; you become more present to yourself and your walking. If you like, think of this shift as the transition from sensation to perception. Before there was a smooth flow of sensations; now there is a focused perception on just some of them.[3]

Such shifts can be abrupt as when your alarm clock goes off or your driving is altered by the sound of approaching sirens. What was a smooth flow of feelings and thoughts in an untroubled state of mind can become the experience of more intense concentration on or perception of sights and sounds. Both the flow and the more intense experience involve what are called "sensitive presentations:" sights, sounds, feelings, smells, and so on. Let this type of consciousness be called the *empirical type of consciousness*. Why? The word "empirical" means "what is experienced," and what you are conscious of at this level are experiences of sights, feelings, motions and so on. These are the sensitive presentations that provide the material for your questioning about what you just saw, heard or felt.

As in the previous example of a sound that awakens you in the middle of the night, the sensitive presentations are often quickly followed by alert wondering and the asking of questions. Without the data that experience provides there would be nothing to wonder about, and without the questioning the data would not be understood. The questioning, however, is a shift to a different type of consciousness. Now you are not only aware of the sensitive presentations (empirical consciousness) but also of your own efforts to understand them. Let this new way of being conscious be called the *intellectual type of consciousness*. How is it distinct? Here you are operating by inquiring, coming to some understanding and formulating what you have understood. This is where detective work flourishes. The clues from the crime scene provide the data, but the task is to make sense of them. Just staring around the crime scene solves nothing. Veteran detectives bring a wealth of prior training and understanding to their reading of the clues. Their questioning already anticipates what they should be asking about and looking for. It is their intelligent questioning that focuses the looking and begins to sort out the relevant from the irrelevant data. Their questioning runs ahead, as it were, of what is known and anticipates the unknown. The what-questions may be voiced or unvoiced, but the detectives are operating on the data, not mindlessly but intelligently. They are trying to understand how the potential clues might be correlated or ordered in a meaningful way, and they have some "ideas" about how to do this. Put more generally, when you tackle a familiar problem, are your perceptions and questions more intelligently focused than when the problem is quite new and strange?

You might think back to the first exercise at the end of the previous chapter. What happened when you played detective? What were the clues you had? How intently did you focus on them? Did your first guesses anticipate types of solutions with which you were already familiar? If you were fortunate, something suddenly came together, the clues "fell into place," and you understood how to solve the puzzle. This "something" is called a direct insight. It often occurs suddenly (directly) and orders the data in your mind in a new way. A sense of satisfaction replaces an earlier frustration, perhaps accompanied by the question, "Why did it take so long to get the answer?"

When a direct insight occurs, there is a further effort required before your operations at the intellectual level come to their proper conclusion. You need to transform the direct insight into some kind of formulation such as is found in an idea, hypothesis or definition. This can require some labor. Think of the difficulty you may have had finding the right words for expressing your answer on an exam. In trying to explain something to a friend, you may have noticed a gap between what you understood and adequate expression of it. Efforts to close this gap are part of effective teaching. Additionally, turning insights into formulations is necessary if you are to test the correctness of your understanding. Imagine the task of trying to verify what someone claimed to understand but could not state in even a minimally precise way.

By paying attention to what you are doing when you are puzzle-solving, you are gathering evidence for understanding yourself as a person who operates with various types of consciousness. Have you ever asked a question, had an insight or understood something? You have (How else would you be able to read this?), so you have been conscious in the intellectual way.

Still, having direct insights and coming up with a formulation in response to a what-question is not the same as knowing. Recall the earlier mapping and the difference between what-questions and is-questions. Bright ideas do turn up, but sometimes they lose their shine after further checking. Why the further checking? As noted earlier, when the issue is something you really care about, you go on to ask further questions: "It sounds good, but is it true?" "Looks like it will work, but does it?" These further questions are signs of a shift in you to a third type of consciousness. Let it be labeled the rational form of consciousness. Here the earlier bright idea or hunch is the focus of attention. In ordinary language people talk about weighing evidence, testing hypotheses, offering reasons for their opinions, checking the stories of suspects against the available clues. The goal is to pass judgment, not on the evidence but on how it is understood. You might think of how a jury operates after hearing the prosecutor and defense counsel tell conflicting stories about the defendant. What must the jury determine? They are expected to determine which of the stories they have received from the lawyers is correct or at least credible "beyond a reasonable doubt." They are to make a judgment about those competing ways of understanding the defendant's relation to the crime. How do they arrive at the judgment? Ideally they begin by revisiting the evidence that has been presented. What does this involve? In simplified form, it involves comparing the different stories about the defendant to the evidence. This reaching for an assessment of the link between story and evidence is a reaching for a *reflective insight*. What the jury reflects upon are the connections or "fit" between evidence and story. Only if one of the stories fits the evidence far better than the other can the jury confidently answer the question before it. Its task is to determine the truth "beyond a reasonable doubt," and doing so requires the reflective insight that grasps either the fit or the misfit between evidence and story.[4]

Perhaps you find the courtroom example unpersuasive. Fine – the earlier refrain returns: "Don't believe a word of this." Take yourself as a specimen of what all this talk of types of consciousness is about and test these claims against your own efforts to settle questions of fact. Exercises at the end of this chapter will ask you to do just this. There will be puzzles and questions and so a searching for direct insights and their formulation into hypotheses or definitions, but your first formulations may be inadequate. Judging whether this is the case depends upon having reflective insights which will then make it possible to judge whether the hypothesis is correct. But find this out for yourself – and possibly find something wrong with this text?

To summarize this section: its examples of persons trying to settle questions of fact identified the first three types of conscious operation (empirical, intellectual, rational), but you also make decisions about how and when and whether to act. If these operations are not aiming at settling what is the case but at determining what will be the case, you expect there to be additions to the first three ways of being conscious.

Decision-making is about what ought to be the case. Its focus then is on the future, on what could become but is not yet a fact. There is then a reason to speak of further types of consciousness that are concerned with possibilities. Consider your own routine planning of vacations or semester schedules. You are not trying to determine what is currently the case but what would be good to bring about. When you succeed in your decisions, do you feel satisfied with how you have turned a possibility into a reality? Do you take credit or responsibility for such smart planning and acting? Let this new distinction be termed *responsible consciousness*. Perhaps not a very attractive label, but it does point to and approximate something important in human living. Here persons are deciding what to make of their lives, what inherited situations to change, what futures are worth creating.[5] These are the activities that commonly are called moral acts, and so here is what ethics studies. More details about this distinct type of conscious operation will show up below and in Chapter Five. Perhaps you are ready to expand the earlier mapping of Chapter Three.

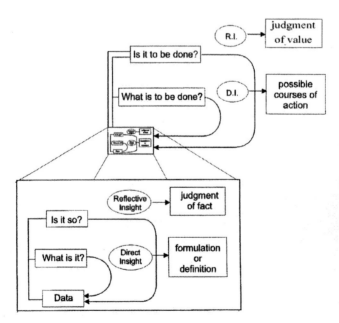

While the diagram is a useful summary, some further comments on its details may be helpful. Two interrelated patterns are distinguished. The first, the structure of wonder, maps the movement from data to the judgment of fact. The pattern includes three contexts for operations and, in total, seven elements or parts: data, what-question, direct insight, formulation or definition, is-question, reflective insight and judgment of fact. This first pattern provides the material to be processed in the second pattern, the structure of concern. The latter (labeled above as responsible consciousness) can be divided into two distinct contexts or parts: *deliberating* and *deciding*. To the earlier seven elements you can add six more: what-question (What is to be done? or What can be done?); direct insight; identified options (possible courses of action); the question for decision (Is it to be done?); reflective insight; judgment of value.

Notice how both patterns include direct and reflective insights. They include direct insights (formulated as guesses about what may be the case or as options, i.e. guesses about what can be made the case) and reflective insights about those guesses (yielding either judgments of fact or judgments of value). This should not surprise you since you use the same thinking process to discover and to evaluate both what is the case and what should be the case.

What is different about the two patterns are the mode and end of questioning. In the structure of wonder thinking is oriented primarily by the demands of curiosity. The desired end is an understanding and judgment about what is in fact the case. Think of a scientist developing and testing a theory as a typical example of this pattern. In the structure of concern the desired end is understanding and judging possibilities worth making realities. Curiosity, which dominated the structure of wonder, now serves the desire to do the right thing. The dominant concern is identifying and adopting worthwhile courses of action. Your daily practical planning is a typical instance of the structure of concern in action.

THE STRUCTURE OF WONDER

If you track how you operate in all five contexts, you may discover these dynamic and recurrent patterns in your own living. This much is an addition to your self-knowledge. You can find proof of the addition by checking for patterns in your efforts to solve puzzles and to make choices. What you gain is more familiarity with how you routinely operate. For example, have you become more aware of all five contexts and so more aware of yourself in moving from one to the other? Contrast your experience of hearing a pleasing melody with your activity in trying to solve a math problem. The former is an activity in the empirical or experiential context – the pleasure evoked by sounds is what you experience. Struggles with math problems occur in the intellectual context and involve more than the data of sense. In fact, you ignore the size of the print and whether you are pleased by the shapes of the numbers. Both are irrelevant to finding a solution and so a distraction from your purpose. And once you have a hunch as to the solution, your purpose shifts to determining whether you have it right. Then the focus is on fitting the answer to the clues you have available. In addition, when the issue involves not only finding the right answer but doing the right thing, the further question of responsible choice arises. You could have all the facts in the world, and still they would not settle the question of what you should do. Think of times when the choices were pressing. Suppose you are thinking of proposing marriage to someone. Your future is in the balance. Listening to pleasing melodies and solving math problems seem trivial in comparison. All of you becomes involved in deliberating and deciding. Your conscious awareness is much more intense. What does this tell you about differences in how wondering and questioning occur?

You may have enough insights into your own conscious operations to recognize why they form "structures." A structure is a set of interrelated parts making up a whole. If you are trying to understand what you are doing when you are reaching for understanding, you will have noticed some "parts." Broadly sketched, understanding is a process of movement and rest in which the movement occurs through raising questions and the rest arrives through answering them. You have tracked this process of questioning and answering across a series of successive contexts. The empirical context supplies the data for your questioning. The latter occurs in the intellectual context as you try to make sense of the data of experience. Judging or verifying what sense you have made is an activity occurring in the rational context. Here your questioning is, first, about what you can do and, second, about what you should do. But you may wonder how these "parts" are related among themselves and why they recur in a somewhat orderly manner?

Does it make any sense to you to talk of the parts as "internally related" among themselves such that each part is what it is by virtue of its relation to other parts?[6] Think of how a what-question is related to a sensitive presentation. The latter evokes the former since, without something to attend to, what would you have to puzzle about? Likewise the perceived presentation as an object of your interest stands out from the flow of indeterminate sensations because of your focused wondering. Keep going: Why do is-questions arise? If you have no previous answers or guesses to evaluate, then why would this second type of question occur to you? You ask it because you have a hunch you want to check, and you want to do some checking because you have a hunch. Sounds circular? Welcome to one meaning of "internal relations" among objects or among activities. Since the focus here is on acts of meaning, the internal relations are among operations (or parts) that are dynamically related. That is, the operations or mental activities presuppose one another, occur because of one another and build on one another. The "parts" assemble themselves in to a whole.

Put another way, the operations do not follow one another arbitrarily but occur in a fairly well-ordered sequence. You might find helpful analogies in some forms of dance and music. Are you familiar with some musical compositions in which the parts follow a prescribed order and lead up to an anticipated and conventional type of ending? Do you know of some traditional forms of dance that also have an internal structure of prescribed steps in an ordered sequence? Perhaps the dancing you are familiar with is less prescribed in its motions; you can pretty much move in any of a number of ways and still be dancing. However, the way you proceed in trying to understand follows a more formal pattern. Your operations are purposeful (you want to know), and the individual acts contribute to this purpose; they play their parts in reaching toward the goal. This is what accounts for their recurrence in a somewhat orderly manner.

Perhaps these remarks on "structure" are still too obscure. The remedy may be to pause and to reflect on your own experience in puzzling. For example, have you ever been driving along and suddenly recognized the smell of something burning? Your first guess (and hope?) is that the smell is coming from outside your car. How do you check this guess? Continuing to drive, hoping that the smell goes away, is one way of checking. What if the smell continues? What do you do next? Even if this has not been your experience, you might conjecture about what you would do. Is there any order to how your imagined responses occur? Is there a completeness to the scenario when you find the source of the smell and decide on what to do about it? If so, then you have some sense of a structure in your reaching for understanding. The "parts" are activities; they complement one another in pursuit of a completeness or "whole;" their occurrence is not just any sequence but follows a relatively stable order.

What moves you along from one type of activity to another? The types of questions are the explicit signs of shifting from one context of conscious operation to the next, but the implicit dynamism is your own wondering or desire to know. Is this at all plausible? Can you make any sense of the claim that your wondering is structured? Again, do not accept such claims on faith but check them against yourself as a specimen of wondering.

METHOD IN ETHICS

Maybe you have discovered five distinct types of conscious activity in yourself and maybe you have recognized a pattern among the various operations. There still is the claim that the operations are recurrent. What might this mean? Suppose the process of reaching for understanding yields results; you find answers to your questions. Do you retain in memory at least some of these results? Obviously, yes; otherwise, you would have to keep learning the same things over and over again. What you learn becomes part of the habitual context of your living and thinking. In other words, your previous understanding provides the means for your future searching and deciding. This much is uncontroversial. Once you learn to ride a bicycle, you leave behind all the clumsy falls and brave choices to try again. Once a recipe works, you can rely on it for a different dinner party. The point is that further questions and learning do not occur in a vacuum; they build on what you have already achieved. If this were not the case, then talk of development in your understanding, both factually and morally, would be very puzzling. But if you have had some insights, made some judgments of fact and decided some actions are better than others, then you have become a "context" for making new judgments and decisions.

"Context" is a useful label for thinking about the role of habits in human living. Familiar examples of habits include the routines people follow in getting up in the morning as well as the predictable responses shy persons exhibit in public speaking. The strategy of self-attention calls for a heightened consciousness of such routines and a deliberate reordering of some of them since "bad habits" do become established patterns in living. In this text you have heard mention of random questioning as a routine open to improvement. Everyday thinking tends to be a "messy" and unpredictable activity, but some improvement is possible through reflecting on the activity and discovering how to do it better. Sports analogies may come to mind. Professional golfers videotape their swings, watch the tapes and learn to spot and to correct problems. Baseball players do the same. In time the "contexts" out of which the players operate change. They develop new habits that are a basis for adjusting to and improvising in new situations. Can the same be true for how persons set about questioning, judging and deciding?

This chapter has invited you to make explicit your own structured wondering. Ideally the examples and comments have led to some insights into how you make sense of situations and opportunities. If so, then your context has changed. You now are more aware of your own mind-in-act. So what? Recall the earlier remarks on personal and pragmatic reasons for self-attention. Self-knowledge is not incidental to leading a richer life; at least that was the implication of the Socratic maxim. The pragmatic rationale was less remote from common-sense thinking. If puzzling and understanding and deciding are all ingredients in moral choosing, then understanding those operations is a first step toward improving how you make moral choices. The point is uncontroversial when you are hiring plumbers or electricians – you expect that they know what they are doing. Why not have the same expectation about moral decision-making? Should it not be the case that moral deciders know what they are doing?

The preceding sections of this chapter were an introduction to some of the ways in which you arrive at decisions. The hope is that, with further reflection, you will gain even further insight into how you operate; you will gradually know what you are doing. Slowly you may find it easy to shift your attention back and forth between a problem that intrigues you and the mental activities that you engage in to solve the problem. This habit of divided attention does not come easily, but the effort to acquire it seems worthwhile. Are you convinced that it is? If you need further convincing, consider two brief arguments. First, what is the alternative to having an adequate understanding of your own performance in decision-making? You might recall the remarks in the Introduction on multiplicity. If you are unfamiliar with what you are doing in understanding and deciding, there will be no shortage of writers who will tell you what it is you are doing.[7] Of course, they do not agree among themselves, so you can either listen to the "babble of voices" or try the alternative route of self-attention.

Second, think of the apprentice plumber who has few clues on how to proceed; now contrast that individual with the master plumber. Which one would you hire? Shift your focus to moral decision-making and ask whose views are worth listening to: the unreflective individual who has strongly voiced (borrowed?) opinions on many topics or the person who has spent years reflecting on how to make careful choices and then actually making them?

All of this effort to familiarize yourself with your own performance in thinking and deciding aims at expanding your understanding of how you operate in being morally responsible. Do you know some of the "parts" of this process and how they are related? Can you track their occurrence in your own life? If so, then you have the beginnings of a method or procedure for analyzing and evaluating a range of yet unmet puzzles.[8] The emphasis should be on "beginnings" since this method is not something one is comfortable with after a few weeks, a semester or even several years of reflection. But you have to start somewhere. As the cautionary note in Chapter One stated, you should not expect in climbing to leap past setting up the initial base camp.

The next chapter will propose some further climbing. Before then some puzzles may help you identify, label and differentiate some of the basic acts that occur when you are problem-solving.

EXERCISES

Reading about a strategy of self-attention is not the same as practicing it. The earlier mapping and naming of various acts and types of consciousness will remain just information until you can refer those terms to an emerging understanding of your own performance. In the puzzles that follow, the primary goal is not to solve them but to identify as clearly as you can what you are doing in reaching for solutions. Ideally you will gain more confidence in practicing the strategy of self-attention, but expect some frustration at first. You might also expect old habits still to be present: the answer becomes the goal and the process leading to it gets neglected. Try to resist.

1. Identify the basis for the ordering of the following letters:

OTTFFSS....

2. Identify the pattern among the following letters:

$$\frac{A \qquad EF}{BCD}$$

3. Dickens, Einstein, Freud and Kant are professors of English, Physics, Psychology and Philosophy (but not necessarily in that order). Match the professors to their fields using the following information:

(a) Dickens and Freud were in the audience when the psychologist delivered his first lecture.

(b) Both Einstein and the philosopher were friends of the physicist.

(c) The philosopher has attended lectures by both Kant and Dickens.

(d) Dickens has never heard of Freud.

4. Try to find a shortcut for adding the numbers 1, 2, 3, 4, 5... up to 100.

CHOOSING WHAT'S GOOD

5

CARE AND MORAL CONCERNS

The last chapter added further details to the earlier mapping of how you operate in puzzle-solving and deciding. This chapter will focus on that part of your structured wondering concerned with choosing what to do. As before, questioning is the key datum of consciousness that will distinguish one way of operating from another. Besides what-questions and is-questions, you have also noticed questions for deliberation and questions for decision. The first two types of questions occur as you try to discover what is the case. The last two are forms your curiosity takes when the issue is what can and should be done. If the central puzzle in ethics is about the right way to live, then these two questions specify some of the steps in reaching an answer to that puzzle.

When persons ask these questions, they have to desire to bring about something good or to prevent something bad from happening. The earlier Roman maxim may come to mind: Care is the mother of all things. Without care not much happens in our lives. This is especially true when indifference accompanies the experience of decision-making. Have you ever played out the old scene between friends: "What do you want to do?" "I don't know; what do you want to do?" "I don't know"?

What is missing in such a scene are sufficiently strong feelings for or against a course of action. Until they are present, decisions are likely put on hold. But perhaps you have heard that careful choosing requires you to put aside feelings in favor of more detached deliberation. If you ever sit on a jury, you may hear advice to that effect. A judge will instruct you to consider only the facts in the case and not to let your feelings for or against the accused affect your verdict. Or perhaps you have had the experience of feeling that you just had to buy that fantastic outfit; you purchased it but then reached your credit card limit well before your next paycheck. In time you may start giving yourself advice about not acting on feelings or impulses.

All the same, feelings are what give flavor and momentum to your living. As one philosopher wrote:

> Because of our feelings, our desires and our fears, our hopes, our joys and sorrows, our enthusiasm and indignation, our esteem and contempt, our trust and distrust, our love and hatred, our tenderness and wrath, our admiration, veneration, reverence, our dread, horror, terror, we are orientated massively and dynamically in a world...[1]

Does this seem true to you? The earlier account of Helen Keller's life seems to square with this view of the role of feelings in living. Her feelings of frustration and anger motivated her struggle to discover a way of communicating. Recall her experience by the well when she grasped the meaning of language: "That living word awakened my soul, gave it life, hope, joy, set it free." Those feelings of liberation and joy stayed with her throughout her life and supported her efforts to overcome her disabilities as a deaf and blind person. Eventually she learned to read and to write; she attended college and even learned how to speak. Without the intense desires within her, these achievements would have been unlikely. So is the advice to leave feelings out of your decision-making erroneous? Clearly great efforts need the motivating force of strong feelings. Perhaps the question is not whether to exclude feelings but what feelings to include, what desires to follow.

A distinction between "motivations" and "orientations" may help in answering this question about feelings and desires. Without a long digression on the reasons for this distinction, an analogy may pin down the differences in meaning between the two terms. Imagine a multi-storied building with its boiler room in the basement and its executive suites on the top floors. "Motivation" corresponds to the feelings, urges and impulses that well up from the lower floors. For good or ill they appear in human living. "Orientation" corresponds to the top-down direction of such feelings by executive decision-making. So your motives are sometimes intense feelings that spur you to action. But recall the remarks in Chapter Four on deliberation and on cultivating self-knowledge. You have had experiences of pausing to reflect on options and of delaying your responses to your likes and dislikes. With some development in self-understanding comes an estimate of your readiness to discriminate among competing desires and to use your best judgment in cooperating with some and resisting others. From such experiences you can estimate how much and how often you are at home in the executive suites. When your orientation to what you feel and judge to be good is habitual, then you routinely decide to pursue worthwhile ends by thoughtfully selected means. In contrast, if there are occasions when your choices have been at odds with your best judgment, you might wonder who is in charge of what goes on in the building of your life.

Hints about different orientations were present in the section in Chapter Two on "Horizons of Caring." It offered a preliminary description of different goods worth pursuing. That subject will turn up in this chapter as well, but presumably your viewpoint will be more developed because of the intervening insights into yourself. Let's begin with the orientation corresponding to the first meaning of "good," i.e. what is in the interests of "me and mine." Imagine you are driving home from class and you notice smoke on the horizon. You assume there is a fire somewhere but drive on not too concerned. But suppose as you get closer to home the smoke appears to be coming from your neighborhood. Besides a more intense interest in the smoke, do you also drive faster? Why? The thought that it could be your house on fire and a feeling of fear are what absorb your attention.

In this scenario a shift occurred from mild curiosity or wonder ("What's burning?") to intense concern. If wonder drives persons in the pursuit of knowledge, concern is what drives moral living. Your concern about family, home and belongings came to the forefront when you thought maybe it was your house on fire. Your speeding up was not so much to settle a question of fact as it was a response to caring about yourself and others. They are worthy of concern, and so these feelings are good to have and to act upon.

Is it plausible, then, that moral living is motivated by concerns, by persons responding to what they call good? You may have some reservations. For example, just because a person calls something "good" does not make it good or worthy of concern. Recall the basic insight that what seems good is not automatically the same as what is good. How do you tell the difference? This is a what-question asking you to care about settling a question of fact. It is further evidence that your moral living, motivated by feelings, does not go its own way indifferent to the search for knowledge. Developing an orientation toward what is genuinely good requires such a search. But identifying what should concern you and be the object of your choice may not always be clear, and so you will have to settle questions of fact. Sometimes what you need to do is rather simple and straightforward, but other times you need to give it a lot of thought. At a minimum, you probably should give some thought to what you prize as really important and to the likely consequences of pursuing it. Whatever choice you make, the result of action (or of inaction) will be a change in what is the case (or a preservation of what is already the case). Either may be good, but rarely is it enough just to wish for good outcomes; you need to act in ways that make them more likely. But what do you know about future outcomes? Unless you are very good at crystal-ball gazing, the future remains unknown to you, and so risk is a feature of most serious decision-making. This is especially the case when choices are pressing, time is short and all the desirable information is unavailable. An old maxim in foreign policy-making holds that, when the crisis demands a response, the needed information is insufficient; but, when the information is sufficient, it is often too late and the crisis is beyond anyone's control.

The maxim may apply to your own experience. Have you ever had to make a difficult decision? Did your feelings pull you in different directions? Did you dodge the hard choice, procrastinate and hope the situation would resolve itself? Later on did you regret not acting? Did this regret change how you faced hard choices in the future? You probably have read about cases of nurses who privately questioned the decisions of physicians. On the one hand, they wanted to voice their doubts about the wisdom of a doctor's decision, but, on the other hand, they were reluctant to challenge their supposed superior in the workplace. Sometimes they hesitated and hoped the situation would resolve itself without harm to anyone. But on occasion the outcome for a patient was devastating. Then the previous silence gives way to regret and a resolve to speak up the next time. Out of such experiences can emerge a new willingness to take responsibility for anticipating good things persons can achieve and bad things they can prevent.

THE STRUCTURE OF CONCERN

As the preceding section suggested, both feelings and careful reflection are relevant to moral knowing and decision-making. To act responsibly is not simply a matter of "going with the flow," but neither is it only a matter of rational calculation. How are your feelings and your thinking related? The earlier mappings in Chapters Three and Four offered a preliminary outline of the structure of wonder and the structure of concern. You may have noticed that the pattern of operations that leads to understanding what is good to do is similar to the pattern of knowing what is the case. The differences lie in how your focus shifts from understanding what is the case to deciding what should be the case. Just as the result of puzzling about sensitive presentations, making guesses and judging them can yield knowledge, so the result of operations of responsible consciousness can yield knowledge of what is good. Of course, the result can also be a poorly formed opinion about what is good. How can you detect which outcome you have reached? This question is what motivated the earlier remarks on method in ethics. How do you go about sorting out the multiple opinions that occur to you or that others suggest to you about what is good to do? Your structured performance in answering these questions is the method basic to determining the difference between good sense and nonsense and the difference between responsible choices and irresponsible choices.

The recurrent pattern in your own experience takes the form of questioning. You begin by deliberating over ends. You ask what are worthwhile objectives and you try to figure out which to pursue. Once you make a judgment and settle on the end, you ask how you can achieve it. What is possible in this situation? What are your options? Depending on your past experiences and powers of imagination, you may envision any number of possibilities. What you are doing in asking these two questions for deliberation is comparable to asking what-questions in the context of intellectual consciousness. There you were trying to organize the data into an intelligent guess. But the possible ends and means you seek when operating as responsibly conscious are first reached by guesses about what could become the case, not guesses about what is already the case. Think of the differences among (1) asking whether you have dented a parked car; (2) wondering how you can identify the owner of the parked car you have just dented; (3) asking whether or not you should admit your responsibility for denting the other car.

Once you have possible courses of action, your next question is likely, Which should I choose? Here again there is a parallel between the is-question and the question for decision. With rational consciousness the is-question leads to a judgment about whether your understanding is a grasp of fact. With the fifth type of consciousness, the question for decision pursues a judgment about whether your understanding of some possible end or course of action is an adequate grasp of what you should do. A whole series of questions may be relevant to answering this question. For example: Is this worth attempting? Am I likely to succeed? Will anyone suffer harm? Do I feel right about doing this?

These and other questions may randomly occur to you as you try to puzzle out a right course of action. As will show up in the last three chapters, it is possible to put some order into the questions that are usually relevant to moral decision-making. This ordering of questions can serve as an instrument for guiding your reflections, but its origin lies in those structured operations recurrent on the various levels of consciousness. In abbreviated form, careful decision-making is a matter of being attentive to the situation and one's feelings; being intelligent in the puzzling one does about the situation; being rational in the judgments one makes and inventive and responsible in choosing ends and means to them. Operating in these ways is not necessarily free of doubts and uncertainty, just as raising an ordered series of questions is no guarantee of answering every question and resolving every dispute. Still, there is an advantage to understanding the relevance of some questions to careful deciding. If you have bothered to raise and to answer them with some thoroughness, your confidence in your judgment about what you should do is likely to be much higher than if your approach was much less organized. As well, the more confidence you have in your decision the greater the resolve you will have to follow through with your plans.

FEELINGS AND CHOOSING WHAT'S GOOD

Moral questioning is a pursuit of an understanding and effective embodiment of what is good. Feelings play a role in that they are responses to what "may be good." Why the qualifier "may be good"? A quick look back at childhood experiences may suffice to find an answer. Were your early likes and dislikes infallible measures of what was good? All the same, feelings are relevant to the process of deciding what is worth doing. Care is key to making human living better and to preserving what already makes it worthwhile. But there are different kinds of feelings. One distinction is between "nonintentional states and trends" and "intentional responses." You might think of exhaustion, uneasiness and bad humor as instances of nonintentional states. These are not so much chosen responses as states-of-mind you find yourself in because of lack of sleep or an upsetting event. *Nonintentional* trends are such desires as hunger or thirst or sexual excitement. Trends have goals. To be hungry is to want to eat. You do not need to imagine food to know that you are hungry. The feeling of hunger comes first; pizza fantasies come second; and then the delivery man brings satisfaction.

Feelings as *intentional* responses are reactions to what you perceive or intend.[2] For example, a flag waving while a bugle is played may evoke feelings of sadness associated with military funerals. Images of the Twin Trade Towers on fire may evoke similar feelings. Norman Rockwell paintings once evoked a sense of nostalgia. There is the famous literary example of Proust's character biting into a pastry and suddenly experiencing a flood of memories of a world that had passed away. Notice that both what is good and what is bad are apprehended in feelings. Or, to reverse the relation, you respond positively and negatively to different sounds, images and tastes. Imagine your response to a friend's smile after a long separation or your reaction to the renewed barking of your neighbor's dog at midnight. Advertizers know of such reactions to images and sounds, and they manipulate them quite deliberately to market products.

Mention of advertizers brings up a conventional distinction between two types of goods: *instrumental* goods and *terminal* goods. The former are things such as money, power or status which are means or instruments for achieving some other good. For example, money may buy security from threats to survival or power may ensure freedom from invasions of personal privacy. In contrast, terminal goods do not serve as means to some other good but are thought to be worth pursuing for their own sakes. For example, appeals to human rights are often claims that some goods should never be ignored no matter what the situation. You may have heard some arguing that torturing prisoners or alleged terrorists to extract information can be a justifiable way of saving lives. Have you also heard the objection that doing this makes persons merely means to other ends? Kant's name showed up in an earlier chapter, and you saw a reference to his Categorical Imperative. One version of it states that persons should never be treated merely as means but always as ends-in-themselves. In the background of talk of human rights and of Kant's imperative is the assumption that persons have intrinsic worth or dignity and so should not be treated as mere instruments to other ends. This may seem vague, but have you ever complained that somebody was just using you? Have you ever objected to being treated as just a "number" or one more anonymous customer with a complaint? What did your objection assume about yourself? Why not extend the same to everyone else?

The last question may revive memories of the earlier remarks on horizons of caring. It is possible to care just about yourself and those you closely identify with, e.g. family and friends. In time, however, feelings for and care about wider populations may emerge. The earlier suggestion was that such an expansion of care was an instance of moral development. Recognizing this is a step toward gaining some reflective control over feelings. Initially you may feel strongly about what you think is good or bad, but gradually you may come to understand that first reactions are not necessarily the best reactions. Think of the destructive cycle of jealousy and resentment of others for imagined wrongs. Escaping this pattern of self-destructive feelings may not be easy, but, if you succeed in escaping, this expanded understanding of and control over your own feelings can lead to a higher viewpoint on your relations to others. What once was unquestioned and seemingly justifiable suspicion of others may become a feeling you question and try to control. Feelings are spontaneous; in one sense you cannot help what you feel. However, once feelings arise, you can approve or disapprove of them, curtail or assent to them.

This shift from spontaneous reactions to reflection back on them reintroduces the three distinct uses of "good." Sometimes persons respond to something solely in terms of whether it is satisfying or dissatisfying, i.e. whether it causes them pleasure or pain. On other occasions, they respond more reflectively, even affirming what is painful as something good. Consider the patient facing surgery or the parent confronting the child about suspected drug use. Sometimes both satisfaction and higher goods coincide; doing the right thing may feel good. For example, being in love can be both a terminal good and satisfying. However, doing good does not necessarily lead to satisfaction (i.e. pleasure) just as being satisfied does not necessarily mean you have done the right thing. For example, breaking off a relationship may be the right thing to do, but it may also be painful. When a soldier dies for others, the survivors call the act "heroic," but they do not describe it as a pleasant experience.

Since this distinction between satisfaction and higher goods may still be confusing, you should pause here and try to identify how this difference has shown up in your own life. The exercise is not trivial. Some ethicists believe that moral living is a matter of rising above satisfactions and routinely showing a concern for, being orientated toward, higher goods. The "lift" or rise may begin when parents teach children to control outbursts of anger, to think about the feelings of others and to distinguish between what seems good and what is good. The "lift" for adults may be more self-directed. Moral development means more than assimilating the moral rules and customs of one's community. It requires your emergence as an "authentic person" who carefully decides what is right and wrong. The contrast here is between being an individual member of some group and being your own person. You were born an individual but can become your own person. Individuality is merely the material difference between you "here and now" and another individual "there and then." The process of becoming your own person begins in socialization (as you believe in and adopt the beliefs and practices of some group), but ultimately growth continues through your deliberate efforts to know what is good to do and to act on that knowledge. Another way of putting this: you were not born with good character but had to acquire the habits (virtues) of routinely knowing and doing the right thing. Can you think of examples where this process of moral development has been left far from complete? Can you locate yourself in this process of development? What, again, is a purpose of this text?

MULTIPLE GOODS

You probably have little trouble finding examples of competing goods and feelings. Think of the earlier description of the tension between the desire for adventure and the desire for rest. More familiar may be the importance you attach to friendship. Does it sometimes conflict with your attachment to honesty? Do you know of persons who put the desire for money first when you would rank some other good as more important? The general insight is that not all goods are of equal worth in every situation. One implication is that decision-making is often a matter of *ranking the goods* you could pursue.[3] For instance, you may like to play a particular sport, but do you ever have to forego a game because of commitments to family or work? Being aware of how your decisions reflect a ranking of goods is an important step in gaining self-knowledge.

To claim that some goods are objectively more important than others is a source of controversy among ethical theorists.[4] Again, this text tries to enter such debates indirectly. That is, it encourages you first to know yourself as a moral decider and only later to review what other people say goes on in making and evaluating moral choices. There is no shortage of viewpoints; what is usually missing is the prior climb to self-knowledge that would provide an experiential basis for evaluating different theories.

As part of that continuing climb, a new map may prove helpful. Talk of "terminal goods" is more understandable if you have some way of ordering or classifying the different kinds of goods people often mention. *Vital goods* are a first type. Good health and adequate shelter are easy examples of preconditions to living well. You might also think of some of the arts and the development of grace in movement and facility in speaking as contributing to living well. *Social goods* are means of preserving and promoting social order. Love of family and devotion to country promote a willingness to sacrifice for some good greater than one's own self. Honesty in the workplace and careful driving are ways of promoting social harmony. *Cultural goods* provide meaningful ends for much of human labor. If you do not go to work or to school every day for the sheer pleasure of either, you might wonder why anyone does? If someone suggests people work to earn a paycheck or students go to college to get a good job later on, you might ask why they want the money or the jobs. Unless a pathology is present driving someone to amass money for its own sake, most people will begin to talk about the good things that they will be able to afford. Some will mention luxury cars and new homes, but others will have dreams of world travel, becoming a patron of the arts, acquiring the leisure time to develop artistic talents they are now too busy to cultivate. Cultural activities explore the meaning and purpose of our daily lives. They are a development of our creative capacity to make meaning. Through culture humdrum daily lives are enlivened by the symbolic expressions of art and religious ritual, by the dramatic action on a stage, by the expressive words of poetry, by the liberating rhythms of dance and music, by the fantasy of film, by the demanding inquiry of the scientist or scholar.

Personal goods refer to the intrinsic or terminal worth of persons and their close relationships. Here you may locate those appeals to human rights that supposedly trump other goods, including the good of a specific social order. Persons as ends-in-themselves are not resources to be exploited by employers or manipulated by governments. Kant's Categorical Imperative asserts this good is never justifiably subordinated to some other good.

Religious goods are thought by many to be the ultimate ends of human living. You might think of cases in which persons risked their lives by refusing to do the evils commanded by civil authorities, and their rationale was that what came first in their lives was the love of God, a love betrayed by the doing of evil. In Chapter Seven a section on types of conversions will return to this type of good.

This listing of five types of goods may help you get your bearings in talk about the varied goods people pursue. (You might pause here and try to find your own examples of all five types. In doing so, can you identify which are instrumental goods and which are terminal goods?)

Even with this simple map, you can expect to find much of the talk about goods and values confusing. One of the intellectual muddles you may encounter is talk about whether any good is *objective* or whether they are all *subjective*. These labels themselves are very imprecise. At a minimum, a speaker may think all goods are subjective because it is subjects who desire and choose them. Presumably objective goods would be good even if no one desired them. A subjectivist position is that all goods are dependent on or relative to those desiring them. If freedom of speech is held up as an objective good, the response is that it is good relative to a particular political tradition but not necessarily good independent of that tradition and its adherents. In contrast, others will argue that some goods are not relative to subjects but are the measure of the rightness of human actions independently of particular traditions. The debates tend to be inconclusive and provide an example of what the Introduction termed "multiplicity." Do you recall the strategy for handling this babble of contentious voices? Paying attention to your own performance in choosing what is good to do will give you some clues on how to begin sorting out such debates. Already the section on "Social Dialectic" should have suggested some problems with the assumption that goods must be either dependent on social traditions or independent of them. Why might this either-or stance be mistaken?

MORAL DEVELOPMENT

Most of us grow up believing in and borrowing from some tradition. The story need not end there. What you initially borrow you may later reject or what you first take on faith you may come to know and to appreciate for reasons of your own. Your original state of complete dependence may lessen as you achieve a limited degree of independence. At least these are implications of social dialectic. If, as part of the exercises in Chapter Three, you located examples of such changes in your own life, these assertions will not seem vague.

But how do you know such changes are ever "changes for the better," i.e. instances of personal development? The section on "Horizons of Caring" in Chapter Two suggested one way to assess changes in moral understanding by appealing to the criterion of comprehensiveness. But further insights into moral development are possible. The general assumption already appeared: what begins spontaneously in you as caring about understanding and caring about others can expand. In short, moral development involves an expansion of mind and heart, of understanding and feeling, ordinarily leading to changes in personal performance.

The expansion of understanding may be as commonplace as learning how to solve a problem that inherited solutions are ineffective in solving. Quite a few years ago police reports in U.S. cities showed a significant rise in muggings and mailbox thefts during a three-day period each month. It was known that delivery of government checks for Social Security and welfare recipients occurred during this period. What could be done? A creative solution was what today millions take for granted: direct bank deposits of government checks. The pattern here is uncomplicated. Someone notices a problem, has a bright idea about a solution, tries it out and finds the results an improvement. Others grasp the benefits of this new approach and adapt it to their own local conditions. The widening efforts in effectively caring about others succeed because someone first cared about understanding. Of course, mistakes can also be a source of learning and a spur to improved performance. In the late nineteenth century, the high mortality rates in the maternity ward of a German hospital were the incentive that eventually improved the antiseptic practices of physicians.

You should be able by now to track the pattern in similar cases. Someone detects a threat to human well being. Intelligent persons generate questions and possible diagnoses. In response to is-questions, they settle on a diagnosis. Then they deliberate over ends, decide which is worth pursuing and go on to ask what remedies are available. After deliberating over the possible remedies, they eventually try one of the options. If the results are favorable, others facing similar problems may decide to imitate what has been done. Gradually what was first a possible improvement becomes a real improvement in human living. But notice as well the change in individual subjects. Acting intelligently to improve living can become a character trait such that a person is both intelligently and affectively better able to meet new threats to human well-being. Instead of being a person with one bright idea, the individual may become a source of many new ideas and a discerning or "wise" adviser to others. At least some may seek out such a person because they believe they have found a caring and intelligent model embodying moral and intellectual development.

But what is development? As noted before, development involves change, but change does not necessarily mean development. The earth is in continual motion, constantly changing its position relative to the sun. As a result we have day and night and the seasons of the year. However, no one calls the motion of the earth a development; it is simply a repetitive cycle. In contrast, think of changes in plants, animals and human beings. Talk of development in these cases refers to an understanding of changes as occurring in successive stages of growth. Seeds once planted develop into flowering plants that eventually produce new seeds. This cycle, though repetitive, produces something new – the seeds grow into mature plants. The same occurs in animals. In four stages butterfly larvae become caterpillars, develop into pupae and finally emerge as mature butterflies.

There are general features common to all kinds of development. First, something new happens. Second, development builds on what preceded it.

For instance, the emergence of the mature butterfly depends upon the prior stages of growth. If a prior stage does not take place, no butterfly appears. Finally, development tends toward greater differentiation and specialization. The butterfly is structurally more complex than the larvae. Evolutionary history provides numerous examples of the gradual emergence of more differentiated and specialized entities. The human species is vastly more complex and specialized than the simple one-celled animals that were its predecessors millions of years ago.

What have you noticed about your own development? The easiest examples are of physical growth, the development of motor skills, e.g. your learning to walk as a child, and the sexual changes beginning in puberty. In addition, previous chapters may have helped you recall cases of intellectual and moral growth. Understanding develops because persons have a spontaneous wonder that leads to the emergence and refinement of structured operations. Imagine how your problem-solving skills have improved over the years. Moral development builds on the same structured operations but expands their range by applying them to new possibilities for living. Has your range of caring about others expanded over the years? Can you now envision better ways of interacting with other people that did not occur to you in the past?

The literature on human development provides clues to finding examples of your own growth. Suppose you read that something called the *operator* is what initiates change and that the operator in human development may be biological, psychological, intellectual or external. Sounds vague at first? Suppose operators of the biological type are events producing changes in the life cycle. For example, changes in the production of certain hormones initiate the onset of puberty which initiates, on the physiological level, the shift from childhood to adulthood. Operators of the psychological type are those basic needs, more accurately called neural demands, which seek conscious expression. Vague again? Suppose you have spontaneous neural demands for affection, adventure, security, sexual expression. The demands for affection and adventure may have led you to seek out new friends while the demand for security may have made you hesitant to leave home and a comfortable circle of acquaintances. How easily did you make up your mind about which university to attend?

Operators of the intellectual type are active in your different kinds of questioning. Perhaps there is no need to revisit how they lead to developments in understanding and in moral living. Finally, changes in external situations operate as challenges to present ways of thinking and acting. In the best case scenario, a person responds successfully to the challenge, not only surviving but becoming more resilient because of the effort. You might think of your first week on a college campus as the challenging new environment and the first semester of classes as the departure from earlier ways of thinking. How well did you respond? Have you done more than simply survive? Are you a stronger and more resourceful person because of such experiences?

Since the types of operators are diverse, you might expect that their demands are not always compatible with one another. In terms of personal living, have you found yourself operating at cross purposes? In one sense you are a unity since you talk of yourself as the same person who has gone through years of changes. In another sense you find yourself divided within. Classical philosophy made use of all sorts of dualistic terms or binary sets (e.g. mind and body, reason and the passions) to capture this experience of inner division. The basis for such terms is the common experience of tension between intellectual operators and psychological operators, or between intelligence and sensitive living. The latter demands immediate satisfaction and follows established routines to reach the desired goods. Human intelligence, however, learns the benefits of delayed gratification, detects when old routines no longer succeed and often finds the goods of sensitive living inferior to higher goods. For example, physical development initiates a demand for sexual expression in sensitive living. The teenager encounters conflicting demands and, absent strong role models, may stumble along in a confused state unsure of what to do and doing some harm along the way. The difficulties are not unique to the adolescent years. While puberty and the conflicting messages from a pluralistic society magnify the tension, adults experience plenty of instances where the desire to do the right thing is at odds with other desires. Because moral living requires intelligent and responsible choices between competing pulls or desires, paying attention to this tension in your life is an important part of moral development.

The demands of sensitive living are insistent, and how persons respond to them is a test of moral character. Demands for sustenance, security, affection, sexual expression evoke a variety of responses, but not all of them are equally good. It is one thing to enjoy eating; it is another to stuff oneself. Securing the necessities of living is important, but devoting all of one's time to the pursuit of money and possessions can be a form of personal impoverishment. Still, these are claims you should check against your own experience. Are you acquainted with persons whose submission of all else to the goods of sensitive living has produced a life you prefer not to imitate?

So far human development appears to arise from a variety of operators and to be accompanied by tension between different demands from different operators. The next question is how balance or harmony among conflicting pulls is possible? Suppose there is a second element to human development; besides operators there are *integrators*. What might this mean? When development occurs in one area of your living, adjustments may be required in others. For example, development of physical coordination puts an end to your once excusable eating habits as a child. Similarly, development of social graces calls for some restraint in saying the first thing that comes to mind when talking with others. Have you witnessed the naive honesty of a child's question (e.g. "Is that your real hair?") that may embarrass a parent but, if asked by an adult, would be taken as an insult?

Integration means persons try to catch up to the development occurring in their lives. The process may be slow and painful. For instance, you may know that a grandparent has died. Intellectually this is beyond doubt, but emotionally you may be in turmoil. What the mind quickly acknowledges, feelings may only slowly accept. One reason to allow for an indeterminate length of time for grieving is to permit feelings to catch up with knowing. If persons skip the grieving process, their pain is buried but not eliminated; it may resurface later in strange ways and disrupt their living.

In very general terms, the operators pursue change; the integrators seek stability. When you move to a new environment (e.g. your freshman year in college?), there are opportunities for growth. The challenge is to change your life in ways that meet the demands of the new situation. Still, you do not become an entirely different person. Besides change there is continuity. If the new situation requires too much change, too radical a departure from your past, then there is the risk of psychological crisis and, in the extreme, breakdown. Perhaps you are familiar with studies of the effects of war or civil upheaval on persons whose lives are torn apart by acts of violence. Overnight their familiar worlds vanish, and integrating the new circumstances they face becomes a nearly impossible challenge.

Besides the tension between sensitive living and intelligence, there is a tension in living in community. What in the individual is a tension between change and habit is in society a tension between innovation and tradition. Both individuals and communities must continue to grow or they will stagnate; but just as personal habits resist uprooting, so traditional patterns or customs may linger after their time has passed. The puzzle about integration reappears here. There is a time lag, a difference in pace, between the emergence of new ideas and adjustment to them. Can you think of cases when new ideas challenged the accepted ways of doing things? Can you identify practices that are environmentally unsound but which persons cling to despite mounting evidence of long-term disaster? Such time lags may help you understand yourself as well as obstacles you meet in public policy debates. Someone once remarked that, when a dramatically new idea is introduced, it is first dismissed as absurd, but after awhile more people see merit in it. Eventually everyone claims to have known it was right all along. Of course, as John Maynard Keynes quipped, in the long run we are all dead; so some challenges, if left unmet, may prove fatal.

Finally, the question of human development requires some attention to *predispositions*. So-called conservatives value tradition and want change to occur slowly if at all. So-called liberals favor innovation but tend to under-estimate the force of habit and the need for continuity. Reformers and social visionaries are usually impatient with the slow pace of change. Whatever your predisposition toward change, have you ever felt a tension between demands for development and demands for stability? You might pause again and try to locate a specific experience of such tension in your life. How did you resolve the tension? Does this retrieval of a past experience shed any light on your own predispositions?

EXERCISES

1. Identify some things about which you feel strongly. What "goods" are your feelings responding to, e.g. what brings you joy and what evokes anger?

2. Review your answers to the second and third exercises at the end of Chapter One. Does the "mapping" of five contexts of conscious opera-tion help you detect how being "careful" or "careless" can occur in dif-ferent ways?

3. What experiences can you recall of efforts to control your own sponta-neous feelings? How successful were you in guiding how you responded to those feelings?

4. What experiences can you recall of a tension between the demands of sensitive living and the demands of intelligence?

MORAL GROWTH: OPPORTUNITIES AND OBSTACLES

6

MORAL DEVELOPMENT: A DEVELOPED VIEWPOINT?

You may have heard someone make the following claims:

> Moral beliefs are just opinions based on personal preferences. Since preferences vary, there is little chance that moral controversies will end. In the short run, some agreement or consensus has to be present for a society to function; yet, even with some limited consensus, controversies will continue unless, in the struggle for power, one side overwhelms all opponents. But such imposed agreements turn out to be temporary, so we should expect controversies to return.

Rather than respond to these claims directly, you might want to consider a background question often left unasked: Why are there different moral beliefs, whether you call them preferences, opinions, or something else? What are the *sources of diversity* in moral beliefs? This question is worth pursuing through several chapters. Not one source but several will appear. The first source is consistent with what the preceding chapter suggested about moral development. If different people are at different stages of moral development, you might expect them to hold variable opinions about what is good to do. After all, you do not assume that the child's ability to make sound judgments is as developed as the adult's. But is there any reliable way of identifying and evaluating differences in ability and outcome?

Researchers, especially those versed in theories of psychological development, have noticed some patterns in moral development. The earlier remarks on "operators" and "integrators" will help organize these claims about patterns in moral growth. Suppose moral development involves the following series of stages: adaptation, assimilation, adjustment, increased differentiation and, finally, mastery. What might these words mean?

Try the example of learning to play the piano. Young persons were moving their fingers long before sitting at a piano. Adaptation occurs when they adapt their finger movements to the new challenge, i.e. playing the keyboard. In doing this they draw on previously acquired skills (e.g. counting toy blocks on their finger tips) and so assimilate to the old skills the new exercise of hitting the piano keys in succession. In a period of adjustment, usually marked by trial and error, the piano students learn to modify and to expand their previously acquired operations. All the hours of practice aim at such expansion in understanding and flexibility. In time the young persons can play scales and simple tunes. The earlier processes of adaptation and assimilation begin to yield results.

What does "increased differentiation" mean here? The piano students learn to distinguish and study slow and fast tempos, to play different time signatures (e.g., 4/4 time for a waltz, 6/8 time for a jig), and to perform different styles of music. With more practice (care still being present?), their repertoire increases. If time and talent cooperate, they may achieve mastery of the instrument. With mastery comes the ability to glance at a complex musical score and quickly recognize how to play the music.

Can you apply the same pattern to your own history of moral development? Have new situations challenged you to adapt your caring about others to those who previously were outsiders? Were you able to show them the consideration that you previously had reserved for a smaller population? Did it take time to learn how to get along with newcomers and to build bonds of trust? Was there differentiation occurring as you learned different ways of interacting with different individuals depending on their personalities and habitual responses? Do you have an expanded repertoire of social skills for dealing respectfully with all persons, not just with close friends but also with "difficult cases"? Mastery may prove elusive, but what might it mean as a goal of moral development? Perhaps you should pause to think of examples of heroes who embodied what you consider to be admirable qualities or virtues. They, more than anyone's theory about moral growth, are persuasive that moral excellence is possible. But who are your heroes? What makes them heroes in your eyes?

Back to the less dramatic talk of patterns of moral growth. What might a researcher mean by talking of "stages" of development? Presumably there is a change that amounts to more than adding something to what one already has or is. A more dramatic change, a leap, occurs that becomes a basic shift in how one thinks, in how one is orientated toward other people and oneself. One researcher, Lawrence Kohlberg, tracked some of these shifts in orientation by studying the reasons people gave for doing things. He sketched and tested a theory about three levels of development in moral reasoning, each with two distinct stages.[1] A brief summary of his theory offers a further mapping of possible lines of personal growth. It also offers an opportunity to "correlate" his theory with the mappings presented in previous chapters. Can you identify similarities and differences? Again, since you can expect there will be rival theories about moral growth, the point is to relate Kohlberg's understanding to your own. Does it help make sense of your experiences? Is it at odds with what you know about your own development?

Kohlberg's three levels are: the Pre-Conventional, the Conventional and the Post-Conventional. These are the broad features of his map. Reflection on the stages may be more enlightening. Why is there movement between stages? Using the terminology of the last chapter, you can speak of questions as the "operators of growth." New problems turn up that you cannot adequately handle with the integrated responses or habits you have already mastered. The problems evoke new questions, and growth is likely when new answers and new ways of understanding emerge. You might link this to the earlier comments about challenges and obstacles: a problem that really stumps you may be your best opportunity for growth.

In Kohlberg's account of moral development, the earliest stages depend on the emergence of certain cognitive skills. In the first stage persons are orientated toward satisfying personal needs by obtaining particular goods. (Can you recall the first meaning of "good"?) The physical consequences of their actions determine, to their way of thinking, the rightness or wrongness of those actions. The general outlook is that good acts bring pleasure and bad acts bring pain. As a consequence, their reason for doing what is expected of them is to avoid punishment. This is the moral outlook of the young child who does not yet grasp any non-instrumental reasons for acting one way rather than another. (Can you recall the third use of "good"?)

At the second stage of the Pre-Conventional level, good choices are ones that produce personal satisfaction and sometimes the satisfaction of others. At this stage children learn how to negotiate to get what they want. They understand that getting what they desire sometimes means finding out what others want. If they are to play together for any length of time, they must give some attention to what others like and dislike. Imagine a child learning how to trade baseball cards or toys with other kids. Bargaining skills may emerge rapidly as a solution to an early form of economic exchange. No grand economic insights here, just the simple insight caught in the maxim: "I'll scratch your back if you'll scratch mine."

Why expect more than this pragmatic attitude of doing good to others so they will do good to you? Both stages of the first level reflect a self-interested or self-centered orientation. Have you ever heard someone claim that the only reason anyone does something is out of self-interest? Have you ever tried to persuade an audience of this? How did they respond? A common response takes the form of examples from family life. For instance, imagine parents beaming proudly as their son or daughter crosses the stage at college graduation. Why are they so happy? If you enjoy arguing for universal self-interest, you may want to suggest that having a college graduate in the family enhances their social status as successful parents or adds another way of protecting their financial security in old age. Maybe you should just surmise they are happy that the deadbeat will soon be out of the house and no longer a financial drain.

What may be missing from such arguments is the new way of thinking that Kohlberg associated with his Conventional level. Instead of thinking of a particular person as the reference point for each decision, some children grasp early on that a group is the reference point for evaluating options. The family is such a group with a number of members having their own roles and functions. Rather than thinking only of individual desires and the particular goods that satisfy them, the child abstracts from the particular to grasp the idea of a whole that operates to ensure the well-being of its members. Sacrificing one's own immediate interests for the good of the group becomes a reasonable and responsible act, especially if the parents have set a positive example for the child. At stage three children tend to measure right and wrong by whether something helps or harms the family. Initially the attitude is one of obedience and conformity to the rules of the family, but eventually the child may be orientated to act out of concern for the family's welfare. Are you familiar with the old story of the child willing to break the piggy bank to rescue the family from financial crisis?

Knowing what is good for one's family will not settle every question about what is good to do. You already have identified with groups other than your family. They may have been neighborhood friends, classmates, or members of a sports team. Were there ever conflicts between the rules and expectations of one group and those of another? The easiest cases to cite are probably conflicts between the rules set by your parents and the demands placed on you by peers. Once again a new problem arises that cannot be handled by the integrated habits of the obedient member of just one group. Here is where Kohlberg suggests a transition to stage four. The change in thinking begins with an insight that the laws of a larger society function to mediate disputes among groups. A type of pragmatic thinking is present: upholding law and order is what is in the best interest of everyone since, without social order, all goods are endangered. Respecting public authorities and fulfilling legal duties are seen as ways of doing what is right. The law, in short, is the measure of right and wrong, but it remains an instrumental good.

Why did Kohlberg's research turn up yet a third level with two more stages? Did you ever think that obedience to authority or social conformity was the sum total of moral living? Two sorts of questions probably bothered you years ago. What if there are multiple authorities and they disagree? Also, what if the laws are unjust and the political leadership corrupt? How are you to make decisions in such circumstances? What do you appeal to in choosing which authority to trust or in judging a law to be just or unjust? These are tough questions that could lead you back to the Introduction and its puzzle about multiplicity. For now, let's sketch Kohlberg's Post-Conventional level and its two stages.

As you recall from Chapter Two, besides the good of order, there is a third meaning of "good." In Kohlberg's terms this third meaning is suggested by reasoning according to moral principles that have a universal validity and so are not relative to the varying interests of groups or social orders. In the terms used in this text, you might think of the earlier distinctions between belief and knowledge and between social heritage and your capacity to raise questions. Are you capable of making sound judgments about inherited customs and current laws? Are you capable of responsible decisions based on those sound judgments? Can you be both a source of and an orientation toward terminal goods? A sketch of Kohlberg's two stages of the Post-Conventional level may provide hints as to how you might answer these questions.

One problem that evokes a new way of thinking about right and wrong is, again, the recognition that current laws and practices need changing. Think of the Civil Rights movement in the 1960s, the defiance of apartheid in South Africa during the 1980s, the protests against the death penalty in the 1990s, the objections to the Taliban's treatment of women in the first decade of the new millennium. On what did the advocates of change base their complaints? If you subscribe to a standard *utilitarian* argument, then the complaints were that some greater social good was being blocked because of such laws and practices. For example, when women are denied educational and employment opportunities, a greater economic good is being denied to the entire society. Without educated women in the workforce, a society operates with far fewer "human resources" than it might otherwise employ for its benefit. The principle of maximizing the good of the greatest number is not being met by such practices, and so they should be changed.

According to Kohlberg, this way of thinking rises above the conventions of a society to hold them accountable to some higher standard, and so it is a distinct fifth stage. The measure of right and wrong is what promotes the good of the greatest number. You may have experienced this way of thinking when faced with a choice between an option that benefited a few but harmed many and an option that helped many but harmed a few. Were you taught that some choices are not between good and evil but between two evils, and that the proper choice was the lesser of two evils?

Can you think of situations in which the responsible choice would be to choose to do neither the lesser nor the greater evil? Here you may find examples of what Kohlberg admitted was a rare way of thinking about moral decisions. His sixth stage is perhaps the ideal outcome of the human search for how to embody what is good; its attainment may be rare and fleeting. Still, there is some evidence that it can be embodied. Perhaps one of the heroes you thought of earlier exemplified such rare attainment. If you know something of Gandhi or of Michael Collins, of Martin Luther King, Jr. or of Malcolm X (before his conversion experience in Mecca), then you may have some sense of the contrast between stages five and six. All four sought what was good and sought to defeat institutionalized or "structural evils" in their societies. Yet the latter individual in each pair was willing to fight evil with evil, to meet violence with violence; but the former in each pair rejected such means – not as ineffective in the short run but as contrary to their conviction that morally evil means should never be used to attain good ends. It may not have escaped your attention that both examples divide along the lines of religious convictions. More on this in Chapter Seven, but a couple of comments are in order. At times all persons seem to fail or at least falter in doing what they know is good. Moral growth seems to be a precarious achievement with individual moral choices being more events than permanent ways of living. Such experiences are the basis for the claim of many religious traditions that persons need "outside" help or a relation to something transhuman. Ironically Nietzsche's phrase applies here: if we remain "human, all too human," then growth is hardly sustainable.

The chart below may help you review Kohlberg's theory of the stages of moral growth.

I. *Pre-Conventional* (orientation to particular goods)

    1.   Obedience to avoid punishment

    2.   Self-interested search for satisfaction

II. *Conventional* (orientation to the good of order)

    1.   Search for group approval

    2.   Promotion of law and order

III. *Post-Conventional* (orientation to terminal goods)

    1.   Maximizing benefits for the greatest number

    2.   Adherence to universal goods

Kohlberg's theory offers one way to map moral development. He measures moral growth by the level of reasoning skills a person exhibits, but he assumes that reasoning is equivalent to skills in logic. Do you find this restricted notion of reason questionable? If you reflect back on your own performance in understanding and judging, you will notice that your reasoning and deliberating involve more than skills in logic. While logic is a technique for ensuring the consistency of the concepts within an argument or a system, there is more to moral deliberation than the logical consistency of judgments. For example, judging and deciding occur in the context of human caring. But horizons of care expand, and the transitions between horizons are not matters of logical consistency but of displacements from one way of thinking to another.

A further reservation about Kohlberg's view of reason arises from the remarks on nominal understanding in Chapter Two. A person can be logically consistent in an argument without having any serious understanding of what the words used mean. For example, what do you mean by the word "person"? Since Kohlberg probably was indebted to Kant for his linking of reason to logic, let's consider Kant's use of this word. In his Categorical Imperative, does the word "person" refer to an understanding of something as having intrinsic worth or to an understanding of something as an instrument to be used simply for other ends? Kant obviously meant the former; still, the question of what you or someone else means by "person" cannot be settled merely by appealing to logic.

Despite these reservations, Kohlberg's mapping of moral development is on target in stressing how the development of skills plays a role in the improvement of moral deliberation. The focus of the last three chapters of this text will be on a procedure for analyzing and evaluating moral choices. You can become skilled in such a procedure, and doing so will improve your chances of being more careful in decision-making.

LIMITATIONS ON EFFECTIVE FREEDOM

The preceding section opened with a question about the sources of diversity among moral beliefs. Presumably different levels and stages of moral growth provide a partial answer. This section will describe further sources of diversity. Specifically, four types of *limitations* on *effective freedom* are sources of differences in moral judgments and practices.[2]

The moral persons that Kohlberg found operating at his Post-Conventional level seemed to base their deciding and acting on personal moral convictions. They exhibited what traditionally is called "moral autonomy" (*auto* meaning "self" and *nomos* meaning "law;" hence the notion of a person as self-governing). In more familiar terms, you may have heard talk of using your "best judgment" or about being a "self-directed individual." What do you think people are assuming when they reject the following excuses? "Don't blame me; I was just following orders." "They made me go along." "He hit me first." The common expectation seems to be that adults are free sources of decisions and actions and, as such, should take responsibility for them as opposed to shifting the blame elsewhere. Of course, expectations may not be met. To quote T.S. Eliot: "Between the idea and the reality...[f]alls the shadow."[3] Put another way, moral freedom is not something persons are born with. At best it is a potential that may or may not be realized. Just growing older offers no guarantee that a person becomes morally autonomous. Some people just grow taller.

Suppose we make a distinction between *potential* and *effective* freedom. All persons are born with the potential to be free. However, we are only as free as we are effectively able to act on that potential. Effective freedom is the degree of freedom we actually have. Recall how moral growth occurs as persons learn how to exercise more intelligent control over their deliberating and deciding. In contrast, very young children are at the mercy of physical responses to pleasure and pain, and for the most part parents make the decisions. As children's intelligent grasp of things expands and their moral skills develop, their range of control extends beyond immediate gratification to embrace the concerns of various groups and to contribute to the good of order. With maturity comes an increasing measure of moral independence, and intelligent and responsible choices occur with greater likelihood. Then persons' effective control over what they make of their lives and world is greater. But the process is not automatic or smooth. All sorts of limitations or obstacles will be encountered.

Consider the different forms these limitations on human development take. The easiest obstacles to identify are *material* or *environmental limits*. Can you think of how natural and social environments set limits on a person's capacity to do good? Natural disasters such as earthquakes, floods or drought may come to mind. They can prove to be barriers to providing for one's family and sustaining the well-being of one's community. You may have read reports of doctors watching many patients die of curable diseases because, in their impoverished country, the needed medicines and hospital facilities are in short supply. Suppose you meet a homeless and unemployed mother with her three children. You give what you can, but you know your small handout is not enough to solve this family's financial problems much less make a difference in the social and economic conditions that produce such cases of distress. Even if you were a President or Prime Minister and wanted to provide more federal assistance to homeless families, you could encounter obstacles if political opponents opposed increased spending and refused to shift funds away from programs they favor.

A second type of barrier to doing what is good is seen in *psychological limitations*. Do you know of cases where irrational fears, delusions or neuroses blocked a person's exercise of freedom? A parent who suffers from panic attacks or manic depression may unwillingly neglect a child. Petty tyrants in the workplace are often victims of their own psychological disorders. They may dislike themselves and cannot believe others would like them; so they treat others with suspicion and distrust. Of course, their own suspicions and hostility will eventually evoke similar responses from others and so provide evidence that other people do not like them. You might reflect on examples of "peer pressure" to locate psychological barriers to following your desire to do what is best. The competing desire to be accepted and the fear of being excluded can be so intense that most persons will go along with the peer group even if they know better than to do so.

Intellectual limitations provide a third type of obstacle. Just as a lack of economic resources can restrict the range of freedom, so limited intellectual resources can block efforts to do what is good. Imagine parents frustrated by a misbehaving child. If they are not familiar with the literature on strategies for avoiding child abuse, they are less likely to keep themselves under control and to avoid doing what they would detest at a calmer time. You may be familiar with legal aid clinics and their clients, e.g. parents at a loss on how to appeal a cut-off of food stamps or an eviction notice. The clients are dependent on the intellectual resources of others to solve their problems and to prevent harm from happening. What if not enough lawyers are doing *pro bono* work? Then material and intellectual limits combine to set even higher barriers to doing good and to avoiding evil.

A fourth type of obstacle is *volitional limitations*. What if persons have sufficient economic resources, they are psychologically unimpaired and are sufficiently intelligent so they know what they can and should do – will they do it? Most of us can cite examples of our failures to do what we knew we could and should do. It may be less embarrassing to seek examples in other people's lives rather than in our own. The source of embarrassment need not be public exposure of our failings; we may be our own silent accusers. Think of the opposition within your own consciousness: you know what can and should be done and yet are not willing to do it. Why not? The why-question is inappropriate here. Why? Notice that the why-question anticipates an answer, a reason or justification for what you did or did not do. If you are trying to understand why you failed to act according to your "best" understanding, are you trying to find a "better" understanding than that best understanding? Might the effort be in vain? What sense can you make of failing to act in a way that you understood would make the best sense? Should you pause to puzzle over the last few sentences?

If you have rushed on to this paragraph without pausing, here is another puzzle. Why do we make excuses for ourselves? You can find examples of excuse-making without much effort. The child's "She hit me first" does not work with the parent. Surprisingly, governments do much better with "They bombed our cities first." But did you ever catch yourself making excuses to yourself? It is easy to understand excuses made to others – you do not want them to think badly of you or to punish you. But what purpose do excuses made in private serve?

You may think people show an almost endless creativity in excuse-making. "Rationalization" is the conventional label for this common exercise in trying to invent reasons for irrational behavior. The recommended pause may have led you to this insight. The inappropriate why-question anticipates a reason where there is none to be found. Rather than accept this absence of an answer, we may carelessly accept nonsensical answers. Indeed, one non-technical meaning of rationalization is "giving bad reasons for bad behavior." The nonsense apparently escapes detection. Have you ever read news accounts of the trial of a serial killer? After a court finding that the defendant is morally and legally sane, the news reporters usually proceed to speculate about childhood trauma as the reason for the horrible acts attributed to the defendant. But if the person on trial was sane and so knew better, what meaning is such speculation trying to find?

The volitional limits on the range of freedom are the hardest to understand because the experiences that exhibit these limits contain an element of the absurd or the unintelligible. This element frustrates a questioner's spontaneous reach for a positive understanding of why something happened. But then notice the benefit of having paid attention to yourself as a specimen of decision-making. If you are aware of your own moral failures and of the creative dodges of excuse-making, you may be on guard against the tendency to search for reasons in the wrong places. At least you might learn to be sceptical of news reporters when they try to make sense of acts that are unintelligible.

One implication of the preceding obstacles to increasing the range of our freedom is that, though we may talk of moral freedom as expected of adults, it is not something that adults automatically possess. Its reality depends on an ongoing struggle against limitations inside and outside of ourselves. The need for such a struggle was a reason for the focus of traditional ethics on character formation and self-control. Parallel to the distinction between potential and effective freedom was Adam Smith's contrast between "natural liberty" and the moral freedom that citizens must acquire if a free society is to flourish. Smith argued that a key role of institutions (e.g. the family, churches, schools and even government) was to tutor and shape natural liberty.[4] You might think back to earlier remarks on socialization and the examples of learning table manners and how to share toys with other kids.

Your early years of character formation required that you co-operate with others, but the process was largely under the control of others. More self-control is expected of adults. Again, a useful analogy is a multi-storied building with executive suites on the top floors. The question of self-control is whether anyone is habitually at home on those floors. In the absence of executive decision-making, what goes on in the rest of the building may be an upsurge of competing desires, but their purposes may be at odds and their outcomes unacceptable. This image of top-down formation of character is a clue to the importance of knowing yourself. A further step to that end begins with the question of whether you have blind spots. That is, do your habitual ways of thinking and deciding contain flaws that you simply do not notice? The next section on four forms of bias may help you detect some blind spots.

FORMS OF BIAS[5]

You already know that, as used in this text, the word "horizon" means the range of questions you can raise and find significant even if you cannot answer them. Now what if there are obstacles to raising further questions, to expanding horizons? Will they leave us with blind spots? One type of blind spot is a psychological deformation which blocks questions relevant to deliberation. For the person suffering from such a psychological block, the blind spot usually goes unrecognized. The original deformation may have occurred in childhood and resulted in the adult's repressed desires and unreasonable fears. As a simple example, consider the use of pesticides to control the insects in your garden. An inordinate fear of spiders may prevent you from wondering whether spiders might have a positive role to play in controlling insects harmful to your flowers. The question does not occur to you, and, even if someone suggests spiders are useful to gardeners, you are unlikely to entertain the possibility. The block here is a form of *dramatic bias*. This form of bias affects the range of questions and of courses of action persons will consider. Stage fright and extreme shyness are instances of dramatic bias where fear can so overwhelm persons that they fail to develop in their own self-understanding and in their acquisition of skills.

What of other forms of bias? If a bias is a barrier to detecting further relevant questions, it will be much like the four types of limits on effective freedom, namely, a barrier to being effectively intelligent and responsible in thinking and acting. With the exception of most cases of dramatic bias, the new twist is that this type of barrier is a failure to ask questions, not because persons do not think of the questions but because those persons prefer not to ask them. The link here is to the earlier insights into the range of caring. One's caring about others may stop at concern for personal satisfaction or at concern for the good of some group with which one identifies. Bias, then, is a deficiency in the development of caring about understanding (some questions are pushed aside) and in the development of caring about others (the effects of one's actions on some populations are not considered). An inverse relationship between the three meanings of "good" and the next three forms of bias may be apparent.

An easy beginning is made with *individual bias*. Most of us are familiar with the so-called egotist or self-interested individual whose sole concern is with self-advancement. Perhaps you have met very intelligent and resourceful persons who are adept at solving their own problems and promoting their own agendas. What you may have detected is that they fail to consider whether what is good for them is good for others. The Golden Rule is not part of their mindset. The good of personal satisfaction seems to be their sole norm for evaluating options. Why should you complain that this outlook is too narrow? Perhaps you repeat the Golden Rule as your basis of complaint. But is the egotist's mindset wrong because it violates a general rule?

Suppose the mindset is deficient not because it ignores a rule but because it blocks the expansion of a person's own spontaneous caring. Usually to get what they want, egotists need to study and to understand other people, just as the child who wants to bargain for baseball cards or toys needs to anticipate others' likes and dislikes. But such pragmatic attention to others stops short of having sympathy for them and having any interest in their well-being. Usually there is a background rationalization for this lack of sympathy, e.g. other people are inferior, stupid, or suckers waiting to be swindled. In the extreme you may encounter a mindset that divides persons into sheep and wolves (though wolves hardly treat each other so badly and do not deserve a reputation better suited to some human beings).

What evidence is there that the egotists are deficient in their own development? Again, there is development in caring about understanding and caring about others. In regard to the first, why should you want to understand what is good for persons other than yourself? Think of what scientists routinely do in research. In reaching for understanding of some type of object or event, they study individual specimens; yet their goal is to understand an entire class of objects or events. They want to know what is probably true about all similar cases, not just true of the specimens at hand. So what egotists do in halting questioning prematurely is to block the occurrence of further insights about what is good for others like themselves. As a result, they block their own further development in understanding. The understanding they do have is devoted to acquiring rewards from others and evading a fair return.

Can you identify examples of individual bias? Try to specify what further relevant questions are missing. For example, if legislators are asked to vote on campaign finance reforms, an incumbent probably is aware of the loss of public trust in elected officials under the current ways of financing campaigns. Still, the only question the incumbent may take seriously is, Will the reforms help or hurt my reelection chances? What further questions may be relevant?

We can describe *group bias* as egotism writ large. A little background information may help. Social classes multiply because creative individuals invent ever new specialized tasks and disciplines. The members of each class tend to develop group loyalties and to distance themselves from non-members. Cooperation among groups occurs, but there are also conflicts, e.g. management versus labor, city versus suburb, citizens versus immigrants, trial lawyers versus physicians.

Group bias appears when, in response to social problems, one evaluates any proposed solutions solely in terms of their likely effects on one's own group. Questions about their effects on non-members or on a much larger society receive little, if any, attention. The usual failure here is to consider whether a solution might be good even though it lessened the dominance or harmed the interests of one's group. This favoring of proposals that protect or enhance one's own group, even if they are harmful to many others, is an instance of the second type of good, the good of order; so why count it as a deficiency in moral understanding?

The analogy to scientific research applies here as it did in the case of individual bias. How is it that intelligent persons block the further questions about whether some proposal would be good for all the members of a population? Again, rationalizations may abound: "Charity begins at home;" "If we cave in at the bargaining table, they'll just demand more concessions in the next contract." "No nation is required to sacrifice its economic interests for the sake of non-citizens."[6] Can you find your own examples of group bias and some of the commonly used rationalizations? You might want to think about controversies over funding for public schools and over closing military bases. Closer to home you may have had experiences in high school of "in-crowds" that excluded non-members from social events and belittled them as unworthy of consideration.

The cumulative effects of prior biases is one way of accounting for *general bias*. If bias is the failure to ask further relevant questions, what happens if this failure occurs repeatedly? Since understanding depends on raising and answering questions, when the relevant questions are not asked, a person's understanding of a puzzle or problem will be inadequate. If the situation involves social problems that need solving, then there will be a faulty diagnosis of what the problems are and so an unreliable basis for deciding what needs to be done. But then the actual decisions that are made and the policies that are adopted will be defective. In time, if the gap in understanding is not closed, the flawed actions to remedy the misunderstood problems may worsen the situation. The result will be an increasing unintelligibility of both the situation and the policies in place. No one may really understand where or why things went wrong or how to undo the mess. Instead, an entire society may stumble from crisis to crisis, just hoping to muddle through and to survive the deteriorating situation. Since desperate people tend to do desperate things, the "final" answer to the worsening round of crises may be the use of force to untangle the baffling situation.

Can you think of examples of such descents into social disorder and confusion? The history of Russia in the last century could provide you with plenty of materials. Much closer to home you might think of government policies to combat illegal drugs or of repeated efforts to "save" the Social Security System and to "fix" national health care programs. There is no shortage of seemingly intractable social problems. The general pattern of the descent can be summarily stated: just as intelligently designed methods tend to yield cumulative and progressive results, so biases tend to produce cumulative and regressive results.[7]

The preceding remarks offer background for another account of general bias. Faced with intractable personal or social problems, many may assume that the unintelligible situation and their common-sense understanding of it is all that can be. The immediate situation may be terribly flawed and unintelligible, but "such is reality, and realists must deal with world the way they find it." For example, a few idealists may talk about sacrificing for the "common good," but the realists believe that political life is an ever shifting power game among different classes and interest groups (or their lobbyists). While pragmatically restrained from admitting as much in public, the realists expect nothing more of persons than factional strife. A few may admit that they wish things were different, but they leave it to idealists to dream of a better world and devote themselves, instead, to working out the compromises that will allow them to see another day.[8]

What, if anything, do you find deficient in this stance? You may have noticed that the starting point is an acceptance of, a facing of, the "hard facts." Did you also notice this was an act of resignation to facts that are unintelligible? What kind of "fact" makes no sense? You might revisit the previous section with its remarks on moral failures and the puzzling absence of answers to some why-questions. Is the resignation of the realist really all that realistic? Are there further relevant questions you have? Perhaps the pragmatic idealist in you objects that the realist makes the mistake of taking the current level of historical achievement – with all of its failings – as all that persons should ever expect to achieve. Maybe you ask: Should we give up hope for providing people with a better time?

You may have detected the danger in accepting this type of realism: it leaves many *structural evils* both unchallenged and unchanged. Can you think of practices worth challenging? Perhaps some examples come to mind: the recurrent exposure of migrant farm laborers to pesticides; the locating of chemical plants near impoverished neighborhoods; continued reliance on local property taxes for public school funding; policies that blame the poor for not having good jobs, a good education, and adequate health care insurance. Or maybe the examples have been more personally experienced: years of schooling that offered little more than nominal understanding; the "churning" of textbook editions to keep royalties flowing; the downsizing of companies to maintain during a non-expansionary period the profit margins experienced during an expansionary period in the economy.

What can persons of good will do about such ongoing practices? Tough questions and decisions face those in the present who have inherited the accumulated nonsense of past failures to ask the right questions, to be careful in inquiry and to care enough about others. If all that well-intentioned persons bring to the analysis and evaluation of this inheritance is their inherited common sense, then they are likely to remain trapped in the general bias that is part of the mess. You may recall the description of common sense as a mix of good sense and nonsense. More than this mixture is required to sort out the tangled web of mistaken beliefs and flawed practices. As the next chapter will point out, a different horizon of inquiry called theoretical understanding offers an alternative to relying solely on common sense. It promises much but requires years of effort, and with both the promise and the time-consuming effort common sense is very impatient. This impatience manifests the basic form of general bias: if ideas are too remote from current thinking and their implementation too much at odds with current practice, then they must be false or perhaps "merely academic." With that dismissal, common sense claims that it alone is competent to deal with the crisis at hand.

What can you do about all this? Well, you are reading this text, and it points out some of the overlooked questions and barriers to asking them. Later chapters will introduce you to some of the skills that can help you understand and evaluate moral issues. By themselves these pages will not change any structural evils, but your reading them may improve the odds of your asking further relevant questions, detecting the presence of bias in proposed solutions and not resigning yourself to the "facts" as you find them. Even this slight shift in the odds does not depend on a textbook but on the dynamism of care in you. It is the precondition to your understanding and acting carefully. Absent its energy, the reading is largely a waste of your time.

A CASE STUDY

Previous chapters have sketched *maps* to help you find your way or get your bearings in moral decision-making. The fundamental map in Chapter Four outlined the structure of wonder and concern. You were invited to check it against your own experiences in puzzling and deciding. Such self-attention is a first step in finding your way around in your own mind. How confident are you that you can now track your own performance in diagnosing situations, deliberating over options and making decisions? If the exercise of self-detection is still brand new and confusing, you may have to take it on faith that the effort is worthwhile. Perhaps some evidence of the benefits to be had can be found in working through a case study. In what follows you will find instances of general bias both in a situation that contains structural evils and in the responses to a proposed remedy for those evils. The question is whether you can spot the general bias in the reactions to the proposed remedy. Be forewarned; none of the national news broadcasters spotted it. Can you do a better job?

Let's take a quick look back at examples of one form of general bias, namely, "political realism." The following claims exhibit this "hard-headed" facing of the facts: "In competition for international trade, any nation that refuses to do business with corrupt and brutal regimes is only hurting itself by a unilateral restraint its competitors will not exercise;" "Whatever violent means a state employs to defend itself from internal or external attacks can be justified because, if the attackers succeed, they will do even worse things to those they have defeated." Supposedly these are some of the facts nations must face. The first purpose of the case study is to suggest that the "facts" may not have been what the realists thought they were, that in fact the realists were at odds with reality.

Presumably you know something about the history of South Africa in the twentieth century, in particular some of the details of the apartheid policies of the white-dominated government in that country. The black majority and other non-white minorities in South Africa were restricted in their access to education, housing, employment and political participation. When resistance to the government's policies grew after the middle of the last century, the regime's response was to impose further restrictions and to meet dissent with criminal penalties and indefinite jailings. Eventually government officials responded to a worsening crisis (and increasing international criticism) with even harsher measures including "extrajudicial killings" and the torture of suspected dissidents.

You may have heard of Nelson Mandela and read about his eventual release from prison and election as the first black President of South Africa. The situation he inherited included demands that those government officials, military officers and police personnel who had tortured and murdered during the period of apartheid be brought to justice. Survivors of torture and those whose loved ones had "disappeared" demanded the guilty parties be punished.

Archbishop Desmond Tutu is the other key figure in this case. As a long-time dissident and Nobel Peace Prize winner, he was a widely respected figure in the new South Africa. He endorsed a compromise reached by the major political parties that a Truth and Reconciliation Commission be established. This proposal included some surprising features. Most controversial was the recommendation that anyone, on either side of the previous conflict, who was guilty of human rights violations and who voluntarily and honestly confessed to these violations at the publicly televised hearings of the Commission would be granted amnesty. The initial reaction to this amnesty proposal was that it would not work. Too much brutality and oppression had claimed too many victims for the survivors to allow the guilty parties to escape punishment. However, when President Mandela lent his support to the Archbishop's endorsement, their combined prestige made the Commission a reality.

The public confessions began; the details of officially condoned murders, bombings and torture saw the light of day; the perpetrators received amnesty. As the international press followed the proceedings, the attitude shifted from "It won't work; they'll never accept it" to the question, "Why grant amnesty to murderers and torturers?" The common-sense answer of the national news broadcasters was that this was a way of "putting the violence of the past behind them and moving on." Can you do better than this cliché? Do you need some clues? Were the broadcasters clueless?

Why did the proposal require confessions in front of the cameras and a live audience? One reason may quickly come to mind. Survivors of the "disappeared" deserved to know what had happened to their loved ones and to know whether their remains could be found. Another reason: the truth about what government officials had done needed to be revealed to the whole world; their lies and crimes needed to be exposed for all to see. Can you reach for a third reason for the public testimony? It may help to know that a recurrent theme of those testifying was that they had felt justified in doing horrible things to their opponents. Repeatedly they testified that they believed they were using violence to prevent even greater violence. Their common prediction was that, if the oppressed groups in South Africa came to power, then they would do to the white minority what had been done to them. If that were to happen, the white minority would have only two options: the suitcase or the coffin, i.e. either leave the country or be murdered. To prevent this, they chose to violate their own laws and to "do unto others before they do unto us."

Are these enough clues? Will it help to remind you about political realism and its resignation to ugly facts? Did the opponents in coming to power turn out to be hate-filled monsters bent on blood-letting and settling old scores? What do you think about the common-sense realism of the officials who assumed victors always exact vengeance and who assumed their violence was necessary to prevent greater violence? What "facts" did the amnesty proposal challenge? What "facts" did the operations of the Commission prove false?

Back to the earlier question: Can you think of a third reason for the public confessions? What if the realists who predicted "this will never work" had blocked the creation of the Commission? What "facts" would then still be beyond doubt? Would you have any evidence of a better alternative to the realist's fatalistic prediction of the age-old cycle of violence and retribution? If the clues and pointers still leave you puzzled, please keep puzzling. What is at stake in this brief case study are needed changes in minds and hearts that are resisted by age-old habits in the human species. A simple test provides some proof of this resistance. Try to go for twenty-four hours without blaming anyone for something bad that happens to you. Check back tomorrow on how well you did on this test.

EXERCISES:

1. Describe your own examples of moral reasoning that reflect the differences among Kohlberg's six stages.

2. Provide specific examples of the four types of limitations on effective freedom.

3. Describe three instances of decision-making that exhibit three out of the four types of bias described in this chapter. Identify what further relevant questions were left unasked.

7

TRANSCENDING LIMITS

PROGRESS AND DECLINE

The preceding chapter began with a question about the sources of diversity in moral beliefs. Is this your question? Have you noticed that different college students hold different beliefs about what is right and wrong? Of course you did not need to take an anthropology course to discover diversity in moral beliefs and practices. But why all this diversity? The last chapter identified three sources. Kohlberg's theory suggests that persons at different *stages of development* will reason differently about what they should do. The four types of limits on *effective freedom* (with Kohlberg's variations in reasoning falling under the "intellectual" category?) describe further sources of diversity in moral understanding and doing. Finally, the four *types of bias* point to variable obstacles to understanding and to doing what is right.

Note the personal challenge of this incomplete listing of sources of diversity. Are you sure your moral reasoning is as developed as it can be? Do you recognize in yourself any of the limitations on effective freedom? How would you go about detecting whether bias is present in your thinking about what you should do? If you do envision further personal development beyond present limitations and biases, how do you set about changing your life?[1] If there were a simple formula or road map to follow, the drama of your life would be far less complicated. Would it be far less interesting? In any case, could someone at least give you some hints as to how to begin changing your life? Perhaps you have already received too many hints. Recall the much earlier puzzle about multiplicity. Advice columnists, pundits, preachers and counselors abound. For good or ill they impart their versions of wisdom, but what you quickly discover is that their messages are often at odds with one another. You may feel as if you are going in a circle here since you are now back to the opening question about diversity: Why are their messages so different?

The question of the sources of multiplicity is worth your attention, but you may recall a related question: How is anyone to sort out this babble of voices? This question is also part of the personal challenge to detect your present limits and blind spots and to develop beyond them. Where might you make a beginning in meeting this challenge? Perhaps you have already begun – did you accept the invitation to practice self-attention? What is the basic condition for further moral and intellectual development? Presumably the answer "yes" is no longer so puzzling. You have some understanding of your own structured wonder and concern, so you have made a beginning, and further progress is possible.

What will further progress require? Machiavelli cited two preconditions for being a successful prince, and, with some modification, both are relevant here. What you need are favorable *opportunities* and a particular type of *character*.[2] Favorable opportunities are an indefinite number of conditions, e.g. enough leisure time, luck in reading a particular book at just the right time, role models who offer encouragement, formal schooling that leaves your childhood curiosity alive. What of the particular type of character? Well, it helps to be a curious and reflective type of person. Perhaps you need no convincing on this point. All the same, consider the following argument as at least a review of earlier chapters.

Your caring about understanding, your curiosity, is what gives impetus to your questioning. The latter is part of a dynamically structured process made up of distinct but related operations. When you are operating well, you gain new understanding and wind up acting according to your best judgment at a particular time. Because the process is recurrent, you can ask new questions on the basis of past insights and respond to new situations on the basis of how you have habitually handled similar situations in the past. Ideally, if all persons were always intelligent and responsible in their living, things would continually improve. Whenever a new challenge arose requiring new insights into both what was occurring and what should be done about it, intelligent persons would diagnose the situation, carefully check their understanding of it and pursue responsible courses of action. As a result of their actions, there would be an improved situation which, in turn, would be the occasion for a new round of challenges and intelligent responses. Both personal moral growth and the moral improvement of social orders seem to be possible.

Of course, you see the problem. Persons are not always operating intelligently and responsibly. "The road to hell is paved with good intentions" is a familiar saying about failures of well-intentioned persons to be sufficiently intelligent. In addition, the complaint, "They knew better than to do that," points out a failure to act responsibly. Both sayings reflect the commonly experienced gap between human aspirations and actual performance. You might revisit comments on general bias in Chapter Six that distinguished between progress and decline. Briefly put, progress is a consequence of repeatedly making intelligent and responsible use of freedom; decline is a result of repeatedly doing the opposite. Just as individuals can improve or go downhill, so entire societies can develop or decline.

So where do these remarks leave you? The question was what type of character is a precondition to further moral development. Besides the general statement about being curious and reflective, what more can you say? Perhaps the comments on progress and decline suggest a further description of the needed *character type*. Since progress seems to depend on some correspondence between aspiration and actual effort in being intelligent and responsible, the needed character will reflect a repeated or habitual consistency between the desire to know and to do what is good and the actual performance of a person. You might think back to the earlier categories of "operator" and "integrator" where the desire is the operator that pushes for moral growth and where specific decisions and acts are the integrators that effect changes in your life. If the changes are consistent with the desire, then they are changes for the better, and some further integrated development is taking place in you. However, if the changes actually occurring are at odds with what you understand and judge to be true and good to do, then what is being integrated is some mixture of frustrated aspiration and flawed performance. Rationalizations may show up to cover over the failures and inner tensions. Indeed, a type of moral resignation may set in: "What do you expect of me? I'm only human."

So two general possibilities for *character formation* are present. You can cooperate with the basic forms of care or blunt their impetus toward growth. Which possibility you will actualize is undetermined, i.e. you are free to pursue or to block your own development. If there were not these two broad options, your living would be far less dramatic and unpredictable. What you may surmise at this point is that the previous remarks about human development and about progress and decline belong to an unfinished story. Applied to yourself, the previous comments are guesses as to what directions you may take tomorrow, next month, next year. They invite you to take a *dynamic*, as opposed to a *static*, view of your life. Can you think of yourself as an unfinished work of art? More broadly, can you think of your tribe or society as a work in progress? Even more generally, what might the broad canvas of human history portray?

The last two questions exceed the limits of an introductory text, but they can be questions for anyone whose "horizon" has expanded beyond the concerns of everyday living and immediate acquaintances. Are they at all your questions? If not of interest now, can you envision yourself becoming puzzled about what is happening to your own "tribe" in this century? Can you imagine a time when your curiosity will extend to wondering about the historical process in which whole tribes and civilizations come into being and then pass away? Such a range of questioning may now be remote from your interests, but the questions of progress and decline are intertwined with just such remote puzzles. Once again, then, you encounter a source of diversity in moral viewpoints: certain questions are of pressing interest for some persons, and others pay them no attention. Their "horizons" differ. The next section will further specify what this may mean.

FURTHER SOURCES OF MORAL DIVERSITY

If personal development and social progress require favorable conditions, you will expect that, since opportunities vary, individuals and groups may differ in their moral beliefs and practices. The remarks on material and environmental limits on effective freedom implied as much. Some examples may help specify how material and cultural conditions can affect your understanding of what is good to do.

Presumably you believe that the elderly should be cared for when they are unable to care for themselves. You may have read news accounts of the abuse of the elderly in some nursing homes. How did you react and why? But suppose you read about a nomadic people living in an extremely harsh environment who routinely abandon any aged member who is no longer able to make the annual trek to winter feeding grounds. Might the harsh material conditions that lower the group's chances for survival make this practice justifiable? What opportunities are not available to them?

As an example of cultural conditions affecting your understanding of what is good to do, think of how you assume freedom of religion is a good thing. What sense, then, do you make of the wars of religion you read about in a European history course? Why did the combatants not realize their societies would be better off practicing religious tolerance? But what if the benefits of religious tolerance were not always apparent? Arguably the idea arose only after political and religious differences emerged in the same society and presented people with the limited options of either tolerating diversity or coercing consciences. Many groups chose the latter option, and only after experiencing the horrors of repeated wars did they slowly recognize the benefits of the first option. However, prior to the emergence of cultural differences, the practice of religious tolerance was of no concern to anyone within the culture. When everyone around you believes as you do, the question of tolerance does not come up. Later, in a time of transition from cultural homogeneity to heterogeneity, the idea of tolerance first appeared to be a dangerous and unnecessary innovation. It took endless squabbles and bloody conflicts to effect a change in people's minds and practices.

Of course, some people will refuse to change their minds no matter how overwhelming the crisis becomes. Their resistance to new ways of thinking and acting stands in contrast to the type of character required for further development. Can you be more specific about this precondition to progress? Suppose some advances and declines are correlative to the presence and absence of certain *differentiations of consciousness.* What might this mean? Recall that your caring about others has expanded over the years. Initially the range of your caring was limited to family and close friends. Historical studies turn up cases of a similarly limited range of caring. The ancient Egyptians had a single word for "human being" and for "Egyptian." What does this tell you about their understanding of and concern for non-Egyptians? In anthropological studies of rites of passage from youth to adulthood, a repeated theme is how a youth is expected to make the transition by shedding human blood. Of course, the victim must come from a different tribe; to shed the blood of one's own kind is forbidden.

What do you make of these two examples? Does it seem arbitrary to you to reserve the name "human being" to one particular population? Do you think murder becomes justified ritualistic killing as long as the victim comes from a different tribe? Your reservations about this name usage and this ritual arise from a "differentiation in your own consciousness." Sounds vague? Think of how you might be concerned for the victim, the outsider, as a "human being." Why do you believe the victim has that status? Presumably you can differentiate between tribes and nationalities, yet you have grown up in a culture that both identifies these differences and recognizes a more fundamental commonality. You have taken for granted that rules protecting members of your tribe from violent assault should protect others as well. You differentiate then between differences among persons that determine, for example, whether they can vote and a common humanity that should guarantee all persons protection from avoidable evils regardless of their tribal identity.

What did it take historically to arrive at this change in mentality? One suggestion is that persons needed to learn to ignore some empirical differences as mere matters of fact. The general historical insight was that tribal identity, while important, was no longer definitive of what it meant to be human. A new understanding of persons as deserving of respect and protection from harm encompassed more than tribal members because the notion of "person" had expanded beyond a previous understanding. But how did this change happen? Perhaps developments in religious and scientific understanding[3] contributed to this shift from a tribal mentality toward a more universal notion of persons as having worth independently of tribal identity. In retrospect you can observe that, prior to the shift, rules protecting insiders from murder did not apply to outsiders. Today that way of thinking, absent group bias, seems quite strange to you.

So you have changed in comparison to an earlier mentality. Do you consider it a change for the better? If you assume all persons have the status of moral equals, then you are mistaken according to the previous tribal mentality. Perhaps the notion of equality is just part of your tribe's preferred way of thinking. Just how would you justify belief in the moral equality of persons?

Besides differentiations of consciousness, there are other changes in consciousness that are sources of moral diversity. Suppose character types differ significantly depending on the presence or absence of certain *conversions* or radical displacements from previous ways of thinking and feeling. This is the most controversial of the claims about the sources of moral diversity, but there is no avoiding the basic issue. Persons carrying out inquiries have the insights that are later the basis for their decisions. But persons may be more or less committed to inquiry, more or less willing to be moral, more or less at home in a world that contains manipulable resources as well as transcendent mystery. Consider these questions: What can you know? What should you do? What can you hope for? Will different answers make any difference in how you live your life? The claim here is that they will because differences in intellectual, moral and spiritual commitments make a difference in how you understand, judge and decide. The medievals were more succinct: *Quidquid recipitur ad modum recipientis recipitur.* Roughly translated this means: "one understands according to one's capacity to understand." Since understanding and judging are acts of specific persons and are the basis for subsequent acts of deciding what is good to do, variations in "capacity" do matter. The point is uncontroversial if the question is whether you have the capacity to read a German novel in the original or to fix a malfunctioning computer. Clearly some persons will be better able to do one rather than the other. But differences in skills are one thing; saying that persons have changed for the better because of "conversions" is more likely to evoke puzzlement and even argument.

The controversial issue here is whether various conversions are preconditions to improving a person's understanding, judging and deciding. To get at the controversial issue, let's revisit two simple examples of *intellectual conversion* that turned up in earlier chapters. Do you remember the example of the two children breaking glasses? Do you agree that intellectual development occurs when a child no longer evaluates actions solely in terms of the quantity of harm done but begins to count intention as a relevant measure of moral responsibility? Do you recall the example of the child learning to think in terms of the good of the family as a group? Do you agree that a type of intellectual breakthrough occurs when persons are able to think about what is good in the nonpalpable terms of social order and bonds of trust? Instead of confining their thinking to immediate and tangible goods, they affirm goods that are due to the mediating but invisible operations of promising and trusting – without which social order collapses. Absent this intellectual conversion, a person's moral judgments about economic policies and political programs are likely to remain focused solely on particular goods and personal consequences. Why, again, is individual bias an instance of underdeveloped understanding?

How does something like *moral conversion* become a source of differences in moral understanding and deciding? Recall the remarks on political realism with its moral resignation to the "facts" that must be faced and the evils that must be done if one's group is to survive. In contrast, a morally converted person has a horizon of concern that expands beyond the welfare of a single group. What secures the latter's interests and even one's own safety is at best a relative good that may be trumped by the good of the alien within one's borders or the good of some population beyond them. Have you met or heard of persons resisting political realism and the mantra of "My country right or wrong"? Did you find their actions admirable? If you have seen the movie "Schindler's List," what was Oscar Schindler's change of heart about? Why would anyone risk his or her life for those who at first are anonymous and alien individuals? What must such rescuers be thinking to risk their lives for complete strangers?

How does something like *religious conversion* make a difference in moral viewpoints? Recall Archbishop Tutu and his endorsement of the Truth and Reconciliation Commission. If legal systems are just, responsible officials should ensure that victims of murder and torture are avenged, so how is justice served when the murderers and torturers receive amnesty? Do some people think justice is not the highest good? Many persons have wondered about the pacifism of Quakers. Does their rejection of violence make any sense to you? Were you ever puzzled by someone's refusal to fight back in self-defense? Perhaps you have read something by Sister Helen Prejean on the death penalty. Why would anyone be opposed to executing mass murderers?

In all these examples you may have noticed a willingness to forgive the oppressor and evildoer. But why forego justice and extend mercy? If you try to answer this question by using some utilitarian calculus of benefits and costs or by seeking some fair trade-off between rights and duties, you may be looking in the wrong places. Ethical theories that rely on principles of utility or try to find a fair balance between individual rights and social obligations are missing the basic religious insights supporting this willingness to forgive. The issue is not which theory has the best arguments on this question; what matters are the basic insights and judgments of those who have experienced some type of spiritual transformation.

To sum up: there are variables in material and cultural conditions, in differentiations of consciousness and in conversions. These variations are sources of multiplicity in views about moral acts and human flourishing. More fundamentally these are variations among moral operators, among moral subjects, who to varying degrees are open to further moral insights and so to a more developed understanding of what is good to do. But does this make any sense to you?

RELIGION AND MORALITY

Talk of "conversions" suggests questions about how religious traditions are related to morality. This brief section surveys how religious beliefs play a role in orientating people's decisions about how to live.

Religion has historically played several roles in human living. It has played a *psychological* role in offering comfort to the bereaved, reassurance to the fearful and hope for those striving to do good. It has filled an important *sociological* role in unifying communities around common beliefs and practices. Think of the function of churches in helping families to educate a new generation in the customs of a particular society. Religion also has served an *explanatory* function in offering its adherents an account of how their lives fit into a much broader cosmic drama. Depending on your background, you may think of examples of how a religious tradition answered your questions about where you had come from and where you were going. Did the answers include a story about how all persons belonged to a drama much larger than their individual lives?

It is not uncommon to hear that religion is of "value" because it plays such roles and that, without religion, social order is endangered. Have you heard some variation on the theme: "What's wrong with this society is we've lost touch with the moral and religious values on which it was founded"? Did the speaker go on to recommend a return to "traditional values" as the way to solve current social problems? On the other hand, some will say that religion has been a source of social friction – recall the earlier references to wars of religion or consider current debates over allowing prayer in public schools. They may quickly add that religion also fails to do an adequate job in its psychological role since it imposes on people standards that are impossible to meet and so generates guilt and unhappiness. (In the last century Freud took this view of the burdens imposed by religion, specifically Christianity, on its adherents.) Some critics will go on to suggest that contemporary science has undermined the explanatory function of religion by debunking its narratives about human origins and destiny.

What are you to make of such claims for and against religion? Welcome back to the experience of multiplicity and to the puzzle about how to sort through all the contending voices. Some clues may help you sort out a few of the claims. Suppose you distinguish between the first two functions of religion (i.e. offering psychological comfort and preserving and transmitting social mores) and its third, explanatory, function. Why make the distinction? Is it plausible to suggest that the first two roles are *pragmatic functions* relative to human needs? What might this mean? Imagine how you feel about a summer thunderstorm: if it allows you to skip watering the yard and so saves you work and money, then it is a good thing; if it ruins your plans for a picnic, then it is a bad thing. In either case the rain is evaluated in terms of how it affects your interests. Have you met people who took a similar pragmatic stance toward religion? Some may have held to inherited religious beliefs because they felt reassured; others may have dismissed religious practices since they felt bored. Again, in both cases religion is evaluated in terms of how it affects persons and their interests.

How is the explanatory function potentially distinct from the two other roles? The thunderstorm example is a place to start. Imagine a child asking a parent what rain is. A typical response uses any of a number of synonyms, e.g. "a form of precipitation," "water falling from the clouds," or even "the earth taking a drink." (Of course, after the age of sixteen, you may be convinced that it is the result of your having just washed your car.) Are these adequate answers to the child's question? Do you recall the much earlier remarks on nominal understanding? If so, then you recognize the child's question is about what makes rain rain – why does it rain? Here we are back to the basic wonder that drives the child's questioning. While probably settling for synonyms as a child, the adolescent may arrive at high school and encounter a textbook synopsis of the hydrological cycle with its classes of interrelated events, e.g. heating, evaporation, condensation and so on. Suppose the adolescent still has further questions, e.g. why does water evaporate or why does it condense? The adolescent may suspect the response, "first it is heated and then it is cooled," is part of the old game of nominal understanding.

How is any of this connected to the distinctiveness of the explanatory function of religion? Note that it is possible to think of rain solely in relationship to yourself: it feels wet, it cools you on a hot day, it wastes your labor in washing the car, it waters your lawn. But the child with a why-question was pursuing something more. Initially beyond the grasp of the child, the explanation of why it rains will be available later in terms of relationships among classes of events. In such an explanation the inquirer finds no pragmatic reference to how rain makes persons feel or even whether it serves human needs. The focus is on understanding events in their relations among themselves, not in their relations to us. Now what if the aim of the explanatory function of religion is to reach such an understanding of how all things are related among themselves?

You may already have some of the background insights for this understanding of religion. Think about your own careful questioning when some issue really mattered to you. It may have been a sudden increase in your water bill or the smell of something burning in your kitchen. If you did not find an answer right away, you kept questioning since the issue was important and because you assumed there had to be an explanation. Notice how your efforts to understand only make sense because you do not assume things just happen; they happen for a reason.[4] Recall, if you will, the earlier claim that the range of your questioning is potentially unrestricted, i.e. you can raise questions about anything. Some inquiries will be quite pragmatic; others will be more remote from everyday living and involve theoretical reflections on scientific puzzles or the so-called "big questions" of life. When children ask where they come from, parents offer a variety of answers, but suppose what they are asking is why they exist. Inchoately they are asking the philosopher Leibniz' question: "Why is there something, why not nothing?" The reach then is for an ultimate explanation for everything. When theologians write of God as "a complete act of understanding," they are affirming that such an ultimate answer to why-questions exists. Note that they do not claim to know what that complete explanation is; they usually acknowledge that by "God" they mean a mystery beyond their own comprehension. Still, the explanatory function of religion is a reaching for some understanding of this mystery, and the roots of that reaching are in you, in your own spontaneous desire to understand. Is this at all credible or is it incredible? You might revisit the claim above that you only make the effort to understand because you assume something. What is it you have been assuming when you have been asking questions?

Much the same claim is made about your spontaneous concern for doing what is good. When you try to decide what is worth doing with your life, are you assuming the effort makes sense? You may not have recognized the assumption until you have encountered both good and evil in the world. Have you witnessed good persons victimized and bad persons victorious? If you have, then you probably have wondered what kind of world you live in where virtue is punished and vice is rewarded. Here are some of the "big questions" belonging to the explanatory role of religion. Do you live in a friendly universe or is it alien to human well-being? Do human beings belong to a universal order that ultimately sides with what is morally good or are they an evolutionary anomaly in a universe that is indifferent to human existence? When Gandhi was asked why he was willing to risk his life for India's independence, he supposedly said he was convinced that good will ultimately win out over evil. His response rested on a belief that the order of all things "conspires for the good," and so human efforts to be moral are worthwhile. In contrast, others have believed that there is no intrinsic intelligible order to the universe and so persons should accept that human history is ultimately without rhyme or reason. You perhaps have read some of the literature of the absurd from the middle of the twentieth century and so are familiar with such claims.

Once again you face the fact of multiplicity. Is it worth sorting out these rival claims? Will it make any difference in how you live if you believe that the world is ultimately absurd or if you believe there is an ultimate explanation for everything? Will caring about understanding seem a "useless passion" with the first option? Pragmatic goals aside, why would you want to keep asking "why"?

RELIGIOUS CONVERSION

In the second section of this chapter, you read that the most controversial of the listed sources of differences in moral decision-making are types of conversion. The references to intellectual and moral conversions may be less controversial than talk of religious conversions. Still, the question of what, if any, religious convictions a person brings to deliberating and deciding is a relevant question. To dismiss it as not worth asking may remind you of the basic meaning of "bias." So let's ask: What, if any difference, does religious conversion make in moral decision-making?

First, what sense do you make of talk of "religious conversion"? Typically the talk is about a "change of heart." In some cases the change is a turning away from former ways of thinking and acting and a turning toward something believed to be far better. The analogous experience you may have had is that of falling in love. The experience revises old outlooks and practices and energizes your new way of thinking and feeling. One of the relevant texts in the Christian tradition is Paul's description of conversion as the experience of God's love "flooding our innermost heart." (Romans 5:5) In fairly traditional terms, the love of God moves persons to respond in ways that imitate this transcendent love, e.g. by loving both God and neighbor and showing as much in word and deed.

Presumably religious conversion makes a major change in a person's conscious affects and understanding. In terms used in the preceding section, the religiously converted person feels and affirms the goodness of the ultimate order of things. Saying "Yes!" to reality in this way is not a single event but an ongoing challenge since the sayer is not necessarily living in harmony with that transcendent good. The traditional religious terms of "sin," "repentance," "self-denial" may sound strange to contemporary audiences, but they once referred to a common experience of persons being at odds with what was best in themselves and of understanding they needed to change.[5]

But what difference would such a change of heart make in how people lived? Think of how a religious person or community may rank various goods in a different order than others who do not share their faith. Previously you may have puzzled over the pacifism of the Quakers or the improbability of Archbishop Tutu's call for amnesty. You may also have wondered how ranking justice lower than forgiveness of an oppressor could possibly make sense. In debates over the death penalty and military actions, the voices of critics often appeal to religious beliefs. This may not surprise you since you are aware of how religious traditions have shaped moral traditions. For example, those who argue that the courts should not uphold "right to die" statutes believe that suicide is morally wrong. In many cases this stance reflects an inherited Christian tradition with its beliefs that life is a gift from God and that it continues after death. In contrast, ancient Roman and traditional Japanese cultures found suicide acceptable if the purpose was to save one's honor or the honor of one's group. The loss of either was an evil far worse than death.

So once again multiplicity appears, but things can get even more complicated. To the general remarks on religious conversion you can add remarks on levels of development within religiously converted individuals. The evidence for such levels turns up when persons speak about how their religious convictions affect their choices. You might think back to Kohlberg's theory in Chapter Six to help track some of these rationales for choices.

You have no doubt heard of "fire and brimstone" preachers who motivate listeners to change their lives by threats of damnation and eternal punishment. A milder approach may encourage listeners to lead good lives so as to enjoy rewards in heaven. Either type of appeal seems to work on some people. After all, the believers just need to be pragmatic in protecting their long-term interests; by following the path shown to them, they can avoid eternal pain and gain lasting rewards. Still, you may wonder if there are any "higher" reasons for leading a good life. Is there more to religious consciousness than a calculus of rewards and punishments?

Consider how early religious education introduces young persons into their community's beliefs and customary practices. They learn what the group prescribes and proscribes and sometimes why. Initially threats of punishment and promises of rewards may accompany the "lessons" on how to live. But this is one more instance of a social dialectic in which what persons first borrow or take on faith they may later question and revise. So in time young persons may understand and cherish a group as worthy of their voluntary support and sacrifice. They may originally have believed that honesty, hard work, devotion to family and church were all good things to promote in word and deed because everyone else said they were the cornerstones of social order; but in time they may assent to these same beliefs as a matter of personal experience and conviction. As part of this process, religious conversion can be a voluntary turning away from selfish desires and a turning toward the good of some community. Talk of being loyal to God, church and country resonates with those who believe these higher goods are worthy of dedicated service, even if such service requires personal sacrifice and loss.

Of course, the dialectic here can show up as a negative relation. Since religious institutions are in the hands of human agents, they can exhibit all the symptoms of bias, moral fault and corruption witnessed in human history.[6] When religious leaders betray the mission of their offices, the loyalty and trust of many are shaken. Scandals reveal, among other things, whether followers believed and trusted out of personal experience and conviction or had been conforming to group beliefs and practices simply as part of earlier socialization. Scandals come unexpectedly and painfully to the latter; for the former they bring pain but less surprise.

Since you are already familiar with Kohlberg's developmental theory of moral reasoning, you probably expect there to be a further level of religiously converted consciousness. Besides the good of your community, are there more all-encompassing goods deserving of your care? Have you ever put aside pragmatic calculations of personal and group benefits in deciding what you should do? The section in Chapter Six on forms of bias (especially with its critique of political realism) may have prepared you for these questions. How you answer them now may depend on what situations you have encountered in your life; how you answer them ten years from now may be different. In time your own living may provide further evidence for the claim that different levels of development in religiously converted persons are a source of moral diversity.

The personal challenge of this text reappears: Have you further growth ahead or is your capacity for caring about understanding and about others already at its limits? The title of this chapter posed these questions indirectly. How you answer them concretely is a matter of recognizing personal and social limitations and struggling to overcome them in daily living. Perhaps you have detected that, in thinking about ethics, many persons are too quick to focus on failures in moral development. For example, do the case studies in the ethics textbooks emphasize corporate fraud, political deceit and marital infidelity and neglect instances of moral decency, not of a dramatic or heroic nature but everyday instances of acting responsibly as a matter of routine?

Whatever your estimate of your own prospects for further growth, can you adopt a long-term, possibly hope-filled perspective on the prospects for the human species? From this expanded perspective, can you think of ethics as the study of the slow emergence of excellence in the lives of persons and the social orders they construct?

EXERCISES

1. What have been two instances of progress and decline in the history of your country? How do your examples reflect the presence or absence of recurrent acts of intelligence and responsibility?

2. Provide an original example of moral conversion and relate it to Kohlberg's developmental model.

3. Describe an original example of religious conversion and relate it to Kohlberg's developmental model.

4. Describe three examples of religious thinking each of which parallels one of the three "functions" of religion cited in this chapter.

THE STRUCTURE OF THE GOOD

8

THE QUESTION OF OBJECTIVITY

The primary question in the preceding chapters was, What are you doing when making moral decisions? In this chapter the leading question is, What are the "objectives" of moral decisions? The earlier chapters laid the ground-work for answering this question, but before taking it up, there is a preliminary question about your moral choices: Can they be objective? The meaning of "objective" may be puzzling. You may already have wondered about its meaning since the question of objectivity in moral decision-making showed up in earlier chapters. Recall the references to received opinions and clichés about variable preferences. Given the fact of moral diversity, both personal and cultural, should you even expect to find objectivity (whatever that may mean) in a field like ethics?

Answering this question requires background preparation, and that is what the preceding chapters provided. Answering the question about your own operations in moral decision-making ideally prepared you to answer the question about objectivity. How so? The strategy of self-attention should provide you with data for checking your developing understanding of how you go about making choices and for evaluating anyone's theory about decision-making. If attended to with care, the data are not only evidence for expanding and checking your claims about decision-making, they are also materials for critical reflection that may lead to more careful performance and better self-understanding. For example, previous descriptions of trial-and-error approaches to problem-solving presumably fit your experience, whether in auto mechanics or computer repair. Did the further descriptions of more methodical approaches to problem-solving remind you of alternatives to haphazard guessing? If so, can you envision providing yourself with a more efficient way of doing things? Your experience may include attention to your study habits and how you might improve them. In business you may encounter all sorts of efforts to enhance average performance through incentive programs, more efficient technology, zero-inventory schedules and so on. In the sciences you may witness careful design of double-blind experiments and deliberate efforts to calibrate testing equipment for ever greater precision. What all this suggests is that you may be developing some understanding of how you and others have been operating and how you may improve your own performance. Learning about your own mind-in-operation can be the basis for understanding how the results of such operating can be objective.

Rather than review the content of preceding chapters, let's emphasize several earlier puzzles that, if they were taken seriously and so occasioned hours (or days, even weeks?) of puzzling, may have led to some basic insights. Think back to the prism-goggles experiment or the remarks on nominal understanding in Chapter Two. The challenge to common-sense views of reality may be a dim, barely felt memory. Intact and unshaken may be your view that what is real is what you sense "out there." Because you see, feel, smell what is out there, it must be real, i.e. not just what is in your mind. "Objectivity" then is a property of things as they really exist out there. If you worked on the "thick glasses" experiment, do you remember the problems with identifying the "out there" with what is real? Perhaps it is time to revisit the earlier puzzles. Again, pausing to puzzle is the key to moving ahead – unless getting ahead is a matter of reading without really understanding?

Though not stated explicitly, the assumption of earlier chapters was that objectivity is primarily a *correlation* between your own structured operations in inquiry and what you are trying to understand. What does this mean? Your spontaneous wondering lies at the beginning of inquiry and gives rise to all sorts of questions. The dynamic process is a reaching toward answers you hope to find but do not yet have; so the process amounts to an anticipating of discoveries yet to occur. What are the correlates of these operations? The simple example of the noise that disturbs your sleep in the middle of the night already provided some clues. The noise is the sensitive presentation that arouses you and evokes attentive questioning, "What was that?" You question because you expect there is a reason for the disturbance, so you are anticipating finding a reason. The what-question has its initial correlate in the noise, but it anticipates discovering what caused it, so the second correlate is intelligible possibility. Do you recall the two examples of replies? "Maybe it was the neighbor's cat, but maybe there's an intruder in the house." Since this second possibility is of some concern, the guesses need checking. The is-question has its correlate initially in the guesses that need checking, but it anticipates settling the issue of fact. So the final correlate of the completed operation of judging is not what you guess may be the case but *what in fact is the case*. The following chart may help you track some of these correlations among operations.

SP <–> What-Q   (A sensitive presentation is whatever evokes curiosi-
                 ty and gives rise to a what question. A what-question
                 is what is evoked by a sensitive presentation and
                 anticipates intelligible possibility.)

What-Q <–> U   (A what-question anticipates understanding, and
                 understanding is what responds to a what-question
                 and may be formulated as a hypothesis or definition.)

U <–> Is-Q   (A formulated response to a what-question evokes
                 reflection on its correctness, and the is-question
                 anticipates settling the issue.)

Is-Q <–> F   (An is-question anticipates understanding what is the
                 case, and "fact" is the correlate of the operation when
                 the question is answered correctly.)

Your puzzling about "correlates" can continue in regard to questions for deliberation and for decision. Try to figure out the terms for these two correlations. Where does "possibility" reappear? How does the is-question show up and what does it anticipate? Again, is there a difference between what "seems" good and what "is" good?

Attention to such exercises can shift your reading from a fairly passive absorption of what someone else says you are doing to an active reach for an understanding of your reaching. It is the latter type of reading that provides the persuasive evidence of objectivity. For example, when have you invested time and energy in solving some personally significant problem? Maybe the issue was whether to continue in a relationship or to break it off. Perhaps the pressing concern was whether to change careers or to stick with a job that was unsatisfying but offered security. Whatever the case, why did you make a serious effort to evaluate your options and to project the consequences of possible choices? Again, as with the nighttime noise, you were not satisfied with a guess or hunch about what you should do because too much was at stake. Now the earlier claim was that objectivity is primarily a correlation between your own structured operations in inquiry and what you are trying to understand. Put another way, objectivity is what you are reaching for in your is-questions and questions for decisions. They are operations that complete either a process of discovering what is *true* or a process of determining what would *be truly* good to do.

If all this is still vague, consider the much earlier claim that it makes a difference whether you are careless or careful in doing work. If you are attempting to settle a question of fact, do you expect to have more confidence in your answer if you have given a lot of time and attention to the inquiry? A simple test of confidence-level is to reflect on how you have produced any number of papers for your college courses. Did you throw some of them together the night before the due date? Did you construct others more carefully, revising and polishing them well in advance of the due date? In which papers did you have more confidence? Why were you more confident? Was it because you expected to get a better grade? Perhaps you believed that your research and formulation of results would stand up to criticism. Why believe this? If your assignment was to study a dispute over a question of fact and to defend your answer, your confidence may rest on your belief that you have answered the relevant questions correctly. If so, then you presumably have reached your goal, namely, a correct understanding of what is the case.

Perhaps simpler examples are in order. As a matter of fact, you have experienced years of making correct judgments about all sorts of things. You first were just guessing when you tried to ride a bicycle or a skateboard. Your first efforts to use a computer were hardly an example of instant mastery. Perhaps a chemistry lab class in high school challenged you to identify the components of some liquid, and your first surmises were wide of the mark but later on target. Pause to locate your own examples – the simpler the better. The question is whether you have ever understood anything correctly. If you have, then you have known something about reality; you have known something objectively. But how did you achieve this "objective"?

It takes some careful self-minding to keep in focus the claim that objectivity is not a property of things "out there" but a feature of how you, the inquirer, are related to what you operate on. Revisiting the prism-goggles experiment or Oliver Sack's account of Virgil's struggle to recognize what he was seeing may help steady your focus. Where was the cup – on the right or on the left of the goggles wearer? Where was the doctor's face when Virgil's bandages came off? Did looking by itself settle either issue?

If you are somewhat familiar with debates about objectivity and subjectivity, you know that one of the recurrent issues is how reliable judgments can be.[1] You do not have to search very far to locate examples of judgments, some of which are more reliable than others. Are you reading this text now or are you fast asleep and dreaming the whole thing? When you drop the pen in your hand, does it float upward or fall downward? Are wars among nations now impossible because a global economy makes war contrary to the self-interests of every nation? Are your answers equally reliable?

Why are some judgments more reliable than others? What determines reliability? Again, there are long-running debates over how to answer this question.[2] Rather than review those debates, let's refocus on you as a specimen of judging and ask what you are doing in *making reliable judgments*. Before judging you are questioning: Is something the case or not? Is this worth doing or not? How do you go about answering such questions? You may be stumped on how to reply, but your routine performance can supply clues to what you already have been doing even if you have not explicitly understood why you were doing it. Return to the simple case of the noise in the middle of the night. Your listening for more noises or the act of getting out of bed to check around the house is a searching for more clues. In the back of your mind you already understand that determining whether the noise came from a cat or an intruder depends on detecting certain things. If you listen and hear a meow, does that more or less settle the matter? If you get out of bed, walk downstairs and see the front door open (not to mention a shadowy figure in the kitchen!) does that settle the question and give rise to new ones? Note how your doing follows from your anticipation of what will count as relevant evidence for or against your two guesses. In more formal terms, you have already made a *prospective judgment* that guides your doing. Why "prospective"? Are you anticipating that, if the cause of the noise is the neighbor's cat, you should hear more sounds made by cats? If the cause is the presence of an intruder, do you expect to hear different sounds and to find signs of a break-in? Your listening and looking are intelligent and focused ways of checking your guesses because you already have a sense of what conditions need to be met if your judgment is to be reliable.

So what determines the reliability of a judgment? The general reply is in terms of how many of the relevant conditions of the prospective judgment are fulfilled. Still too vague? Try thinking about how a police detective handles potential suspects in a crime. Motive and opportunity usually head the list of relevant considerations. If a potential suspect has an ironclad alibi and so had no opportunity to commit the crime, then the detective's judgment is the person is no longer a suspect. Can you think of other relevant conditions that need checking before settling on who the guilty party might be? Why are detectives interested in fingerprints, DNA traces, gun registration records, eyewitnesses and so on? Interest in these matters depends on a prior understanding of what conditions are relevant to determining a question of fact. To the extent the detectives find those conditions satisfied or unmet, they will be making more or less reliable judgments about suspects.

What seems clear about detective work may seem less clear when the question is about the reliability of your moral decisions. You can imagine how someone could prove that a suspect was guilty beyond any reasonable doubt, but are you equally confident about having made the right decision in recommending what sentence the a convicted defendant receives? Assume that you intend to do what is good, but how do you know what it is? About many decisions you may feel untroubled and even confident. Years ago you learned that what seems good is not necessarily what is good. Throwing food at the dinner table or talking while others were speaking once seemed good, but others taught you table manners and respect for others. Today you take such things for granted. Still, on more complex issues, how do you know that you are not just following the conventions of your society and conforming to its variable understanding of what is good? Are you interested in knowing what is good to do regardless of such variable conventions?

The earlier remarks on social dialectic are worth recalling here. What you inherit are the beliefs of your "tribe." Reading this text can be an exercise in this dialectic since you have been asked to believe a number of things but also invited to check them against your own developing understanding. Accepting the invitation may prove crucial in pinning down how your moral choices could ever be objective. It is one thing to affirm or deny someone's arguments; it is another to identify in your own life evidence that supports your denial or affirmation. In the previous chapter talk of moral and religious conversions invited you to reflect on yourself as a specimen or non-specimen of such breakthroughs. Even earlier talk of three different levels of moral reasoning was less about sketching Kohlberg's theory and more about tracking your own ways of moral reasoning. Does the question of objectivity in moral decision-making need your experience as a reference point?

Someone may quickly object that this approach turns ethics into a study of *subjective feelings* and the innumerable variations in individual biographies. This hardly seems a promising approach to the question of objectivity. The objection has merit. Think of how your prospective judgments about what you should do reflect your own personal history. Again, your prospective judgments identify what you anticipate are the relevant issues for arriving at a judgment. For example, suppose some students with no background in advanced mathematics were asked if a particular route was the most efficient path for garbage trucks to take through a neighborhood. Do you think they might be at a loss where to begin? Did their educational background help or hinder their asking the relevant questions? An example closer to home occurred at the end of Chapter Four. If you worked on the alphabet puzzle, did you anticipate that the relevant data would form some kind of mathematical sequence? Was this an educated guess reflecting your past schooling? Did you eventually discard this prospective solution? Extend this dependence on prior learning and development to moral judgments. What if persons have little understanding of or empathy for a group within their society and they have to evaluate policies affecting this group? Will they make prospective moral judgments that include the well-being of this group as a relevant or weighty consideration? Even if they do not, others may, and so there can be different judgments about the merits of the policy.

The question of multiplicity and the remarks of the last two chapters on sources of moral diversity return. Perhaps this section on objectivity gives you a different slant on these two puzzles. As a matter of fact, people make different moral judgments. Does that mean all of these judgments are equally defensible, equally reliable? Consider the possible variations in feelings and understanding among jury members in a death penalty case. Suppose all the jurors have concurred that the defendant is guilty of first-degree murder. What happens next if they have to choose between a life sentence without parole and the death penalty? Think of the possible variations in what they bring to their deliberations. Some may think, if he is guilty, then in fairness to his victim he deserves death. Others may believe that, even if he is guilty, so long as he poses no further threat to society, he should receive a life sentence. Still others may favor a life sentence because it offers a chance for the individual to reform his life. Just punishment and public security are important, but the thought of writing off any human life as beyond redemption is at odds with their felt convictions about what is best. Notice how easily the first group's two conditions (guilt and fairness to the victim) are satisfied in making their judgment on the proper sentence. As you move to the next group, however, a new condition appears (future security); and with the third group, there is yet another condition thought to be relevant (moral conversion). If you like, imagine representatives of all three groups in the same jury room. For starker contrast, imagine Archbishop Tutu and a governor of Texas serving on the same jury in a capital case.[3] Will they give the same weight to all the preceding conditions in making their decisions?

The jury example highlights a regular feature of decision-making. Different people with different beliefs enter the jury room and so are likely to form different prospective judgments, but the group's deliberations may challenge and change some of those beliefs and judgments. Has this been your experience in less dramatic discussions with family, friends and classmates? With some frequency serious conversations raise new questions, detect hidden complexities and identify overlooked details. You may have had the experience of a discussion with others that allowed you to uncover blind spots and faulty assumptions in your own thinking and in that of others. If so, you and others had an opportunity to let go of some of the accumulated nonsense previously borrowed and to adopt a more intelligent and responsible stance.[4]

Public debate can have a positive role in moral decision-making. Conversing with others can shift the odds that your prospective judgments will expand to include a wider range of conditions.[5] In that case conversation makes a contribution to the objectivity of your moral understanding and deciding. Can you recall occasions when others persuaded you to think differently? Did it occur to you to thank them for helping you develop?

This long section needs summing up. It began with a question about objectivity in moral decision-making and suggested self-attention as the path to answering the question. You read that objectivity was a correlation between structured operations in inquiry and what those operations intended. To understand and to evaluate this claim, you were invited to reflect on simple examples of nighttime noises and your late night writing of term papers. The related question of the reliability of judgments turned up. Again, self-study was the recommended path to an answer. Talk of "prospective judgments" was a clue to what you might find in your own experience. In searching for answers, do you draw upon past understanding to identify what will count as relevant evidence? Does reliability in judging become a matter of finding the relevant evidence and satisfying the identified conditions? Try another example. If you go outside, see dark clouds on the horizon, hear the rumble of distant thunder and feel breezes from the outflow of a storm, what do you expect to happen? Now eliminate all these conditions; what do you expect? Do you settle questions about moral actions this easily? Yes and no? Often you have few doubts: it is good for parents to care for their children;

it is good for motorists to be courteous; it is wrong for investment bankers to give misleading information to clients. When moral issues are more complex, your judgments may be more tentative and provisional. Are there any conditions under which the death penalty is justifiable? Is an economic blockade of a country morally defensible if it harms civilians? Fetal-tissue research promises benefits to innumerable individuals; yet, if it depreciates human life, does it risk harming all persons?

What if someone advises you to use your own experience as a "reference point" for evaluating such complex issues? Does this mean your judgments and decisions will ultimately rest on subjective preferences? Has a section devoted to "objectivity" ended with an endorsement of "subjectivity" as the measure of right and wrong? Why add, then, the concluding remarks about conversation and public debate as potential contributors to objectivity in decision-making? Recall the remarks about social dialectic. Perhaps they placed too much emphasis on your detecting nonsense in inherited common sense. But either pole in the dialectical relationship may contain flaws.[6] This allows open communities to learn from individuals in their midst and vice versa. So conversation with others may be a means to detecting your own biases, to anticipating more developed ways of moral reasoning, to envisioning differentiations of consciousness and conversions that you have yet to experience.[7] This prospect may not be strange if you have admired older individuals who seemed wiser and more adept at recognizing the complexity of moral issues. Why did you seek their advice? Was it because you recognized in them something admirable? What did you expect to learn from them? You probably were assuming that, in leading good lives, they had learned something important and would share it with you. Notice how objectivity as a relation between what persons intend and what they achieve may be part of what attracts you to such figures. Your own intending of what is truly worthwhile may find embodiments of that goal in admirable individuals.[8]

If you have been lucky enough to have met remarkably good persons, you probably recognize the potential of such meetings to transform your own ways of thinking and doing. The transformations were not likely the result of formal arguments or theoretical reflection. Indeed, expecting another to persuade you by logical arguments to think and behave differently would probably be a barrier to actually changing your life.[9] But is this not another way of inviting you to find objectivity in a relation to some type of subjectivity?

REVISITING THE GOOD OF ORDER

The preceding remarks on encounters with remarkable persons reemphasized the public context for making moral choices. This section revisits the earlier comments on three uses of the word "good" with special attention to the second use: the good of order. You may now be in a better position to appreciate how moral choices can be a group endeavor to provide everyone with a better time.

Recall that the first use of "good" referred to a relation between needs and their satisfaction. If you are hungry, then food is what you want and call good. You can expand the example to any number of goods and services consumers want. The next step is to realize that a flow of goods and services depends upon a social order. You may think of visible grocery stores, banks and malls as making up such a social order. If you followed up the earlier invitations to puzzle about acts of meaning, then you understand that invisible acts of meaning sustain such enterprises. For example, acts of promising and trusting are the basis for employment contracts with checkout clerks, for bank loans to home buyers and for credit card purchases at a mall. A third use of "good" turns up when persons ask whether particular goods and the social arrangements that provide access to them are truly good.[10]

To focus on the second use of "good," survey your own common-sense appraisals of what is good and bad about your society. Why do you believe that road rage is bad but safe driving is good? Why do you think dealing honestly with customers is good but defrauding them is bad? Why are you suspicious of first amendment defenses of violence in tv programs for children but supportive of reading programs for children? Perhaps there is a common assumption behind all these appraisals: certain ways of interacting with others enhance personal growth and build better societies while others are destructive of both. Why should you treasure the former and object to the latter?

The issue here is having a new insight into the good of social order. Is it enough to believe a social order is good if it "delivers the goods"? Some argue that a social order should be seen as no more than an instrument for satisfying human needs. Does this reduce the second meaning of "good" to the first? Besides the benefits you receive, what other reason is there for loyalty to social arrangements?

If you have grown up in the West, you have probably heard a standard response to the last question. *Classical Liberalism* is still the reigning political theory in much of the West; it certainly was influential in the construction of many western political institutions and their legal codes. Even if you have never studied the theory, you will have heard some of its familiar phrases: "the state's authority derives from the consent of the governed;" "people consent to be governed out of self-interest." The latter claim is a response to the puzzle of why persons would surrender some of their liberties and bind themselves under common laws. The usual response is that persons recognize there is "strength in numbers," and so they submit to public authority because through cooperative efforts they are better able to satisfy more of their needs. Think, for instance, of what your driving would be like if there were not common agreements on how to maintain roads and on how to pay for them – not to mention some common rules governing driving. The "social contract" provides such benefits, and in turn citizens promise to obey the rules that are consistent with the terms of the contract.

Even this thin sketch of Classical Liberalism can cause you to puzzle. When did you consent to be governed? When did you sign a social contract? The standard response within the theory may still cause you problems. It first states what is uncontroversial: the society into which you were born has provided you with all sorts of benefits. Then it asserts a principle of reciprocal justice: "For benefits received benefits are due." The next step is the problem: you have a duty to obey the duly enacted laws of the society that has so benefited you. You may wonder what this entails. If someone does you a favor, is it good to make a fair return? Yes, but does that mean you are obligated to make whatever return your benefactor requests? Think of the possibilities and you might hesitate to accept future gifts. So social orders have claims upon their members, but they are not unrestricted claims. Recall the remarks on a third level of good as the basis for *legitimate dissent* from the commands and practices of some group.

You may have detected a further problem with this reigning political theory in the West. It assumes persons submit to laws out of self-interest. Above the question was, Does this view reduce the second meaning of "good" (the good of order) to the first (the good of personal satisfaction)? So what if it does? Well then your puzzle is how to understand persons who make heroic self-sacrifices to defend their social orders. If they put at risk their careers, their families' security, even their own lives, how are they pursuing their personal satisfaction? The puzzling may get off track here and bog down in the old debate about whether anyone ever does anything except out of self-interest. To stay on track, recall how your spontaneous caring about others is dynamically expansive. Just as the child learns to appreciate the family order as more than a means to individual benefits, so older persons develop all kinds of loyalties to social orders and think them worthy of personal sacrifice. At the root of such loyalties are judgments, a saying, "Yes, this institutional order is good," and a saying, "Yes, I will play my role in it." Why does this happen? Presumably the first "yes" is an affirmation of the worth of the order, and the second "yes" is a voluntary decision to help sustain this order.

Examples are helpful in detecting the multiple "yeses." Think of a family and the periodic sacrifices its members make to support one another. Think of members of the legal profession who see *pro bono* work, allowing the indigent access to the legal system, not primarily as acts of personal charity but as acts of professional responsibility. In other words, they think of their legal profession not as a private career but as a vocation to serve and to protect a complex web of social relations and goods. Finally, closer to home, you might wonder why your professors show up to teach their classes, advise their students and do their scholarly research. But to make the examples "right at home," what "yeses" have you said and to what social orders?

You may have already wondered why this "revisiting" of the good of order follows upon the section on objectivity. What is the connection between the two? For one thing, there is a contemporary notion of objectivity as equivalent to the *publicness of knowledge*. That is, we accept truth-claims that have passed public scrutiny. For example, scientists routinely subject their research findings to peer review expecting that, until colleagues duplicate their findings through their own experiments, the initial results are at best tentative. Only after repeated failures to disconfirm the results does the profession embrace the findings as an addition to the discipline's common stock of knowledge. Similarly in ethics, one test of the justifiability of a moral action is *publicity*. If you are willing to make the reasons for an action and the action itself public, then that provides some evidence of the rightness of both. You may be familiar with contemporary demands for *transparency* in public policy-making. Transparency means that public officials are accountable to a broader and better informed public for how they make decisions. Decisions behind closed doors and secret deals that only a few are privy to are non-transparent and more readily lend themselves to abuses of power.

So "publicness" as a measure of what is true and truly good has merit. Aristotle supposedly was asked by an Athenian father how he could make sure his son grew up to be a person of good character. His response was: "Raise him in a community that has good laws." The philosopher recognized the crucial link between anyone's developing subjectivity and the public order in which such development occurs. Is this a new correlation or does it remind you of the earlier comments on social dialectic?

A cautionary note concludes these largely positive descriptions of social orders. As noted previously, in his famous work, *Obedience to Authority*, Stanley Milgram recounted how ordinary persons reacted to gentle prodding by a supposed scientist conducting an experiment on learning abilities. The basic design of the experiment was to have a volunteer read word sequences and have a second volunteer, strapped to a chair with wires attached to him, repeat them in the same order. If the latter made a mistake, then the former was to administer an electrical shock by flipping a lever on a board that had multiple levers marked from 15 to 450 volts in 15-volt increments. If more mistakes occurred, the reader was to administer progressively higher voltage. It was all a ruse since the second party was an actor, the wires attached to him did not deliver any electrical current and he was not in any danger. The real purpose of the experiment was to determine how far up the shock panel the naive volunteers would go.[11] The actors would deliberately give incorrect responses. After passing a certain voltage level, the actors would begin to say they were in pain and wanted to be unstrapped. If the naive volunteers continued past this point, the actors would scream as if they were in pain. Eventually the actors would mention a prior heart condition. In those variations of the experiment where the two subjects were in separate rooms with only voice contact, the actors would later fall silent as if a heart attack had occurred.

Prior to conducting the various forms of the experiment, Milgram sent out a description of its basic design to numerous experts on human behavior and asked them to predict how many of the naive volunteers would proceed all the way to the 450-volt level. Keep in mind that the purported scientist running the experiment would never raise his voice or threaten any of the real test subjects when they said they were worried about the other "volunteer" and wanted to break off the test. All the lab-coated figure said was the experiment must continue and the test subject is suffering no real harm. Knowing that much, the experts predicted that only one to two percent of the naive volunteers would go all the way to the end – for all they knew killing the test subject. The experts assumed that low percentage reflected the average number of sadists in a general population. In fact, Milgram found far higher rates of compliance.

Rather than survey all the various designs and outcomes of the experiment, let's focus on two extreme cases. In the first, *ninety-two percent* of the forty naive volunteers went to the end of the shock board. While most of them exhibited anxiety and expressed concern for the well-being of the test subject, they did not challenge the authority figure in the lab coat and walk out of the experiment. In interviews afterwards, they were told about the set-up and how they had not actually harmed the actor. What was noticeable were the different rationalizations they offered. Sometimes they blamed the other person for being so stupid; sometimes they said they wanted to quit but the authority figure "forced" them to continue; some remarked that, since they had accepted five dollars to participate in the experiment, they had to keep their promise to cooperate; a few reported feeling satisfied they had done their job.[12]

What of the other extreme case? In it *only ten percent* of the naive volunteers went past the point where the actor demanded to be released. How is this shift from a ninety-two percent rate of compliance to ten percent possible? A simple variation in the design was all it took. In the first extreme case two volunteers, who were really actors, joined the naive volunteer who then simply read the word sequences while the others administered any shocks.[13] The actors were instructed to proceed to the end of the shock board, and thirty-seven out of forty volunteers went along. In the second case (with ten percent compliance), the two actors were instructed to challenge the authority figure and to end the experiment when the test subject asked to be released. Almost all of the naive volunteers went along. So what is the key variable here? In familiar terms, "peer pressure" made all the difference. If the two actors went to the end, only three out of forty volunteers managed to stand up to them and the authority figure. On the other hand, when the "group" broke with the authority figure, nine out of ten volunteers joined them. Of course, in the subsequent interviews, most of the volunteers said nothing about following the lead of the two other "volunteers;" instead, they cited their own concern for the well-being of the test subject and how they knew it was wrong to hurt someone.

So what is the "cautionary note" at the end of this section on the good of social order? Spelling it out would be a disservice to serious learning. Some hints may encourage you to pause and to ponder. Does it come down to a matter of "dumb luck" regarding which actors are around us? Does carefully choosing your friends matter? Is publicness really reliable as a measure of what is true and truly good? If not, what is the alternative? One clue (for which you will still have to hunt) – how were those three out of forty volunteers able to resist their own desire for public acceptance and their own fear of an "ugly scene" in public? What made them exceptional? Given your own liability to succumb to peer pressure and to rationalize this surrender of your developing subjectivity to an ambiguous "objectivity," how do you lessen these risks that originate within you? What can improve your odds? Yes.

THE DIMENSIONS OF THE GOOD[14]

This section reviews the content of previous chapters and offers a new "mapping" of moral decision-making.[15] This time the mapping is not focused on intentional operations but on their "objectives." Recall the opening question of this chapter: "What are the objectives of moral decisions?" So this question is one focus, but there is also the "summing up" or pulling together in one place of some insights and terms from earlier chapters.

One clue to the mapping attempted here is found in the earlier claim that objectivity is primarily a correlation between structured operations in inquiry and what those operations intend, i.e. their "objectives." Your first puzzle may be about the words "intend" and "intentionality." Both express what some understand is a common feature of inquiry; namely, when persons ask questions, they are "intending" or reaching for answers; they are anticipating discovering something about reality or about possibilities that can become realities. Recall how what-questions were signs of the desire to know but also took two distinct forms. Besides asking what is the case, you can also ask the question for deliberation and so "intend" ends you can pursue and means you can adopt. In other words, you can reach for an understanding of what possible goods you can bring into existence and what possible means you can actually use to make a potential good a reality.

Suppose then that human beings have this *capacity* to intend various goods and to act or to operate in various ways to procure them. Not much of a stretch here if you think of someone shivering in the cold, wanting warmth and deciding to build a fire. The fire is a means and warmth is the end or good that meets a human *need*. Here is a clear instance of human concern focused on or intending a particular good as an objective. But imagine the historical account of human mastery of fire and of other forms of energy as means of survival. The need may be recurrent, but the means to satisfying it have changed over time. The *operations* or actions that exploited human capacity and produced heat for cave dwellers required certain *skills*, but over time both those operations and those skills became more complex. The flexibility or *plasticity* of human abilities permitted *development* of new means for understanding and controlling sources of energy. Among the gradually developed means are *institutions* which now supply energy on demand to paying customers. For example, city utility departments are humanly designed orders for delivering basic services providing power for heat in the winter and for air conditioning in the summer.

Routine access to such services is possible only because of the ongoing *cooperation* among persons who fill certain *roles* and competently carry out assigned *tasks* with the required know-how. Think of the interdependence of persons who produce and those who consume energy from public utilities. A vast web of relationships links consumers as bill payers with coal miners or oil drillers and refiners, with truck drivers and storage facility operators, with utility plant employees and managers of city agencies. The network of related enterprises spreads outward indefinitely to issuers of public bonds, road and power-line construction crews, mechanical engineers who design plants and stockholders who fund their expansion.

If all these relationships are routinely and predictably to yield energy for consumers, they must form a stable order, an institutionalized set-up that people commonly accept and agree to maintain, each filling a role in ongoing schemes of cooperation called "institutions." Particular goods will keep flowing as a result of this complex *good of order*. But this order of things acts back on its creators. Institutional roles and tasks require certain types of skills, and this "demand" on human capacities favors the emergence and development of some operations over others. For example, the capacity for and operation of counting will, in some persons, develop along the lines of professional accounting practices; the capacity for social interaction and subsequent social skills will, in some persons, be directed by an understanding of personnel policies. More simply, think of how the child's daydreaming can, in response to market demand, become the varied skills required to make economic forecasts or predictions about labor supplies.

So operations express capacities and meet needs; human plasticity makes possible the development of skills, and institutional roles and tasks both presuppose those skills and evoke the emergence of new ones. How are these relations part of moral living? The social orders that maintain a flow of *particular goods* flourish or decline depending on degrees of cooperation among persons willing and able to fill their roles in institutional frameworks. The vast network of interdependent operations continues to function because persons are able to do their jobs and actually decide to do them. Let enough of them exhibit an unwillingness to play their roles and things begin to fall apart. At least this much can motivate executives to be concerned about employee morale and to design worker-incentive programs.

The social orders that actually result from willing cooperation among countless persons are far from static arrangements. In the short run, institutions may seem unchanging, even inert, but their existence is rarely secure or stable. Why? Think of how dependent institutional set-ups are on prior conditions: the skills available in a given workforce which experiences turnovers; the fluctuating levels of investor confidence; the expansions and contractions of consumer demand; group bias held in check but potentially explosive in political strife, strikes and departmental feuds. Think as well of some of the external threats: political enemies, economic competitors, natural disasters.

So challenges to the survival of social orders are numerous. But why do persons make personal sacrifices to meet these challenges? You have read about the answer of Classical Liberalism. People seem to be loyal to a social order out of self-interest since it provides a flow of goods to meet human needs. But that answer may be incomplete. A social order can itself be a good that is the objective of moral choices and acts. How so? In the first place, do institutions owe their origins to intelligent planning and decisions to cooperate? Secondly, do they owe their survival to the recurrence of such decisions? The negative example makes the point clear. If natural disasters are accidents that can disrupt institutional functions, what of the effects of morally irresponsible choices and systemic corruption? Persons are at *liberty* to choose means and ends, to cooperate for the common good or to conspire for some lesser good. If liberty is used to pursue not what seems good but what is good, then persons are contributing to a set-up that is good and that provides particular goods that are in fact good. But liberty can be used irresponsibly. Suppose an executive is motivated by individual bias to earn salary bonuses and to amass a stock portfolio larger than any rival's. Leveraged buy-outs and accounting practices that inflate a company's net worth may be means of gaining salary bonuses and more stock options. Whether the company's "growth" is sustainable and whether employees and stockholders are at risk are not the executive's concern. What links the executive to others is a narrow concern for personal benefits to be gained and costs to be avoided. But then *personal relations* are being undermined since the legitimate expectations of others for honesty and fair returns on their labor and investments are ignored. Investors and employees are just resources to be manipulated.

Fortunately you can find businesses and public institutions that are run differently. Persons at liberty choose to make a responsible use of their freedom. Executives and employees understand how their cooperative efforts meet both personal and collective needs. Feelings of loyalty to the institution and to its personnel guide choices. Despite disagreements they believe that what they are doing as a group is worthwhile, and so they sacrifice time, energy and self-interest to sustain their common enterprise. Why do they do this? Presumably they are in agreement that some goods are worth the effort, are *terminal goods* worth promoting. These may be talked about as the "values" of financial security for employees, the reputation of the firm and professional accountability. Behind such talk is not only a shared understanding that it is good to promote family life, corporate integrity and personal honesty but also a willingness to make performance consistent with these goods. This willingness of subjects has its intended objectives in terminal goods, but then the operations of responsible subjects have correlative objects that are truly good.[16]

This correlation of personal decisions and objective goods may shed further light on the earlier terms *orientation* and *conversion*. If a person's habitual orientation is toward growing in understanding of what is true and in doing what is good, then efforts to make moral decisions become a pattern of behavior that witnesses few lapses. Recall the old maxim that "the good is what good persons do." On the other hand, if the commitment to understanding and to doing what is good is careless and episodic, decision-making yields mixed results. Moments of clear resolution occur interspersed among longer periods of indifference and inattention to what one is making of a life. Think of persons drawn to better ways of living but also drawn back by feelings of insecurity and a preference for comfortable routines. The tension between envisioned growth and reluctance to depart from old habits becomes a test of human liberty. Will you go forward or rest where you are? The challenge is personal: "What am I to make of my life?" It is also social: "What are we to make of our community?" Care, again, can become the mother of innovations. Or to revisit the question of conversion: How can any of us sustain the orientation to what is truly good? What can make recurrent departures from comfortable but inadequate routines of living themselves routine? St. Augustine offered a succinct response: *"Incipit exire qui incipit amare."* ("One begins to leave who begins to love.")[17] Responding to what you know and feel to be worthwhile and dismissing fears and rationalizations can become habitual if feelings and understanding are integrated and consistently orientated toward making of one's life something genuinely good. Absent that integration, a life of wavering between responsible choices and drifting along on impulses becomes the mediocre alternative.

Recall what the poet Rilke said of this challenge.[18] But who is the operator responsible for either alternative?

To conclude this chapter, the following "map" of the structure of the good[19] presents a summary of this section and also an invitation to expand your own understanding of how your living is entwined with the lives of countless individuals and institutions. Try using the categories to track your routine purchases of commodities, your paying of taxes, your pursuit of a college degree or your choices of friends. The complexity of seemingly simple choices may become more apparent. Attention to such complexity can be a step toward more reflective and responsible decision-making in the future.

Individual		Social	Ends
Potentiality	Actuation		
capacity, need	operation	cooperation	particular good
plasticity	development, skill	institution, role, task	good of order
liberty	orientation, conversion	personal relations	terminal value

EXERCISES

1. Choose either the prism-goggles experiment or the thick glasses experiment and tell how it casts doubt on the common-sense assumption that the objectively real is "what is already out there to be seen."

2. Provide an original example of a "prospective judgment" about some question of fact. Then identify how you would go about determining if the relevant conditions were in fact fulfilled.

3. Identify the "correlates" of questions for deliberation and questions for decision.

9

A NEW WAY OF DOING ETHICS

APPLYING THE STRATEGY OF SELF-ATTENTION

Repeatedly this text has promised that the strategy of self-attention can help you sort out the problem of *multiplicity*. Again, that problem takes many forms, but they commonly feature different and incompatible answers to the same questions. In the field of ethics, competing theories propose different normative guidelines for decision-making. Sometimes the norms, while different, yield compatible results. On other occasions the choices the different theories endorse are incompatible and so give rise to the puzzle about how to judge the opposed positions. If the response to the puzzle is to construct another theory, the list of answers likely grows by one more entry and the puzzle is no nearer being resolved. A promising alternative is to study what precedes answers, formulated meanings and theories. Reflecting on and beginning to understand what you are doing in arriving at answers to questions are the first steps toward this promising alternative.

The test of the promise lies in actually applying the results of your self-attentive inquiry to controversial issues. Are you now ready to criticize contending positions and to detect how to resolve some of the conflicts? This chapter provides examples of controversial questions and encourages you to apply insights from previous chapters in evaluating answers to them. But the issue is whether the relevant insights are now *your* insights. Have you paused at the recommended places and gained some self-understanding? The goal has not been to persuade you to reject one set of theoretical claims in favor of another. Instead, the goal has been to encourage you to use your emerging self-understanding as a basis for evaluating different conclusions. Do you have a new perspective on how to handle the contending positions? Does this self-attentive inquiry prove to be a better way of doing ethics?[1]

The proof for any answer lies in the doing; hence the rest of this chapter invites you to puzzle about debated issues that are usually treated in a quite different way.[2]

Before introducing the first controversial question, we should retrieve some remarks on prospective judgments from the preceding chapter. Two simple examples should suffice. Suppose you ask yourself if it is going to rain within the next half hour. Presumably you take a look at the sky, check the horizon for approaching clouds, listen for thunder in the distance. Why are these predictable operations? Most people have a prior understanding of what to look for in anticipating an approaching storm. This prior understanding guides them in checking for relevant signs; so, when the question comes up, the "careful" and intelligent thing to do is to check for the relevant clues. This checking is guided by an anticipatory understanding that, if the relevant signs are present or the relevant conditions are satisfied, then the question is easy to answer. To generalize: a prospective judgment is the anticipation of what conditions have to be met before a reliable judgment can be made.

Now a judgment may be about a matter of fact or it could be a judgment of value. In a judgment of value pertaining to choice, one is affirming or denying that something is worth doing. Our second example fits this type of judgment. Imagine you are dining out with friends in an upscale restaurant. The waiter brings the menus, and the question is, What should I order tonight? The menu options are numerous, but your habits and tastes narrow the list. (Forget the escargot and any cold soup?) Still, among the remaining options, no one choice is obvious, so you have to give some thought to your selection. What will be the relevant considerations? Notice that anticipating already was present in your established habits and tastes that inclined you to rule out some dishes. They were considerations relevant to a negative judgment of value, i.e. what you would not like to eat. The exercise here is worth a pause. Try to play out the scene around the table as you scan the menu, ask advice from your friends or the waiter. Try to make explicit what counts as important to you in selecting a first-class dinner.

This second example may seem a strange follow-up to a chapter that endorsed talk of "objectivity" in moral decision-making. Could anything be more subjective than tastes in food? As the Romans put it: *De gustibus non disputandum*. We tend not to argue about matters of taste and, instead, leave them to individual preference. We do not expect any compelling argument to sway others into sharing our tastes. This example, then, serves to introduce the first of the questions focusing this experiment in self-attention: Is there ever any such thing as a compelling argument? The approach in this chapter is not to answer the question for you; or better, it is to supply you with plausible reasons supporting opposed answers. With a few clues the following pages will encourage you to find in your own intentional operations evidence for sorting out, for judging, the competing answers.

Question #1: Is there ever any such thing as a compelling argument?

Answers in the Affirmative (A):

(1) Your experience has probably been that some arguments are more persuasive than others. Thus, you recognize that some arguments could be compelling even if many are not.

(2) If being "rational" means assenting to truth-claims for which there is sufficient evidence, then arguments supported by such recognized evidence are compelling. Not to assent to them is to abandon one's rationality.

(3) Any attempt to prove that arguments are never compelling would be self-defeating. That is, if such an argument were successful, it would prove the opposite of what it claimed.

(4) Why would we give reasons for what we claimed was true if no compelling reasons were ever possible? Our performance in arguing presupposes that we believe we are not wasting our time.

(5) Common sense assumes a difference between the delusions of the insane and the findings of scholars and scientists. Unless there are compelling arguments for this difference, the distinction between fact and fiction may be arbitrary.

Answers in the Negative (N):

(1) If "compelling argument" means a reasoned conclusion that is "certain," i.e. one that is impossible to doubt, this sets too high a standard for evaluating arguments or proofs in any empirical discipline. Probable opinion "as yet unrefuted" is most often the accepted standard.

(2) The continuing absence of consensus on how to answer major questions in intellectual history indicates that compelling arguments are, at best, rare. If they were common, far more consensus would have been achieved across the centuries.

(3) The appeal to "compelling arguments" assumes that the decisive criterion of truth is ultimately something "outside" of the judgments of persons. But arguments and formulated reasons are secondary to the rational capacities and operations of variable individuals.

(4) Given a little self-reflection, we recognize that no argument "compels" us since we have a capacity to rationalize, quibble and procrastinate indefinitely. In other words, no matter how sufficient the proof, we can always invent reasons for postponing assent. (Jung was right in asserting that intellectuals made the worst patients.)

(5) Just as understanding what might be the case is distinct from judging what is the case, so judging what is good to do is distinct from deciding what one will do. Arguments that settle what is probably good to do fall short of "compelling" the decision or consent to do it.

How can you begin to assess these incompatible stances? Perhaps you see the advantage in first asking what the phrase "compelling argument" means. In A(2) it seems to mean any conclusion supported by "sufficient evidence" which, when understood by a rational person, would necessitate assent. However, in N(1) the phrase supposedly means a reasoned conclusion which no one could doubt. Despite the argument there that a lower standard of probability is all we should expect, you may wonder whether a highly probable opinion "beyond any reasonable doubt" would be compelling. But, then, N(4) mentions tactics of evasion useful in postponing assent no matter how probable an opinion is. Of course you might think using such dodges scarcely represents us at our finest or most rational moments.

You could pause here to puzzle about the last sentence. What does this talk of "finest or most rational moments" assume? You could also review the affirmative and negative stances and ask what the words "reasons," "rational," "reasoned" and "rationalize" mean. Now it might be a misstep to try to define each of these terms as if that would settle the issue about compelling arguments. Can you anticipate why defining terms might not end the debate?

What alternative is left? Some self-attention may offer a way forward. A few clues can help. So, for example, what has been your experience in operating rationally? (Simple examples are a good beginning.) When and why have you assented to some truth-claims? What has been your experience in rationalizing or evading consent? Have you experienced a "gap" between knowing something is true and accepting it as true? As long as you were operating "rationally" was there a gap? What about judgments of value? Have you ever experienced a gap between knowing what you can and should do and actually consenting to do it? Once again, as long as you were operating rationally and responsibly, was there a gap?

If you are starting this paragraph after a long pause over the preceding questions, then the strategy of self-attention is in play. If you are reading on with no pause, then, to be honest, your old habits are probably still in place. The claim, again, is that you are a specimen of rational consciousness and of rationalizing consciousness. As such you are a source of empirical evidence relevant to the preceding questions. But the implicit prospective judgment regarding whether arguments are ever compelling could include your experiences as relevant conditions. Can your self-study, perhaps as yet barely underway, identify some of those conditions and determine whether they are fulfilled? Again, contending theories and their arguments and appeals to evidence are secondary phenomena; what comes first are the operations of inquisitive and inventive persons. But persons are highly variable, so does this priority undercut any possibility of objectivity in judging and deciding?

With this question of objectivity we have arrived at the second controversy for this experiment in self-attention. Recall how earlier chapters prepared for the explicit discussion of objectivity in Chapter Eight. For example, after exposure to multiplicity (e.g. diversity in moral beliefs and practices), most people find plausible the clichés about morality as a matter of personal opinion or local custom. To move beyond clichés, the text asked you about differences between being careful and being careless in inquiry and about shifts to methodical, as opposed to haphazard, approaches to problem-solving. As well, the notion of social dialectic may have shown you a way of responding to claims that your moral beliefs and practices are wholly due to your social conditioning.

Even earlier (in Chapter Two), the prism-goggles experiment and Oliver Sack's story of Virgil were clues that maybe objectivity is not a property of things "already out there" and objective knowing does not occur by simply taking a close look. All of this was preparation for the hypothesis in Chapter Eight that objectivity is primarily a correlation between operations in inquiry and their intended objects. Setting up the hypothesis required that we first gain some familiarity with intentional operations before raising the question of their intended objects. Once the operations and their patterned relations are named and differentiated, we can ask what are the proper objects or objectives of, for example, what-questions, is-questions and questions for decision. The claim was that, if we ever succeed in answering an is-question correctly, then we know what is objectively true. Similarly, if we ever succeed in correctly answering a question about what is good to do, then we know what is objectively good. But how do we know if we ever succeed at either of these tasks? In response the notion of prospective judgment made an entrance. The initial question was: Do we ever find that all the relevant conditions for answering a question are in fact satisfied? The examples of a jury trial and of predicting a storm were uncomplicated instances of prospective judgments. Still, juries sometimes and weather forecasters oftentimes err, so the prior question about objectivity becomes: Can we ever know that we have identified all the relevant conditions for answering a question? That is, before asking whether the known relevant conditions are satisfied, we need to ask if all the relevant conditions are in fact identified.

Again, the approach in this chapter is not to answer these questions for you. Instead, it asks you to find in your own intentional operations evidence for sorting out, for judging, competing answers.

Question #2: Is objectivity in judging and deciding possible?

Answers in the Affirmative (A):

(1) Public conversations and debates are ways of identifying relevant conditions and so of expanding the range of considerations an individual takes into account. In a society with freedom of speech within the public media, all the relevant conditions for at least some judgments should be identifiable.

(2) The notion of a social dialectic is a corrective to views that make cultural, historical or linguistic variables fixed barriers to objective knowing. The desire to understand and the capacity to raise and answer questions amount to an element of indeterminacy in each person which, in principle, can challenge any inherited determinants of a person's thinking.

(3) If understanding is corrigible and being careful in inquiry is possible, then no matter how limited one's initial understanding of relevant conditions is, in principle all relevant conditions could be known.

(4) Suppose someone asserts that some relevant conditions can never be known. How would this be provable if such conditions were unknowable?

Answers in the Negative (N):

(1) Trying to identify relevant conditions involves raising and answering questions. How can we be certain all possible relevant questions about some issue have occurred to us? We cannot since our knowledge is incomplete; so objectivity in judging remains elusive.

(2) What we recognize as relevant conditions, what we accept as rational argument, what we perceive as real – all tend to vary with culture, history and language. So objectivity seems to require an independence from variables of place, time and language that we do not experience. Our perceptions of our world are always filtered through the variables of our time and tribe. In other words, we cannot stand apart from those variables and judge things objectively.

(3) If objectivity were possible in judgments of fact and of value, should there not be far more consensus in both ethics and public policymaking? Differences, especially incompatible ones, in both fields are evidence that objectivity may be beyond our capacities in knowing and deciding.

Now shift your attention to your capacity to judge these incompatible claims. What makes for a decent beginning is making explicit what objectivity means to you. Are you still wedded to a "first realism" for which objectivity is a characteristic of objects out there which are to be known objectively through careful inspection? Is this the view of objectivity assumed in N(3)? Will it make a difference if you have been "displaced" from that first realism so that what's objectively real is what is known not in looking but in correctly judging? Perhaps that displacement is either barely underway or still remote; nevertheless, are you able to respond to N(2) in terms of a social dialectic? What about N(3)? Because there are enduring differences in moral beliefs and practices, does that fact preclude nonarbitrary evaluations of all moral differences? Recall the earlier materials on the sources of moral diversity. Have you retained any earlier insights about moral, religious and intellectual development?

Do you have any questions about the affirmative answers? For example, regarding A(1), why should you trust public conversations or debates to reveal all of the relevant conditions for settling some question? Are the public media, our courts and political forums open to all voices? If cultural decline is widespread and group and general bias pervade the common sense of the day, what is likely to emerge from public conversations? Will some questions be forbidden as not in keeping with good taste and with being polite? Of course your trust in public debate may survive because of the element of indeterminacy cited in A(2). However, both it and the possibilities cited in A(3) may remind you of the comments on moral autonomy in Chapter Six. What "in principle" is always possible may in fact be rarely achieved given so many limitations on effective freedom.

Again ideally, one or more of the preceding questions will have held your attention and delayed your reading of this paragraph. Have you tried focusing on yourself as a specimen of one term in a social dialectic or as an instance of moral, religious and intellectual development or as an indeterminate experiment in caring about understanding? "In principle" you, and all the rest of us, have the capacity for such self-study, but it does not happen automatically. Between potential freedom and effective freedom are obstacles – which brings us to the third controversial question: As specimens of moral judging and deciding, are we deluded in thinking we are at liberty to choose our own course in life?

You could cite your ability to raise and answer questions as a principle of indeterminacy and make it part of a negative response to this question. On the other hand, the Milgram studies offer empirical evidence for at least overestimations of the frequency of moral autonomy among adults. If those studies demonstrated the rootedness of our actions in social, especially hierarchical relations, others indicate the dependency of behavior on biochemical conditions. For example, by changing colors in a room or by exposing test subjects to certain aromas, one can alter their moods and dispositions. But the latter affect how we operate in inquiry, in relating to others, in being careful or careless in our choosing. Besides any number of preconscious conditions, think of how the propagandist's deliberate manipulation of economic crises can foster a climate of fear and thereby shift the odds that large numbers of decent people will retreat to an ethic of personal survival.

The reference to "odds" introduces a new puzzle about whether moral freedom is an illusion. If we are free, then should it not be the case that the odds are roughly the same between our doing the right thing and doing what is wrong? But right courses of action are fewer in number than ways of making mistakes, so the odds of doing what is wrong are higher. Analogously and more concretely, are there more ways to miss a pitch in baseball than there are to hit the ball? The latter are far more numerous. However, ballplayers, through talent and practice, develop skills that shift the odds of hitting the ball. Can the same be true regarding choices of right and wrong? To be more specific, can individuals deliberately cultivate habitual patterns of behavior? Some habits will be virtues and others vices. If they are virtues, then do persons stand a "better chance" of choosing to do what is good, of cooperating with their best judgments about what is good to do?

The preceding remarks have been circling around questions about our capacity or potential to deliberate and to decide according to our "best judgments." Let this tentatively be the meaning of "moral freedom." Why would anyone object to talk of such a capacity? Any debate should be about whether this potential is ever developed, i.e. whether persons who are capable of morally free acts ever make them. A medieval distinction between natural and obediential potency may be helpful here. Our predecessors assumed persons have natural potencies, e.g. a capacity to socialize or a capacity to understand and to make decisions. But obstacles of many types impede efforts to sustain genuine personal relations or to act consistently according to one's best judgments about what one should do. Despite the obstacles, there are wondrous examples of persons surmounting them. Whether saints or repentant sinners, public heroes or anonymous benefactors, some individuals offer positive evidence that the highest human capacities can be developed.

Now the medievals read such positive cases, and the far more numerous cases of stupidity and moral failure, as evidence of "obediential potency." By it they meant a human capacity that could not be developed without divine assistance, without grace. Now this certainly is a strange topic for a contemporary audience. It appears here as a reminder that for much of Western history ethical questions were not isolated from theological discussions. Also it is a clue to how old the discussion of moral freedom is. You may detect in the few remarks about obediential potency how two types of freedom or liberty were implicitly present. First there is a natural freedom or liberty to judge, decide and so direct one's own life. As a potency or capacity, it is indeterminate regarding its path of development; so the hard question is how to form this liberty so that persons habitually choose to do what is good. In sum, we are born free, but leading morally good lives is not automatic, and this truism is why each new generation poses a moral-political challenge to its social order. Of course, this truism presupposes a negative answer to the following question.

Question #3: Are we deluded in thinking we are at liberty to choose our own course in life?

Answers in the Affirmative (A):

(1) The experts who predicted extremely low rates of compliance among Milgram's test subjects obviously overestimated the distribution of effective freedom in adult populations. The actual rates are empirical evidence that, at best, moral autonomy is statistically deviant.

(2) Like many streams flowing into a single riverbed, antecedents to our actions set the conditions for our present thinking and acting. In our ignorance of most of these antecedents, we overestimate the importance of our present deliberations in how we decide to act.

(3) As noted in A(2), too often estimates of our own freedom proceed from a superficial view of the complexity of our lives. For example, our moods and dispositions affect how we behave, what choices we make. But, in turn, all sorts of preconscious conditions shape our dispositions; so how we act may be due to conditions unknown to us.

Answers in the Negative (N):

(1) What have been some of your experiences in operating with questions for decision? Have you experienced a gap between knowing what you should do and actually doing it? With deliberate effort have you been able to make your doing consistent with your knowing?

(2) Do you live in a universe in which different options, different courses of action, are real possibilities? Do you ever recognize that different options are available to you? Are you sometimes careful in weighing options and in selecting from among them? Have you ever been careless? Did that make any difference in the outcome?

(3) Have you ever struggled and succeeded in altering your moods or dispositions? (Think perhaps of an instance when you forced yourself to smile and appear to be enjoying a social event when the opposite was the case.) Have you ever heard persons "ration-

alize" or excuse their behavior because they were in a "bad mood"? Whose mood was it? Who was in charge?

Once again the preceding reasons and answers are multiple, plausible and incompatible. At least A(1) stands out from the rest because it offers some empirical evidence pertinent to the question. But you will have noticed that all three answers in the negative make an appeal for empirical evidence. This time, however, you are to be the source. But the general claim in A(2) about hidden antecedents and the specific case of the same in A(3) raise doubts about how important reflection and deliberation are to our decision-making. Perhaps preconscious determinants are actually in charge of our lives. What do you think of this possibility? The questions in N(2) and N(3) offer clues as to how you could make a thoughtful response.

NEW PUZZLES

The opening pages of this chapter invited you to puzzle about three questions and to use your developing self-understanding as a basis for evaluating diverse answers to them. This section of Chapter Nine presents three new puzzles and leaves it up to you to evaluate answers and to take a stand. But "taking a stand" does not mean simply expressing your opinion. Instead, it should be your stance supported by evidence you acquired in your own self-study. Again, no one can do this for you, so let's begin with the first puzzle.

Puzzle #1: Why should you treat persons with respect?

First of all, how have you experienced and understood relations among persons? You undoubtedly have witnessed people relating to one another in ways different from how they relate to non-human things. For example, persons driving along a roadway watch out for pedestrians but ignore the bugs that end up on their windshields. Likewise consumers regularly purchase items at stores and then expect to use them as they see fit; but, if they hire employees, there is no such expectation of complete discretion in use. Why are there these differences in relationships? At a minimum you may think that persons are obligated to show respect toward one another, an obligation they do not have in relation to insects and consumer goods. But why do we assume this? To be honest we may not have given much, if any, thought to this question. Simply as a matter of our upbringing, most of us internalized popular beliefs about the rights and dignity of persons as persons. But now we are adults and saying "That's just what we were taught" may not be an adequate answer. So is it possible to give reasons for showing respect for others?

A pragmatic type of reasoning may occur to you: "If I do not show respect for others, they will not show me the respect I expect." Does this pragmatic motive really reflect the sense of respect for persons expressed in talk of human rights and human dignity? You may recall the remarks in Chapter Six on Kohlberg's various levels of moral reasoning. Do you remember the claim for a hierarchy among types of moral reasoning and where pragmatic calculations of self-interest appeared in that hierarchy? What non-pragmatic reasons might there be? Can your experience with self-attentive inquiry provide clues helpful in understanding why you believe that persons are deserving of respect?

Clues for Puzzle #1:

A first clue is available in how you spontaneously operate in making generalizations. Think of your own experiences in generalizing about persons, animals or whatever. Once you think you have understood one case correctly, what do you assume about any other cases similar to it? Do you operate with an unspoken assumption that *similars should be similarly understood?* Of course an important question is whether the cases are in fact similar. Answering it requires insights into individual instances. But, so long as there are no significant relevant differences between cases, there will be no differences in how you understand them. Is it much of a leap to suggest that, if you know two cases are in fact similar in every relevant way, then you should treat them similarly?

A second clue requires some familiarity with the distinction in Chapter Two between nominal and serious understanding. Consider how you could take the time to *describe* individual cases. You could point out the different positions of objects belonging to the same class or remark on how events of the same kind occur at different times. You could note how similar objects vary in size, coloring and so on. However, if you are trying to *explain* what makes them what they are, do you tend to disregard these variations? To be specific, when you are trying to understand why a type of animal behaves in a particular way, is your goal to produce results valid for only the particular specimens you are studying here and now? In reaching for an understanding of the entire class, do you ignore incidental differences among its members?

Puzzle #2: What sense does it make to talk of a "right of liberty"?

J.S. Mill formulated a principle of non-interference which has played a major role in the United States' legal system. Leaving competent individuals at liberty to do as they choose, even if they harm themselves but so long as their choices harm no others, is one way of showing respect for other persons. It may also be a pragmatic compromise because of a lack of moral consensus in a culturally diverse society. This lack of consensus marks many contemporary theoretical debates about rights and duties, entitlements and obligations. You may be familiar with the so-called "rhetoric of rights." Have you heard persons complain that their rights were being violated because someone stopped them from playing music as loudly as they liked or because a landlord prevented them from sheltering numerous cats in an apartment? Have you witnessed examples of tasteless and offensive speech (perhaps on bumper stickers and t-shirts?) and heard the predictable appeal to a right of free speech? Why do appeals to freedom of speech ring hollow when the "speech" is a tabloid's sensationalized attack on the character of a public figure? Or why do appeals to freedom of religion seem less persuasive if the practices being defended deny large numbers of people access to an education or a political voice?

In both the theoretical debates and the popular disputes over "rights," you are witnessing another instance of "multiplicity." Can self-attentive inquiry into your own performance help you sort out and evaluate some of the confusing claims? Again, this chapter invites you to reflect on your own making of meaning as an alternative to the standard ways of arguing about basic issues. Some clues may help.

Clues for Puzzle #2:

The earlier puzzles, beginning in Chapter Two, may have prepared you to think in a different way about rights and duties. Instead of imaginable things "out there" or "in here," you may be ready to think of them as relationships that exist because of how intelligent persons operate. For example, if persons have a capacity to direct their own lives according to their "best judgments," then could the "inner demand" to do so be one meaning of "duty"? Could "right" refer to an understanding (a shared expectation?) that others not interfere with or frustrate the "doing of one's duty"?

What sense can you make of talk about liberty as a "universal human right" and so as more than a customary belief in some societies? If you affirm in yourself an obligation to decide and to act according to your best judgment, should you affirm that all competent persons have a similar responsibility? Were you already assuming as much when you said: "They knew better than to do that" or, "If they had known then what they know now..."? What do such remarks presuppose? Especially the first remark reveals how you assume that to ignore one's "best judgment" is to behave irresponsibly.

The preceding clue concerned your own inner demand for consistency between knowing and doing or, put negatively, the obligation to refrain from making nonsense of those parts of your life dependent on personal decisions. The question then was whether all persons are under a similar obligation. (You may want to return to the clues about generalizing in Puzzle #1.)

Can you think of another reason for endorsing a universal right of liberty? Is moral development in competent persons more likely if they are left at liberty to choose how they will act than if they are coerced into acting as others insist they should? What was your experience in growing up and having more independence from parental supervision?

Puzzle #3: Can you make a case for civil disobedience ever being justified?

Earlier chapters described a progression in the meaning of "good" from benefits for oneself to group interests and then to what anyone would legitimately expect under similar conditions. As well, remarks on moral development indicated that ultimately the claims of any group on our loyalties may be trumped by the third understanding of "good." Appeals to what all are due may be a way of relativizing the claims of any group.

But how can persons turn against their society and break its laws? In the section on social dialectic in Chapter Three, the question arose about how individuals were able to criticize the results of their own socialization and even to act contrary to the norms of their society. What enables them to do either? (Do you remember the answer was "Yes"?) But now what may *justify* them in doing either?

Does it make sense to speak of having "a duty to yourself," of having a self-imposed requirement to follow your best judgment? Perhaps the traditional word "conscience" is worth puzzling over in this context. Just what does it mean to "have" a conscience? Again, is conscience some imaginable property "in here" for you and "out there" in others? Or try puzzling anew about what it may mean to be a morally autonomous person. Recall the etymology of the word "autonomy." Does talk of self-imposed laws make more sense after thinking about "conscience" as a correlation of inner demands and expected responses from oneself and others?

Some will worry that appeals to one's own conscience are fraught with danger since social order would, they fear, be torn apart. Would there soon be as many "laws" as heads? How would you reply to such worries? And what are laws in the first place?

Does it make sense to think of criminal statutes as encouraging citizens to cooperate with their own inner demands for responsible living and as protecting them from the anticipated failures of some to meet those demands? Laws, from this stance, do not bestow "human rights" on persons, but they do codify common expectations about how persons should or should not respond to one another in different types of situations. Put another way, the laws are formulations of what persons commonly judge to be tolerable and intolerable ways of responding to the demands for responsible living. Because some will act irresponsibly due to incompetence, ignorance or moral fault, laws and their enforcing agencies become routine parts of living in society. But what do you say to someone who sees laws as intrusions on rights or curtailments of liberty? What do you say to someone who thinks all lawbreaking is indefensible?

EXERCISES

Most of this chapter has been an "exercise" in self-attention. As part of this experiment you could revisit the reasons for the different answers to Questions #1 through #3 and recast them in the form of "If...then" statements. For example, the first affirmative answer to Question #2 [A(1)] could read: "If open public debate routinely occurs, then the relevant conditions for some judgments will be identified."

Reformulate in this way all of the reasons listed after one of the three questions. Doing so can help you identify the content of a prospective judgment. Being explicitly aware of that content can make your efforts to answer the question more deliberate and even methodical. Is this worth doing? Is being explicit about the content of a prospective judgment a way of learning more about what it means to be reasonable? Again, the proof may lie in the doing, in actually conducting the experiment.

INSTRUMENTS OF DECISION-MAKING 10

SHIFTING FROM OPERATIONS TO INSTRUMENTS

In reading this text you have found both a recurrent question of how to sort out and to evaluate opposed positions and a repeated claim that adding one more theory to the fray makes little difference. The promising alternative is to find a specimen of moral decision-making (you?) and to study it as a way of having an experiential basis for testing theories about moral choices. Ethics textbooks usually do not suggest this, but you should be suspicious of all of the claims in them (including those in this text). Test them against your own growing understanding of yourself as a specimen of moral decision-making.

Admittedly most of us are unpracticed in shifting our attention between a puzzle and how we are puzzling, between the object of inquiry and ourselves as inquiring. It is a new type of learning. Do we need to revisit the first chapter to find a reason for this kind of learning? There the stated challenge to contemporary educators was teaching *how to judge*. The last chapter was an opportunity to practice self-attention in making judgments. The experiment there presupposed your efforts in earlier chapters to learn how you are a source of insights, judgments and decisions and so potentially an informed and critical evaluator of your own and others' meanings, judgments and actions.

How interested should you be in further experiments of this sort? In a democracy, either large numbers of informed citizens actively participate in public decision-making or they leave it all to the "experts." If the latter is the case, then the long struggle in the West to decentralize authority and to allow democratic participation in decision-making ends with most citizens being dependent on the "kindness of strangers." The former option of informed participation depends on schools meeting the challenges of educating citizens about how their economy works, how policy-making occurs and how they can judge others' decisions. But how well are the schools meeting the challenges? What has been your experience?

If till now the classroom efforts have been haphazard or even non-existent, this text may provide a better organized beginning. The first step was to shift your attention to yourself as an inquirer. The exercises in self-attentive inquiry were ways to begin mapping how you operate in making decisions. Ideally the earlier chapters drew your attention to and helped you to differentiate and to name the operations that lead to choices. Gradually there was a sketching of maps as heuristic tools for finding your way around your own mind-in-act. These were initial steps toward taking some control over and improving your performance in understanding and evaluating. Such steps pursue a major goal of liberal education, namely, being able to explain and to defend why you believe what you believe, say what you say and do what you do. Is this a worthwhile goal for you?

With this chapter the focus shifts to *procedures* for analyzing and evaluating moral decisions.[1] Instead of asking how you make choices, you now are asked to evaluate the formulated choices of others. Previously the focus has been on intentional operations, mental acts, the structured performance that precedes and produces choices. This first focus went counter to standard educational practice with its neglect of minds-in-act and its emphasis on their products. Perhaps you now are more aware that "being educated out of your mind" is a serious danger and worth resisting. The new focus has a role to play in being a self-attentive inquirer. When the shift in emphasis is from operations to procedures or instruments, the same culture of neglect is a danger. How so? The study of "instruments" is a traditional part of classes in logic, ethics, psychology and teacher education. Typically in such classes there are reviews of types of arguments, exercises with strategies of moral evaluation, case studies of therapeutic techniques, demonstrations of teaching methods and of ways to measure learning outcomes. All the same, many students enter and leave such courses with little understanding of why these arguments, strategies and techniques work. They may have a nominal understanding of how to do something, but, if asked to explain why they are doing something in a particular way, many will reply: "That's what we've been taught." Even worse, if they apply a procedure and a problem remains unsolved, many will be at a loss what to do next. Information and technical know-how may have piled up through years of schooling, but the creative questioning that produces such "tools" may have become moribund. So attention to instruments is not unimportant and is worth your time, but the continuing challenge will be to keep in mind your own mind.

The broad steps toward improving your use and evaluation of various instruments are: (1) to call your attention to them, (2) to discover how reliable they are, and (3) to differentiate between competent and incompetent uses of them. Let's begin with easy examples. You are familiar with an indefinite number of classifications. Think of how legislatures categorize crimes as felonies or misdemeanors and then add further subdivisions under each category. Or think of the popular labeling of foods as having high or low cholesterol contents. The basic insights behind the labels are that something falls under one heading rather than another because it shares a relevant feature(s) with all the members of the class, and the class owes its identity to this common feature(s).

How can you test the reliability of classifications? What is unreliable about classifying all Irishmen as heavy drinkers, or all redheads as hot tempered, or all victims of the AIDS epidemic as morally culpable for their disease? You already know the classification label for the first two claims. They are called "*stereotypes.*" But why are they flawed classifications? Back then to the preceding paragraph. What are classifications supposed to do? Do you expect them to formulate an understanding of some population as sharing a common feature or attribute? If so, then the reliability of the classification depends on whether that understanding is correct, i.e. it depends on a judgment about whether each member of the population in fact has the relevant attribute(s). Knowing that a particular classification is reliable requires, in part, sufficient study of members of the grouping. If you know this much about the instrument, then you have some control over its use. For example, you know that you can challenge either of the stereotypes: (1) by finding a member of the group without the relevant attribute (so not "all" have this feature), and/or (2) by asking just how much research the speaker has done on this class. In the latter case, you benefit by keeping the burden of proof on the one who uses the stereotype, but in either case you can exercise some control in using and in responding to someone else's use of such an instrument. Try this for yourself in regard to the third claim. All AIDS sufferers share common medical attributes, but do they share common moral features?

Before suggesting further ways of checking the reliability of instruments and before saying anything about competent and incompetent uses of them, this chapter will spend time identifying some of the common instruments used in formulating moral decisions.

COMMON INSTRUMENTS

Most moral controversies are about the future. The usual questions are about what should or should not be done and about what will or will not happen as a result. In many cases the results or consequences that people predict will follow from possible actions are the basis for their choices among those possible actions. But you may wonder how anyone ever makes reliable moral choices if the latter rely on predictions, i.e. on estimates about the future. Just what do you know about the future? If most moral choices require predicting, i.e. answering questions about the future, and if the future is unknowable, is moral decision-making merely guesswork?

The usual response to this puzzle is pragmatic. In your everyday living, you have to anticipate the future, plan ahead and act on the basis of what is unknown. For example, you routinely schedule meetings, preregister for classes, save money to pay end-of-the-month bills and so on. These familiar activities depend on your predictions about the future. But do you believe that some predictions are safer, more reliable than others? Try two instances of predicting:

1. "If I drop this piece of chalk, it will fall downward."

2. "Once we have an integrated global economy, wars between nations will be impossible."

Which of these predictions is more reliable and why? The first is based on your understanding of numerous past experiences, but the second has no precedents and so seems less reliable. Why should the absence of precedent matter? Do you usually assume that similar events or situations recur over time? Do you assume, then, that future events will be at least partly similar to past events? Does this account for your implicit assumption that the flow of events is partly *continuous*? At the same time, do you assume that the future will sometimes be *discontinuous* with the past? Do any instances come to mind? You might try thinking of instances of predictive failure or of the "best laid plans" going awry. But how can you improve the reliability of your predictions? One way is to broaden your study and understanding of past cases. But let's leave questions of improving and testing the reliability of predictions to the next section. The focus first is on identifying the main instruments used in formulating moral decisions, in stating a choice.

Suppose the main instrument used in formulating choices is what some call *theories*. When you hear the word "theory," you may imagine esoteric discussions among scientists dealing with questions remote from everyday living and its common-sense ways of thinking and speaking. (You probably are familiar with the cliché: "It sounds good in theory, but will it work?") All the same, common-sense living does have its "theories." For example, if you want to drive your car to campus, you know that at a minimum you need to have fuel in the tank. What the instrument called "theory" formulates is an understanding of a *causal link* between fuel in the tank and the running engine. In more technical language, a theory expresses an understanding of how two or more variables are linked by a rule such that deliberately changing the value of one variable will alter the value of the other variable(s) in a predictable way. Let the second variable be the car engine; then change the value of the first variable, fuel tank, from "having fuel" to "being empty," and the value of the second variable goes from "running" to "being stalled."

It should be easy to follow up this first example with an indefinite number of your own examples of theories. Think about what you are taking for granted in the routine tasks of using door handles, water faucets, light switches, and handshakes. Without much, if any, forethought, you act in certain ways because you anticipate that doing X is a way to "cause" Y. What is the basis for these unreflective acts? Do you regularly operate with tacit or unarticulated understanding of how to get things done? When was the last time you thought about faucets and light switches? In daily living your attention is usually on getting something done, e.g. getting a drink of water, and the instruments you use are taken for granted.[2] Is this not the vast reservoir of nominal understanding without which much of our living would be impossible? Notice how this background understanding may become explicit when some piece of equipment breaks. Then your routines are disrupted and your tasks frustrated. Think of the faucet that drips in the middle of the night keeping you awake. Or what happens if you flick the light switch on but the lights remain off? Then your focus shifts to the broken instrument, and the question is how to repair it.

Trying to fix the broken tool may reveal the adequacy or limits of your understanding. Perhaps the "theory" you have tacitly been operating with in using light switches amounted to no more than a minimal understanding that flicked switches turned on lights. Further understanding of electricity, wiring and fuse boxes may not be yours. What are your options when the switch fails? Chancing trial and error (not usually recommended around electrical outlets?), consulting a do-it-yourself manual from the bookstore or hiring an electrician may come to mind. Each option reveals that understanding is what is missing, and the sought-for understanding is of how things are causally related and so of how to take action to fix what is broken.

What proves whether or not your "theoretical" understanding is reliable? At the level of daily tasks, the proof that you know what actions will produce which results lies in the doing, not in verbal arguments. Ethics classes usually do not involve new field tests, so defending your choices will usually require appeals to past experience. What you may have discovered is that repeatedly operating on the basis of some "theories" in different situations has taught you to refine your understanding so that you bring a wider and more flexible range of generalized insights to new situations. Think, for example, of how you learned over time to read and to respond to signs of distress in different friends or to hold in check your anger in traffic snarls.

So far this section has offered a few fragmentary remarks about two of the instruments used in moral choosing: predictions and theories. A brief summary of the initial comments on the reliability of both is possible. Your choices about what you should do often follow upon your understanding of what the consequences will be. Thus, you could formulate part of the reasoning for your choices as predictions of those consequences. How reliable is your reasoning? One way to check is to formulate the predictions behind your choice and to ask how reliable they are. What you will find in the next section is that the reliability of your predictions depends on the reliability of the theories that express an understanding of how certain types of actions and outcomes are ordinarily related.

Before turning to the next section, you may want further clues about how to understand the differences among the key forms of expression: *choice, prediction and theory*. One way of distinguishing between theory and prediction is to notice that the latter formulates an understanding of a "particular" relation between two or more events while the former expresses a grasp of a "generalized" relation among classes of events. Put another way, theories state what someone understands about relations among classes of events, and predictions are products of applying that generalized understanding to particular future cases. Notice that theories take the form of a generalization because they refer not to an understanding of a specific case or event but to a grasp of relations between classes of events. Certain words are often clues that help you recognize a statement as a generalization: "Whenever," "Anytime," "All," "Every," "None."[3] After reviewing the following pairs of examples, try to invent your own instances of theories and predictions.

1a. "Whenever a car runs out of gas, it stops." (theory)

1b. "If I forget to get gas before driving to the ski slopes in the morning, I'll be stranded on the highway." (prediction)

2a. "Anytime interest rates fall significantly, the rate of unemployment declines." (theory)

2b. "If the prime lending rate is set below 6% in April, we will see the unemployment rate drop by a full percentage point by June." (prediction)

Just as a prediction is an application of a theory to a particular future case, so the term "choice" refers to how persons might use both in deciding on a course of action. If they bother to explain their decisions, they are likely to state how they believe they should take or not take certain actions to achieve or to prevent certain outcomes. With a little bit of reflection, can you detect how they probably have made two choices, not just one? To continue with the preceding examples:

1c. "I'll write myself a note tonight, so I won't forget to buy some gas in the morning." (choice)

2c. "Politicians should immediately begin demanding a reduction in interest rates and so create more jobs." (choice)

To review: this section has identified two instruments that formulate key components in decision-making. There are others which will appear in the next chapter. For now, notice how the two instruments parallel types of intentional operations. Predictions formulate answers to is-questions. In effect, they are statements: "Yes, this will happen" or "No, this will not happen." As used here, "theory" formulates answers to what-questions. A theory expresses answers to questions about how kinds of events follow from kinds of actions. You might well guess that, since there are other types of operations in inquiry, these two instruments do not exhaust all the basic tools used in choosing. What instruments might parallel operations of sensing and deliberating?

To close this introduction to some of the basic instruments, recall that one aim is to learn how to become a more critical evaluator of your own and others' choices. One step is to identify the tools that people use to state and to defend choices. A mapping of such tools is underway. An initial mapping of what appears in an ideal[4] account of a decision includes three components. First is a statement of the outcome or purpose chosen and the means selected to attain it. Second is the explicit statement predicting that these means will produce this outcome. Third is the explicitly worded theory or theories offering the reasons for accepting the prediction. When the question of reliability returns in the next section, you will already have anticipated that answering it becomes easier if the account of a decision cites precedents as evidence for the reliability of any theories employed in linking actions to outcomes.

THE QUESTION OF RELIABILITY

The first step in analyzing an explicitly stated decision is to identify its key components. The preceding section began this process of recognizing and differentiating the content of a formulated choice. The next step is to evaluate that content. Where do you begin? Perhaps you have already guessed that one option is seeking evidence for the reliability of any theory presupposed by the choice. If a decision assumes a causal linkage between actions and outcomes, then a relevant question is, Why assume this? A theory spells out the answer in terms of what has generally been the case. But what evidence is there for the theory? Since a theory ideally formulates accumulated understanding of past experience, the search for evidence lies in asking if any precedents support the theory, how many there are and of what quality. When persons demand "sufficient reasons" before assenting to some conclusion, they are asking is-questions about the quantity and quality of evidence.[5] Another common is-question about evidence asks whether there are exceptions to the general pattern of relations stated in a theory. More details about these and other critical questions follow below. The practical aim remains the same: to encourage you to develop the "habit" of asking the *right questions* about choices. Mapping the instruments used in decision-making provides a more detailed focus for such questions and a rationale for asking them in a certain order. Asking such ordered questions is a "procedure" that improves your chances of using reliable instruments in a competent way and of detecting the opposite in yours and others' proposals.

Back now to the question of evidence for the reliability of a theory. If someone provides no evidence for a recommended decision, should you dismiss the proposal as unreliable? Perhaps, but sometimes writers and speakers offer no evidence because they assume their reasons for a decision are matters of common sense, i.e. they assume everyone in their audience accepts such reasons as obvious. You may have encountered this reliance on common sense in proposals for harsher sentences for drunk driving. Without ever having heard of the deterrence theory of punishment, most people assume that, as criminal penalties for certain behaviors increase, fewer persons will risk engaging in those behaviors. They, therefore, accept that harsher sentences will lead to fewer fatalities on the highways. So persons publicly advocating such sentences may take for granted that no one will disagree with them, and they see no need to cite evidence or precedent.

The problem is that common sense is actually quite variable and tends to be a mix of good sense and nonsense, with those relying on it alone usually unable to tell the difference. So a defense that appeals to common-sense meaning may still be open to question, even if most people endorse it. For example, cited in the fourth endnote of this chapter was a proposal to increase sentences for anyone trafficking in illegal drugs. Suppose someone appeals to the effectiveness of penalties for drunk driving as evidence for this proposal. You may still wonder if there are significant dissimilarities between drunk driving and dealing drugs. Can you think of any that might lessen the effectiveness of harsher penalties for the second type of crime?

If appeals to common sense are not adequate as a test of the reliability of a theory, what is? First of all, you may already be wary of expecting any theory to be foolproof or certain. Certainty, or the impossibility of error, is too high of a standard for both theories and the choices based on them. Why not demand certainty before deciding? Recall the comments about knowing the future. In addition, do you already expect that even very reliable theories will fail under some conditions? Think about choices of how to prevent bank fraud. If governmental regulations and audits fail to stop all embezzlement from banks, does this mean the regulations and periodic audits are a waste of time? If your efforts to base your friendships on trust and honesty sometimes lead to painful disappointment, do you discard the belief that friendships tend to be stronger when based on mutual respect and honesty? What is it about your choices that allows for generalized beliefs of this type while at the same time being open to exceptions?

Examples of several theories may offer some clues. (Again, theories are statements of how classes of events are understood to be causally related.)

1. "Whenever cold air passes over a warm land mass or warm air passes over a cold land mass, fog occurs."

2. "Anytime the government mandates expensive new safety equipment on automobiles, the cost to consumers for new automobiles rises."

3. "Responding to strangers with signs of trust reduces the risk of misunderstanding and suspicion."

Do you expect exceptions to all three theories? Why might fog not appear even if the stated conditions are present? How might you be able to buy a new car that has the mandated safety equipment and still not pay a higher price? Notice how the theories mention only a few interacting classes of events. In actual cases, other types of events (called "variables") can interfere with how the cited classes of cases regularly interact. Such interfering variables are *limiting conditions* on the reliability of a theory. Predictions based on a theory can fail because of them. Is this what you expect? Is this something you find acceptable? The standard response is: "It depends." If you base predictions on the same theory and they repeatedly fail, then you judge the reliability of the theory to be low. Your options, then, are either to discard the theory or to search for variables that often interfere and build them into the theory. For example, weather forecasters have learned not to predict fog when a warm or a cold front is fast moving or humidity levels are low. To construct an improved theory, they add to the formulated generalization a proviso: "Whenever X expect Y unless (or except when)…" Have you done the same as your understanding of human relations develops? Have you refined your understanding of how trusting you should be with strangers, how careful you should be in maintaining confidences and how loyal you should be to friends? What exceptions have you come to recognize and to accept?

Expecting generalities to have exceptions is uncontroversial. In regard to theories, the basic insight is that they are simplified or *idealized* patterns of relationships between or among only a limited number of variables. While they may take an absolute form (i.e., begin with "All," "Anytime," "Whenever"), people commonly expect exceptions because they implicitly understand that real conditions are often more complex than ideal conditions. You may have seen the phrase *"ceteris paribus"* in a textbook or heard someone use the words, "all other relevant things being equal." Both are ways of remembering that interfering variables, or limiting conditions, qualify the reliability of any theory. All sorts of practical steps are taken in recognition of this. For instance, manufacturers adopt quality control procedures because they expect any number of variables can lead to defects in their final products. Monitoring for quality at various stages along an assembly line is an intelligent response to the anticipated problems. An unintelligent response would be to demand that control procedures reduce the incidence of error to zero. Why is this an unrealistic expectation?

Have you taken a course in statistics? If you have, what did you learn about "chance," "frequencies" and "probability"? It may jog your memory if you think about what the earlier reference to "ideal conditions" meant. If a theory is a hundred percent reliable only under ideal conditions (i.e. when the few stated variables interact in isolation from all interfering variables), you may suspect that such isolation is not always the case. As a result, whether a theory holds true in a run of real cases is far from certain. So what might all the talk of "probability" mean? Suppose theories tell you what to expect when only a limited set of kinds of events interact. Might statistical frequencies tell you how often to expect such ideal conditions to be met in a run of cases? Imagine efforts to identify the frequency with which fatal accidents involving trucks and passenger cars occur on a section of your local highway. Do any single month's figures give you adequate data? Will you have to broaden the time period to determine the frequency of fatal accidents per month? When you compare the figures from different months, are they the same? Are some of the monthly figures far apart? Now shift back to a version of the earlier question: Should you expect that any traffic-control measures will reduce the incidence of accidents to zero?

If you paused and worked on these questions, you may now wonder why anyone would expect the generalized understanding expressed in theories and applied in predictions to be true in all cases. Your new expectation may be that theories and predictions are at best reliable, with "reliability" being a matter of the ideal frequency upon which, in a run of cases, outcomes are expected to converge.[6] But you may still wonder how to determine the strength of any theory. In keeping with the new focus on instruments and procedure, this section offers *three leading questions* that provide a checklist for understanding and assessing theories:

1. Is the theory precisely and unambiguously phrased?

2. If it is a new theory, is it compatible with accepted theories?

3. Has the theory been tested and found reliable?

157

Why these three questions in this order? The first question sets a minimum standard for the reliability of any theory. It functions negatively to weed out theories that are vague, imprecise, or ambiguous. Because of their wording, such theories leave you confused as to their meaning. As products of understanding, they leave you with further questions. Until you have answers, you are unable to rely on such theories. Consider two examples and how their imprecision leaves you unable to use them with any confidence.

1. "To extinguish a fire, add water."

2. "Whenever the will of the people is allowed to rule through free elections, democracy is fostered."

In regard to the first example, you might ask, How much water, delivered at what rate? Will it matter what type of fire you are fighting? In evaluating the second example, you might wonder how you are to understand "the will of the people," "free elections" and "democracy." As they are presently formulated, both theories are hopelessly imprecise, and their usefulness is in doubt. Can you invent a similarly flawed theory? Think of some of the popular advice columns in newspapers and their responses to readers' questions about strengthening family ties. Do phrases like "quality time" and "building self-esteem" show up? Try incorporating some of these terms into a theory. How precise can you make it? What further questions do you need to answer before having confidence in your example?

The second question of compatibility is most often relevant in assessing new theories. If you are familiar with the time and expense involved in longitudinal and/or control group studies of human populations, you recognize the need for simpler ways of assessing the quality of new theories. A test of compatibility is one option. As an example, suppose someone predicts that, if the federal government subsidizes the private development of non-polluting batteries for electric cars, these new autos will reach the consumer market more quickly than they ever would without such subsidies. Since there is no precedent for this type of product receiving public funding, how would anyone estimate the reliability of the theory behind this prediction? What tends to happen is persons draw on their accumulated understanding of similar cases. For instance, many will assume that governmental subsidies offset risky research and development costs to private industries, and so they encourage accelerated development of new products by those industries. A further theory of even greater generality may be part of the background test of compatibility: Investment capital tends to prefer less risky over riskier ventures, all other things being equal. If both of these generalities are credible, do they support acceptance of the prediction about electric cars?

Now try to invent your own case of a new theory that seems reliable because of its similarities to already accepted theories. What will this involve? You will need to assume a causal relation between two or more classes of events. For example, can you link access to undergraduate degrees entirely via the Internet and quality in education or cost savings? What background understanding are you drawing upon in linking these types of events?

The third question about precedents may remind you of earlier questions about classifications: (1) How much past experience can anyone cite in support of them? (2) Are there obvious exceptions to them? Answering either question will involve historical research. Recall the earlier claim that, whenever the prime lending rate falls by a significant amount, national unemployment rates fall. Historical research could lead you to identify those times when the prime rate fell, and then you could check what happened with the unemployment rate in subsequent months. But suppose you find instances when the first type of event occurred without being followed by the second? Should you dismiss the theory as unreliable? "Yes" if the exceptions are numerous, but "No" if the exceptions are few and you are able to link them to unusual conditions, e.g. a worldwide depression in the 1930's or a dramatic transfer of wealth to oil exporting nations in the 1970's. Do you remember how to build such "limiting conditions" into a theory to enhance its reliability?

You have undoubtedly heard of a fourth way of assessing a theory, especially one that lacks precedents. *Pilot programs* are standard ways of testing new theories and the proposed actions based on them. Usually begun on a small scale, such programs include close monitoring of initial results which then become data for judging assumptions about purposes and means. This approach has the advantage of avoiding expensive failures while allowing for new insights on how to revise and to improve a program before taking any more extensive actions. They are ways of "testing the waters" and making adjustments as "you go along."[7]

Most people will recognize the wisdom of pilot programs and the monitoring of local conditions. Many may also recognize that political and economic liberties are significant conditions for effective policy-making since such testing and adjusting need to be left to persons "on the scene" who are able to detect the consequences of programs for local populations. This

159

much is recognized in textbooks on business management. The pragmatic argument is persuasive: If decisions are made only "at the top," then (1) supplying the needed information from local sources will be time-consuming and eventually deliver only condensed information thereby obscuring conditions at a local level; (2) delays in making decisions will be inevitable as information is sifted, but then local conditions may have altered; and so (3) the delayed decisions may be irrelevant to changed conditions. For these reasons the "pyramid model" of corporate decision-making has fallen into disfavor. But you may be able to add a further reason for advocating local input or "microautonomy" in public policy-making. The *principle of subsidiarity* within the tradition of Catholic Social Teaching expressed this further reason: persons should "have a say" in the decisions that affect their lives; out of respect for the dignity of persons, policy-makers should "push" the decision-making down to the lowest level where it can occur effectively. In short, political leaders should show self-restraint and allow their moral equals to follow their own best judgments, *ceteris paribus*.

A further observation: even if people know a theory is unreliable, they still may use it as a basis for their actions,[8] and in some cases justifiably so. The classic example is the flood of policy initiatives during the first hundred days of the American President Franklin D. Roosevelt's first administration. Anecdote has it that someone asked the recently elected but not yet inaugurated FDR whether he would be a good president. His answer was that he would either be a great president or the last president. Innovative programs relying on untested theories were his cabinet's response to the desperate conditions of the Great Depression. Similarly most persons will accept some high-risk forms of surgery when the alternative is death. Of course, burning witches in previous centuries was thought acceptable as a way to cure a plague. So desperate measures by desperate people are usually indicative of a lack of understanding and of sufficiently reliable theories within a public store of knowledge.

Let's end this chapter by noting how a procedure for understanding and criticizing decisions is gradually taking shape. The leading questions that can help you understand what someone proposes as good to do are:

1. What is the preferred outcome (purpose) and how should it be achieved (means)?

2. How will the means achieve the purpose (prediction)?

3. What generalized understanding (theory) is the basis for this prediction?

So far the questions for evaluating a decision are:

1. How reliable is the prediction? (But answering this question depends on the answer to the next question.)

2. How reliable is the theory supporting the prediction? (But answering this question depends on answers to one or more of three other questions about precision, compatibility and precedent, including past results or the current outcomes of pilot programs.)

As a final note, you may want to draw some new parallels between instruments and types of operations. These questions about reliability are questions for judgment, e.g. "Is this theory compatible with...?" Doing historical research to discover previous cases when people relied on a theory is a way of answering questions for understanding, e.g. "What happened and how often?" Finally, a pilot study that generates new data parallels the first component of structured wonder, i.e. sensibility and its provision of data for further questioning.

EXERCISES

1. Describe an instance of decision-making. Compose your account so that it explicitly contains the five basic components: purpose, means, prediction, theory, precedent.

2. Revisit your example in the preceding exercise but this time identify and differentiate the mental operations presupposed by each of the five components.

3. Invent an original example of a theory and evaluate its reliability by using the three questions of precision, compatibility and precedent.

JUSTIFYING DECISIONS 11

CHOOSING AMONG OPTIONS

This chapter continues the review of instruments used in making decisions and offers further suggestions on how to evaluate them. If you have been tracking how the instruments result from different types of operations, you may be wondering what instrument can explicitly guide your search for options. What instrument formulates a procedure for how you can set about answering the question for deliberation, i.e. what can be done? There is, of course, the further question of what should be done, i.e. the question for decision. The second and third sections of this chapter identify instruments reflecting both types of questions. In effect, you will be introduced to standards and strategies for *identifying* and for *evaluating options*.

One way of tracking what is going on in this chapter is to notice how the is-questions change. The question for judgment shifts from asking, "Is a theory reliable?" to asking, "Is a choice of some purpose and/or action *justifiable?*" It is the latter question that turns up frequently in the field of ethics. But ethics is also about "being careful in decision-making," and the careful use of reliable instruments to identify and to evaluate answers is part of making defensible choices.

Just as the question for deliberation precedes the question for deciding, so identifying instruments for detecting what can be done precedes a study of those for evaluating options.[1] So how can you begin to identify options or possible choices? A common obstacle to identifying options is *indifference*. If a person could not care less about a proposed course of action, any effort to find alternative purposes and means is likely to be careless. What usually happens is the person thinks of a couple of options that anyone could imagine; no special effort is made to be creative or to imagine new aims or novel solutions. Instead of taking the quest for options as an opportunity to be intellectually creative and adventurous, the person settles for "obvious" answers. Care or concern is what is missing, but also absent may be the habit of being intellectually imaginative and adventuresome. Has previous education stifled the development of this habit in you?

If you are to push beyond a narrow range of "obvious" options, it helps to have a strategy for deliberately seeking new insights. A relatively simple strategy can assist you in this search. It goes by the traditional name, *"playing the devil's advocate."* As a strategy it can provide a format for detecting oversights, missed options or flaws in known options. It can also serve as a tool prompting the interested user to reach for more creative options. A summary of the steps in this thought experiment may remind you of earlier encounters with this strategy. Let's assume you are trying to evaluate someone's decision that has already been formulated as a proposal. Then, once you have identified the key components of the proposal (i.e. its purpose, means, predicted linkage, supporting theory and any precedents), take the following steps:

1. Even if you are in favor of the proposal, assume an adversarial stance in relation to it.

2. Try to invent objections to the stated purpose and proposed means, i.e. the options already chosen. (Here is the test of your own creative intelligence in trying to find better means or to anticipate overlooked outcomes.)

3. After identifying some alternative means and outcomes, evaluate their merits.

4. If you have found good reasons for objecting to the original decision and for favoring an alternative, formulate a new or a revised proposal.

Before using two case studies to practice this strategy, you might note that playing the devil's advocate is fairly easy to do when the proposal under attack is one you already dislike or one to which you are largely unsympathetic. The adversarial stance is much harder to adopt when you are strongly in favor of a proposal. In the language of an earlier chapter, the strategy requires some skill in *role-taking*. Can you deliberately suspend your own feelings and beliefs about some proposal and think about it from the position of an opponent? Doing so, at least temporarily, calls for an attitude of intellectual detachment and a willingness to be imaginative in inventing objections. How easy is this to achieve? Recall the section in Chapter Six on types of bias. For most of us there are some groups who rarely, if ever, show up on our "radar screens." That is, we simply do not identify with their lives and concerns. If we are evaluating a proposal that has consequences for one of these "invisible" groups, we might believe we are proceeding to weigh alternative means and ends in a detached manner, but our actual practice may be quite flawed. The flaw may not be so blatant as what you have witnessed in political debates and commercial advertizing. Have you observed persons pushing their own agendas and totally ignoring the concerns and interests of others? In extreme cases speakers and writers respond to legitimate objections by charging that all dissent must be due either to ignorance or to base motives. Have some in their audiences remained silent and suppressed their own doubts because of a fear of conflict or ridicule? Far from any attitude of intellectual detachment, both groups may have blocked further questions.

To begin practicing the strategy of devil's advocate, it may help to avoid topics that evoke strong feelings in an audience. Caring enough about mastering the procedure may initially require caring less about the practice materials. So, in the two case studies below, the proposals are not the sort that "push the buttons" of most undergraduates.

CASE ONE

We should abolish any fixed retirement schedules based on age. Age is an inappropriate and unreasonable basis for determining a person's competence to do a job. When you fix a retirement age for everyone in a particular career, you treat unfairly many individuals who can still do good work and who want to continue working.

The analytical procedure emerging from these chapters begins by asking you to identify the basic components of any formulated choice. What is the purpose of this first proposal? What are the means it recommends? It may help to point out again that the stated means will be an answer to a question about what should be done. You can, then, identify the purpose by asking a why-question, i.e. why should anyone do this? In abbreviated form, answering *how* something is to be done provides you with the means, and answering *why* provides you with the purpose. So in the first case the chosen purpose is to treat individuals fairly, and the chosen action is to abolish any fixed retirement schedules based on age. Note how the means could be worded positively: "Let ability and willingness to work be the standards for determining who continues to work."

Identifying the predictions and theories in this proposal is more difficult because they are left implicit. A clue to finding the key prediction is to remember that it will presuppose a causal linkage between actions and outcomes. To make the prediction explicit, you will need to spell out this assumed linkage. In this first case, try to link "abolishing mandatory retirement schedules based on age" with "treating individuals fairly." What might the key theory be here? Presumably mandatory retirement schedules are set by measuring the average performance of a large population. Do you expect many individual exceptions to what is a statistical average? But if similar cases should be treated similarly and if numerous individuals are exceptions to the statistical generality, then are the exceptional individuals being treated unfairly when they are treated similarly? One way of generalizing and formulating the insights here is: "Whenever we restrict liberties of an entire population because of statistical generalizations about that population, we unfairly burden some individuals." The course of action, then, seems clear: remove the cause of the injustice and you will remove the effect. By the way, is any evidence offered in support of the theory? Has any research been done to provide relevant data? Is some appeal to precedent made here? Of course this may be a case of appealing to common sense and expecting no questions from an audience.

Well, you are the audience, and it is time to play the adversary and to invent objections to this proposal. A useful hint in doing this: since most proposals contain recommended actions and promised outcomes, paying attention to each in turn offers a plan for how to proceed in raising objections. Let's begin by imagining objections to the promised outcome of treating individuals fairly.

Objections to the Purpose

(1) You could envision how, without any fixed retirement age, marginally competent and even incompetent employees would hang on to their jobs. Efforts to dismiss them would likely generate lawsuits. To avoid legal expenses, firms either would have to retain these employees or would have to "buy them out" with lucrative retirement packages. But both options would be expensive and harm the "competitive edge" of firms. The outcome would be to treat stockholders or owners unfairly.

(2) Without mandatory retirement, younger employees will experience delays in promotion, but then firms will less readily benefit from their new ideas. This is likely to cause economic harm both to the firms and to the younger employees awaiting promotion. Will the latter have grounds for complaining that they are being treated unfairly?[2]

(3) If you estimate the potential economic harm across an entire economy[3] resulting from this proposal, will more people be harmed with fixed retirement schedules or without them? Should the choice be to select the option that benefits the greatest number of persons? If some portion of a population will inevitably be treated unfairly, should their number be kept to a minimum?

Objections to the Means

(1) Did you notice that the proposal recommends banning all mandatory retirement schedules based on age, but it says nothing about positive means for distinguishing between competent and incompetent job performance. Do you think some effort should be made to identify fair and reliable tests of competence to do certain jobs? Are such tests possible? How would they be administered? What safeguards are possible to prevent biased evaluations? These may be hard questions, but, in omitting them, the proposal is overly simplified and so flawed.

(2) You probably suspect that the proposal should allow for some exceptions, as opposed to a total ban on mandatory retirement. Did you detect some oversights regarding questions of public safety? You probably thought of careers in commercial aviation, the armed forces and law enforcement. Are there relevant significant differences among job requirements that justify treating some classes of employees differently?

The final steps in playing the devil's advocate are to evaluate any objections you have raised and to revise the proposal depending on your judgments about the merits of the various objections. For example, to the initial proposal you may now want to add clauses exempting certain careers. Keep in mind that generating objections is a process of inventive guessing. You need not judge your objections initially. It often helps to suspend judgment until you have a number of guesses about possible flaws in a proposal. Once you have generated some objections, you are ready for the next question: Which option should you choose to support and why? Here the question for decision follows upon the question for deliberation, and a new strategy for moral decision-making will appear at the end of the third section. First, though, let's apply this section's strategy to another case study.

CASE TWO

The criminal justice system is supposed to provide for public security. Defense lawyers, however, too often use trial continuances and legal technicalities to allow their clients to escape justice. If we are serious about reforms that enhance public security, we should do away with defense lawyers except for defendants who are not mentally competent and so unable to present their own case. Otherwise, if innocent, defendants do not need lawyers; if guilty, they do not deserve their help.

Are you having an easier time spotting the key components? Is the purpose here to make the criminal justice system more effective in protecting public security? Are the means to abolish the use of defense lawyers? What exception is allowed? Is it easier now to identify the prediction that links means and intended outcome? Without defense lawyers to delay and to frustrate the administration of justice, what is predicted to happen? The two theories implicit in this case may be harder to formulate. A clue: generalize the relationship between the terms in the prediction. Is one assumed causal link that defense lawyers tend to obstruct the administration of justice thereby endangering public security? What, then, is presumed to be the case if you remove such obstructions?

Is any evidence presented in support of either theory? No precedents are cited though the writer may be assuming that most readers are familiar with anecdotal accounts of "smart" lawyers using legal technicalities to help their clients escape punishment. What if you apply the question of *precision*? The phrase "public security" appears in both theories. What does it mean to you? You might think of freedom from criminal threats and violence, but you also might think of security in the enjoyment of rights and liberties, e.g., being protected from arbitrary arrest and conviction. Can "public security" plausibly be understood in both ways? If so, is a key term in the theories ambiguous? Even though the theories fail the minimal test of reliability, try the question of *compatibility*. Is this proposal compatible with the Bill of Rights? Some legal experts hold that the purpose of the Bill of Rights is to make government inefficient, and that includes its administration of justice. This viewpoint may make sense to you if you are familiar with historical abuses of the state's powers to accuse, prosecute and imprison. In any case, this quick application of the three critical questions about reliability probably makes playing the devil's advocate much easier.

Objections to the Purpose

(1) The proposal puts both innocent and guilty defendants, if they are not legal experts, at a disadvantage. Prosecutors backed by the government's resources would have greater leeway in interrogating and charging defendants. Even if one assumed all prosecutors sought truth and fairness above all other ends, their errors in judgment would lead to more innocent individuals being convicted. How would this be an enhancement of public security?

(2) You might wonder which purpose of the criminal justice system is more important: justly punishing the guilty or protecting the innocent. You may have heard the remark, "Better that ten guilty persons go free than that one innocent person be found guilty." The proposal would reverse the priority here: better that a few innocent persons go to jail than that guilty parties go free. Of course, persons who do not foresee themselves being the targets of false allegations may not worry. Should they still be concerned for the welfare of populations at greater risk of being such targets? (Recall that bias can show up as a failure to ask how actions affect others besides oneself and one's group.)

Objections to Means

(1) The practice of overcharging accused parties to coerce a plea bargain would flourish under this proposal. Political pressures on prosecutors to win convictions could lead to guilty parties receiving disproportionate sentences. Despite its flaws, the current adversary system that relies on the use of defense lawyers at least offers guilty parties some hope that their punishments will fit their crimes.

(2) While the proposal makes an exception for those who are mentally incompetent, it says nothing about who determines which defendants qualify. Presumably the mentally incompetent are not responsible and so should not be prosecuted in the first place. But "competence" to defend oneself is lacking in almost every defendant. The criminal justice system is a maze of procedural rules and criminal statutes in which ordinary citizens would wander aimlessly without the aid of professional counsel. The exception for incompetence, then, should include all those unable to defend themselves in court. But, in this case, only accused legal experts should be ineligible to obtain defense counsel.

After raising objections, your next steps are to evaluate them and to revise the proposal according to your judgments about those objections. In regard to this second case, you may have concluded that it deserves outright rejection instead of revision. Notice that sometimes your choice is between doing something or not doing it. As far as having a positive alternative to a proposed course of action, you might wish you had one, but, if you judge the initial proposal to be beyond repair, then deciding to reject it is a defensible choice.[4]

Before considering a strategy for handling the question for decision, you may want to practice playing the devil's advocate on your own. The following case is one option. (On most editorial pages in newspapers, you can also find examples of recommended choices for further practice.)

CASE THREE

Increasing the penalties for teenage crimes will lessen the chances that teenagers will break laws or recidivate. Since there are reliable correlations between some types of crime and age groups, criminal sanctions that target particular age groups may reduce some types of crime and so benefit society. Which kinds of behavior should receive harsher penalties? No complete list is available since the behaviors that a society finds threatening may change with time. But is there any consensus today on what types of teen crime need special attention? Shoplifting by teenagers is arguably one candidate for inclusion on the list. With billions of dollars worth of merchandise stolen each year and the amount climbing at an alarming rate, we must find effective deterrents. One option is mandatory jail time for any teen convicted of shoplifting merchandise worth more than twenty-five dollars. The threat of even three days in a local jail will be enough to scare most teens away from shoplifting.

The strategy of devil's advocacy begins to merge the two tasks of *identifying* options and *evaluating* their merits. Its primary function is to give the inquirer an organized way of expanding the range of options. Still, in finding fault with any of the options, the role-playing inquirer is well on the way to asking what should or should not be done. The focus shifts, then, from the question for deliberation to the question for deciding. In schematic form, the pattern of operations in deliberating begins with what-questions (What can be done? What are real options?), moves on to creative puzzling and inventing of options, and ends with an is-question (Is this a realistic option?). The pattern in deciding involves a new round of questions. There are what-questions (Which option is best? What is really worth doing?) and puzzling about how to answer them. Then there are is-questions (Is this option really the best? Is this what I should do?). While this schema of patterned operations omits much of the complexity of decision-making, it does provide a way of checking for careless *performance*. Have you found that paying attention to is-questions before assenting to some opinion is a way of discovering the limits of what you really know? Are you more aware now that eloquently packaged proposals may be sound, nothing but sound? Attention to even this basic pattern can be the beginning of more critical listening and reading.

All the same, habits in education change slowly. Most educators continue to focus on instruments and to overlook operations. Most students will find it easier to follow the steps in playing the devil's advocate than to pay attention to how they are thinking about some issue. A traditional ethics text rarely challenges old habits. Instead of focusing on your performance in questioning, guessing and judging, the standard text presents various instruments as guides to moral decision-making. The usual format is a review of four or five ethical theories[5] and a listing of the ethical principles embedded in them. Before reviewing examples and puzzles about such theories and principles, let's identify a different instrument that reflects how persons operate in making decisions.

PRIORITIES

When facing a number of different options, in regard to either possible purposes or means, how do you set about choosing? This section suggests that part of your performance involves a *ranking of goods* and that instruments resulting from this operation can be formulated as *priorities* and *principles*. Examples may help you locate operations and instruments in your own experience.

Suppose you need to choose between competing options. Time and limited resources permit you to pursue only one of them. So what do you do? Presumably you try to understand which option is better than the other. Leaving aside how you determine "better," imagine how your choice involves a ranking of the possibilities. If you bother to make explicit the reasons for your ranking, they could take the form of a priority statement. The term "priority" may seem vague, so here is a case of both the operation and the instrument.

Suppose one day you get an assignment back from a science instructor and the grade is a D. You are surprised since you thought you understood the assigned materials and had worked hard. You decide to see the instructor and ask for an explanation of the low grade. When you show up during office hours, the instructor appears to be upset about something. Your questioning of the grade seems to worsen the instructor's mood, and, after being on the receiving end of a few sarcastic remarks, you can tell you are not getting anywhere. You leave the office confused and a little angry. You know that the school has an appeals process available to students who think their teachers have acted arbitrarily. You wonder if you should try that option. Of course you could accept the grade and try to do better on future assignments. Still, if the instructor is so unpredictable in grading, perhaps you should drop the class and avoid further risk to your GPA.

In trying to decide among the three options, you recognize that you are not the kind of person who easily forgets or accepts being treated poorly. That means you are unlikely to revisit the instructor and risk further belittlement. Your initial preference is to try the appeals route. Still, that can be time consuming, there is no guarantee of success, and you may wind up provoking the instructor and so receive more bad evaluations. There is still the option of dropping the course, but then you will have wasted time and money on a class for which you will receive no credit.

Given these details, what choice and which outcome would you prefer if you were this student? Presumably you would prefer to get the grade changed through the appeals process. But, because there is a possibility of your appeal failing and of further antagonizing the instructor, you may prefer dropping the course rather than waste time on an appeal and risk further harm to your GPA.[6]

This description of preferring one option and/or set of consequences over others indicates what you commonly do in "ranking goods." If you bother to formulate the reasoning that goes into such a ranking, the result could be a generalized statement, e.g. "Don't accept arbitrary evaluations from a teacher whenever the issue is significant to you and when appealing a grade can be done without wasting time and without doing further harm to your academic standing." This is an example of a "priority." Notice that you rarely make the reasoning behind your choices explicit in this way. Everyday choices usually involve routine performance guided by unformulated insights acquired from past experience. Your attention is focused on doing, not on talking about what you are doing. (Recall your use of faucets and doorknobs?) But this new instrument called a "priority" is worth some attention, so here is another example.

Suppose you drive into a campus parking lot, spot an open space (remember this is a hypothetical case!) and pull in. The problem is you pull in too far to one side and hit another car. You get out to look for damage. Your bumper has a few scratches, but the other car has a very visible dent in one fender. You look around and see no one else in the lot. You have heard stories of persons leaving blank notes under a windshield wiper on a car they have damaged to give any observer the impression of an honest admission of responsibility. That is one option. Of course you could leave your name and phone number instead of a blank piece of paper. The first option will spare you an expensive repair bill and an increase in your insurance premiums. The second will result in those expenses, but you are also concerned about being honest and doing the right thing. You know that, if someone hit your car, you would hope the person would take responsibility for the damage. If you choose the second option, can you formulate a priority statement that reflects the ordering of goods you may have adopted?

If priorities are rarely thematized, why bother mentioning them in this text and eventually building them into an analytical procedure? The primary reason is that asking you to formulate such priorities can draw your attention to implicit beliefs that you may not have noticed even though they are part of your routine living. Being aware of your own priorities can make a minor contribution to avoiding an "unexamined life." Then there are two practical reasons for bothering to identify and to formulate priorities. First, if you are criticizing others' proposals and decisions, it may help to generalize the reasoning behind them. Spotting questionable rankings of goods becomes easier if the rankings are expressed as generalized statements.[7] Second, if a decision you make turns out to be a mistake, it is probably too late to take back the action; but what you can change is the understanding that guided your original choice. You may have heard the old quip: "The nice thing about experience is it lets you recognize a mistake when you make it again." But at least sometimes people learn from their past mistakes, and this means they altered their original understanding. In formulating the understanding presumed by a choice, a priority can serve as an explicit focus of criticism, especially if you are trying to diagnose what went wrong.

JUSTIFYING CHOICES

The preceding section on rankings and priorities provided background for a series of puzzles about *ethical principles*. Here are some examples of widely known principles.

1. Aristotle's Principle of Justice ("Treat equals equally and unequals unequally in proportion to their differences.")

2. A Principle of Moral Equality ("Each person is entitled to treatment as an equal, i.e. should be shown the respect and concern of which any moral being is worthy.")

3. Aquinas' First Principle of the Natural Law ("Do good and avoid evil.")

4. Principle of Liberty ("Each person should enjoy the maximum liberty compatible with the same for all others.")

5. J.S. Mill's Principle of Non-Interference ("Society is justified in coercing the behavior of an individual in order to prevent him from injuring others; it is not justified in coercing him simply because his behavior is immoral or harmful to himself.")

6. Kant's Categorical Imperative ("Never treat a person simply as a means but always as an end in himself.")

7. Principle of Human Well Being ("Each citizen is entitled to an opportunity to attain a standard of living consistent with human dignity.")

8. Principle of Direct Utilitarianism ("An act is justified if it produces the greatest amount of good for the greatest number of people.")

9. Principle of Indirect Utilitarianism ("If any person acts according to a rule which, when regularly acted upon, increases the good of the greatest number of people, then that rule dictates what is morally right.")

Given different ethical theories and principles, you may wonder which ones you should rely on to guide your thinking and deciding. A general answer repeats the previous chapter's claim about the reliability of any theory. Since theories formulate the accumulated understanding of past experience, their reliability depends upon the correctness of the judgments made about that understanding. In turn, the correctness of the judgments depends on the fit between evidence and understanding. Imagine, if you will, the amount of time and energy researchers expend in testing for such a fit between their guesses and whatever data they dig up or create by designing experiments. But does this kind of testing by individuals really occur with ethical theories and principles? Recall the distinction between belief and knowledge. In regard to most of what you claim to know, are you dependent more on what others have told you than on what you have tested for yourself? Apply the same question to whatever moral principles you accept. Are these standards of your own making or did you inherit them from some group? Did you accept them because of personal research or did you internalize them as part of your socialization? What standards are already part of your borrowed identity? Rather than repeat many of the earlier remarks about socialization, let's briefly focus on one widely accepted moral principle.

In contemporary Western societies, most persons believe that moral equality is a standard by which to judge many decisions and actions. This belief shows up in outrage over racial and sexual discrimination, in the rationales for food assistance programs and for government subsidized health care, in popular condemnations of public officials who try to be above the law. But the question is why you should continue to believe in the moral equality of persons. Are you willing to settle for "That's just what I've been taught"?

As you know, scholars have tried to find a better answer. Some have appealed to historical experience arguing that societies and governments which denied the moral equality of persons produced policies marked by arbitrariness and contradictions. Their practices often manifested signs of group bias. In contrast, societies with more egalitarian beliefs and practices tended to show fewer signs of group bias in the make-up of their institutions. Other scholars have argued for a reaffirmation of the original theological and/or metaphysical rationales for moral equality.

Today at least it seems uncontroversial to endorse a principle of moral equality. Most people now seem to assume some such notion in evaluating personal behavior. The pursuit of self-interest by egotists, with no regard for consequences to others, is widely censured.[8] Recall the ease with which you detected the missing questions in cases of individual bias. But controversy does appear when the principle comes into conflict with group interests. The familiar cases involve debates over the pursuit of national self-interest and often fall under the heading of *the problem of borders*. While a society may use and honor the rhetoric of human rights and of universal human equality, it still draws lines in the dirt, calls them national borders and presumes they justify differences in how citizens and non-citizens are treated. The former have access to benefits and opportunities which the latter do not. Does this amount to group bias or can differences in the treatment of supposed equals be justified?

Is there a puzzle here for you? You have been taught to believe in the moral equality of all persons, but you have also been taught that citizens have more "rights" than non-citizens. Do you expect your government's economic policies to provide jobs at home even if that means fewer jobs abroad? Do you believe that, in a competitive world of nation-states, each government should put its national self-interest first? You may be uneasy with the implications of simple affirmative responses. Some exposure to recent controversies over trade policies may have alerted you to the problem of borders. There have been so-called "dumping" controversies over the manufacture of goods in one country (e.g. pesticides and flammable children's clothing) which, while illegal to sell in the domestic market, can be exported. You probably have also read criticisms of trade agreements which benefit domestic consumers but which leave foreign workers liable to dangerous and degrading working conditions. Your uneasiness reflects a conflict between an understanding of human equality and practices that expose non-citizens to risks while protecting citizens from those same risks. Is it possible to justify such differences in treatment?

The usual defense of such "differentials" appeals to a version of the *good of order*. The key insight is that preserving an institution requires that there be benefits available to members which are not available to non-members. Why should this be so? The pragmatic response is that the survival of institutions requires that some people make sacrifices to maintain them. Usually there is a reciprocal arrangement so that benefits flow to those who benefit the institution. Think of how taxpayers expect services, dues-paying members of clubs expect access to club facilities, contributors to pension funds expect retirement benefits to which non-contributors have no access.

If equal benefits were to flow regardless if one contributes taxes, dues or pension savings, who would make the needed sacrifices?

Does this pragmatic argument justify differences in treatment? Two reservations may occur to you. The first may emerge from reflection on the good of order as you have experienced it. The second may arise from a worry about group interests becoming the sole measure of what is good to do.

How have you experienced the good of order? Think of family life or of political communities. Have you witnessed individuals sacrificing their own well-being to protect others they love and institutions they cherish? Did they do so either to pay back others for benefits received or to earn future benefits because of their sacrifices? Can you reconcile examples of heroic self-sacrifice with the pragmatic appeal to preserving a flow of personal benefits? In the extreme, when individuals risk their lives defending family or country, are they focused on personal rewards or do they believe something greater than themselves is worthy of such risk-taking? Notice the shift in understanding. Persons esteem and are loyal to some forms of social order, and they treat those who are members of such orders differently. Think of parents sacrificing for their children or fixing meals for homebound members of their church. In doing so they favor some more than others. Perhaps they say, "charity begins at home;" but are they justified in giving some what they do not give others? Should they be *impartial* in choosing whether to benefit a family member or a stranger?

This way of thinking about the good of order dispenses with talk of reciprocal benefits. Do you detect something morally deficient in understanding group loyalties as based on a calculus of personal rewards?[9] But then on what more could they be based? Should you return to an opening chapter on how spontaneous caring for others is an intending of what is good and how this "reaching" can develop? In the "Epilogue" you will find further suggestions about moral development that may help you sort out this puzzle.

There was a second possible reservation about the pragmatic defense of unequal treatment of supposed equals. While expecting your public officials to give priority to the interests of citizens over non-citizens, you may be worried about making the good of your group or nation the ultimate measure of what is good to do. Should national self-interest trump all claims? That is, regardless of any harm it does to outsiders, is a policy that serves national interests justified? Historically some have said yes and then have formulated their reasons as a principle of *raison d' état*. In one version, the principle reads: "Whatever it takes to preserve and to enhance the power of the state is justified." Do you have any problems with this?

You may suspect this principle is no more than an rationalization of group bias. If the sole measure of foreign-policy decisions is this principle, should you expect consequences that will sometimes be arbitrary and contradictory? Have you ever heard of one country condemning terrorist attacks on itself or its allies and then calling similar acts against its enemies "acts of freedom fighters"? Or have you read of historical examples of governments retaliating for attacks on their civilians and then excusing the civilian casualties ("collateral damage") they cause by claiming enemies are shielding themselves behind civilian populations?[10]

The problem of borders will remain a puzzle for years to come. Controversies over immigration and trade policies will continue, but you may suspect that defensible decisions will fall somewhere between the extremes of advocating either completely open borders or *raison d' état*. Despite the unresolved puzzle, this section on justifying choices is not inconclusive. A central assumption in moral decision-making is that you should evaluate options in terms of their effects on all parties, i.e. no group is automatically unworthy of any consideration. Do you agree? Probably in your better moments you agree that even the worst criminals should not be tortured. Still, some differences in treatment may be justified since some differences do make a difference.[11] Just which differences should count as relevant? In some situations you will find it easy to answer. For example, if you are hiring lifeguards for the local public pool, you discriminate between job applicants who can swim and those who cannot. In other situations, answering will prove more difficult. Think of decisions about "downsizing" a work force and the competing claims of employees and stockholders. Or imagine the legal and moral questions about whether employers should be able to fire any employees addicted to drugs or alcohol.

If you accept a notion of moral equality, then a minimal guideline for deciding whether differences in treatment are justified demands *role-taking* in evaluating your options. An instrument that can guide such role-taking takes the form of a thought experiment. Assuming you have already played the devil's advocate and so have identified several options, take the following steps:

(1) ask how any individual or group will be affected by each option;

(2) imagine yourself in turn as any one of the individuals or groups likely to be affected by whatever you choose;

(3) ask which option will have effects on others that you think someone would be justified in imposing on you.[12]

This relatively simple thought-experiment is an instrument that presupposes a minimal notion of equality. Thinking about possible decisions from the vantage point of those affected is a way of showing consideration to others. Stopping to reflect on more than how you might be affected is a way of showing self-restraint. Asking whether you would think others justified in putting you in the position your decision will place others is a way of assessing whether differences in treatment might be morally defensible.[13]

Are these reflective acts still a vague set of operations? One clue: Can you detect how traditional principles of *impartiality* and *reversibility* are parts of this role-taking experiment? The puzzle here is that your decisions can benefit some people more than others or they can burden some more than others. But how are such decisions fair to moral equals? The question shows up in public debates quite often. Despite inflated political rhetoric, not everyone will benefit from cutting taxes, from harsher sentencing of drug offenders, from increasing government spending, from banning ownership of handguns, from financing school vouchers or from enacting "free trade" agreements. While personal decisions and public policies need not be "zero-sum games" in which there must be a loser for every winner, benefits and burdens are usually unevenly distributed.

The question is whether adequate reasons justify differences in how benefits and burdens are distributed. The tendency among ethicists in the West is to fall back on some principle of utility for guidance. Of course, there are other theories besides utilitarianism, so asking which guidelines or principles one should adopt leads to further puzzles.

PUZZLES ABOUT PRINCIPLES

So what are some further puzzles? As worded, ethical principles rarely take the form of priorities, i.e. they do not appear to be explicit rankings of one option over another. Only infrequently is there any mention of an ordering or comparison of possible goods. Instead, the expressions are usually noncomparative in form. In addition, they are often worded as *absolute rules* seemingly valid and binding for all times and in every situation. For example: "Never treat others simply as means but always as ends in themselves;" "Never tell a lie;" "Always give others the consideration due any moral equal." So their given phrasing mentions no exceptions and seems to say that one is never justified in violating them. Is this a problem for you? It may be if you guess that such principles may be analogous to how some theories, as idealized formulations, lack any mention of interfering variables or omit the clause *ceteris paribus*.

The puzzle here has a history. There was a debate in the third century AD about early Christians who had escaped martyrdom by lying when asked if they were Christians. Were they justified in telling a lie to save their own lives? The more general form of the question was whether one was ever morally justified in doing one evil to avoid another. More recently the question has reappeared in times of war. During the Second World War, the French Resistance faced it when deciding whether to bomb German troop and munitions cars attached to civilian trains. "Never harm the innocent" is the principle, but does this principle apply to the U.S. bombing of Baghdad, Belgrade, Kabul? Is the euphemism "collateral damage" a symptom of the quandary? Are you familiar with talk of a principle of "double effect" and its distinction between intended and unintended consequences? Might such debates over principles grow out of a neglect of the *priority of insights over principles?* The absence of a comparative form in the wording of most principles may contribute to the puzzle.

Pursuing these questions would involve you in an ongoing debate between proponents of the two main types of ethical theories: *deontological* and *consequentialist* theories. The former type tends to endorse absolute principles admitting of no exceptions; the latter type notes the variety of such principles and how they may come into conflict; so persons often need to rank goods and to set priorities, usually in terms of anticipated consequences. To most consequentialists "Never do avoidable harm to the innocent" is a generality that has few, if any, justifiable exceptions, but they would be reluctant to say there could never be a set of circumstances where an exception could not be justified. To stress the contrast here, it helps to point out that most ethical theories rooted in a Christian tradition have been deontological. For example, a traditional claim is that one is never justified in doing one moral evil to prevent a worse moral evil or to attain some good. For this reason some Christian ethicists have opposed abortion even to save the mother's life. You may be familiar with the pacifism of traditional Quakers and their opposition to taking a life, even that of an attacker. How do you think they would have responded to the question facing the French Resistance? What critics often overlook in these faith-based positions is the understanding of human history they presuppose. The religious believers are not unaware that by failing to do one evil they may be allowing (as opposed to "causing") tragic human losses to occur. However, they usually accept a theology of resurrection, i.e. they believe that history's victims will be reclaimed by the God of history who asks for moral goodness in people and not victories over their enemies.[14]

It may be useful to end this section on ethical principles by reviewing some of the remarks on them made in Chapter Three. As formulated generalizations they sum up previous insights about how to provide people with a better time. In being communicated to a new generation, they provide some guidance on how to live. But as general rules they are useful only if persons have a series of related insights, e.g. understanding what the principles mean, understanding the details of concrete situations persons face when making decisions (i.e. the diagnosis problem), and understanding which principles are relevant to those situations.

The key insight, then, is that ethical principles by themselves do not settle the issue of how to decide. The "foundations" of moral deciding and acting are not "instruments" of any sort but persons who care enough to raise questions and to act on their moral insights. Are you convinced of any of this? Would it be easier to subscribe to some form of moral-legal literalism so that to know the principles or laws would be the same as to know what you should do? But, in your experience, have these principles and laws been more than ink marks on pages for you when reading or more than sound waves for you when listening?

EXERCISES

1. Describe an original example of someone's decision and then apply to it the steps in playing the devil's advocate.

2. Provide an instance of the "problem of borders" and explain why you think the differences in treatment are justifiable or not.

3. Invent a scenario in which the available options seem to reflect a conflict between different ethical principles. What option would you choose and why?

OUTLINE OF THE PROCEDURE

One of the purposes of this text has been to introduce you to a procedure for taking greater care in making and responding to moral decisions. The last few chapters have identified various "instruments" people commonly use in formulating and arriving at their decisions. A procedure that derives from an understanding of how you operate in deciding and that draws your attention to the common instruments that express these operations provides a checklist for detecting oversights and for judging the reliability of the instruments and whether they were used competently. Testing the worth of the procedure requires applying it to cases and evaluating the results. However, the primary goal is not testing the procedure but "redesigning" your mind. The procedure itself is an instrument and so dependent on any user's interest in being careful in understanding and deciding. All along the invitation has been to alter previous habits in education. The procedure can play a role in this reeducation of feeling and thinking, but, again, the responsibility lies with the user of the instrument.

An outline of the procedure is a way of gathering together fragments scattered across previous chapters. Note the division of the headings into "operations" and "instruments." Entries under the former are especially relevant to tracking your own performance in making a decision; entries under the latter suggest ways of identifying and evaluating the decisions of others that are explicitly worded as proposals.

Operations	*Instruments*

A. What Is the Situation/Problem?

1. Researching -> Guessing	1. Sources of Evidence
2. Judgment of Fact	2. Formulation of Diagnosis

B. *Why Is It a Significant Problem?*

1. Identifying Parties Affected
2. Identifying Claims, Preferred Outcomes & Obligations
3. Judgment of Value

1. Forms of Bias
2. Competing Proposals

3. Formulation of Purpose

C. *What Can Be Done?*

1. Identifying Options
2. Consequences of Each Option?
3. Reliability of Theories? Real Possibilities?
4. Judgment of Fact

1. Playing Devil's Advocate
2. Predictions & Theories
3. Three Critical Questions

4. Formulation of Means

D. *What Should Be Done and Why?*

1. Which Option Preferred /Why?
2. How Are Goods Ranked?
3. Deciding/Choosing

1. Strategy of Role-Taking
2. Priority Statement
3. Statement of Proposal

PRACTICE WITH THE PROCEDURE

In deciding what you should do, you can proceed in a number of different ways. Consulting your own self-interest or protecting the interests of some group to which you are attached are two options. Asking what would be good for anyone to do under a given set of circumstances is a third option. Even flipping a coin can be a way of resolving indecisiveness. The procedure above, with all of its steps, offers yet another option. Why choose it as a guide?

Promises were made in previous chapters that an organized approach to decision-making yields certain benefits, e.g. improved odds of detecting oversights and of having greater confidence in the choices you eventually make. Again, the proof lies in the doing, so the rest of this final chapter presents practice materials. In the first two cases studies, use of the procedure will be quite detailed. Later materials will serve to emphasize parts of the procedure that are more difficult to master. Finally, in the two Appendices, you will find further practice materials to use on your own.

CASE ONE

John Doe works for a firm manufacturing electrical space heaters. His job is to carry out routine safety inspections on the firm's products. One day test results that he quickly double checks indicate a problem may exist. He suspects that during a one-week period heaters with defective wiring were shipped by the firm. Since the defects could cause fires, he immediately brings the test results to the attention of his superiors. After further studies, company officials agree that the wiring problem, if it exists in any units other than those tested, occurred in only one shipment of a hundred units. Slight changes in the assembly process will avoid similar defects in the future. There are lengthy discussions about the shipped units that are already in the hands of unsuspecting consumers. No reports of fires have been received, and the company safety experts appear divided as to whether there is any real danger posed by the defective wiring. The head office decides to avoid the bad publicity associated with a recall, so nothing is done about the previous shipment. John Doe is convinced there is a real danger of fire resulting from the units previously shipped.

What should he do and why?

The opening question of the procedure is, What is the situation or *problem?* The ink marks above provide you with data, and presumably you have an initial understanding of what John Doe is facing. Later questioning may broaden that understanding, but a preliminary diagnosis could run something like this. Unsuspecting consumers are possibly at risk, but management has decided not to inform them of the risk. John Doe thinks the fire risk is quite high though other safety experts appear less convinced of the danger. How he should act under these conditions is his personal problem. The public problem is the tension between consumer interests and management's estimate of the firm's interests. Is this a fair diagnosis of the situation?

Why are either of these problems *significant?* Identifying the individuals and groups affected by management's decision and by whatever choice John Doe makes is a way of understanding the relevant goods at stake. Assume John Doe has a wife and two children (and a sizeable mortgage). Surely they are a group worthy of his consideration. What of the unsuspecting consumers and the owners of the manufacturing plant? How about John Doe's fellow workers at the plant, including friends he has made there over the years? What of the other safety engineers who are members of his professional association? Are these all the relevant parties? Reviewing the types of bias is a way of checking for omissions and possibly expanding the list.[1]

What are the likely preferences or *claims* of these various parties? The financial security of his family may be John Doe's immediate concern. At the same time, he understands that owners of the defective heaters would prefer to know about the danger they face. Management, representing the firm's owners, prefers that employees cooperate with their decisions. Similarly John Doe's fellow employees expect him to be a good "team player" who will do nothing to endanger their jobs. In contrast, safety engineers have a professional code of conduct, and it clearly states that members are obligated to protect consumers from life-threatening defects in any product the members inspect.

So what are John Doe's competing *obligations?* Put another way, what would he judge to be worth pursuing? What are the various good ends he could pursue or bad outcomes he could avoid? Meeting his obligations under the professional code is one purpose he could pursue. Protecting owners of the defective heaters is consistent with this end. Competing purposes are present: showing loyalty to the firm and its managers, maintaining his reputation as a reliable team player and preserving friendships in the workplace. But the most apparent obligation is to do nothing that would harm his family's financial security. Is there any way for him to achieve all of these good ends? Suppose his initial decision is to try to meet all his obligations; how can he do this?

What are his *options?* Here you need to reach for possibilities beyond the "obvious." Do you think there may be a sequence to whatever options he has? That is, are there some actions he should take before others? Suppose his reading of the professional code is that he is obligated to double check his earlier findings by running more tests, and, if the new results are the same as before, he should report them to management and urge a recall. Let this be his first option. But what if he does all this, the test results are the same and management still sticks by its original decision? Then what are his options?

He could easily say that he has met his professional responsibilities by his second efforts. His job is not to make company policy but to report his findings to those who have that responsibility. His second option, then, is to accept the earlier decision as the final word in this case. But, if he is sufficiently alarmed by his findings, he could try one more time to reverse the decision, perhaps by writing memos, talking to other safety engineers, pestering individual managers when he sees them in the hallways at work. All these would be a third option at odds with the second. But what if he tries and fails? Is there a fourth option? You have heard of cases of *whistleblowing,* i.e. when someone goes outside a corporation or governmental agency to report its errors to a larger public. This may be a fourth option for John Doe, but it clearly is at odds with a number of the things significant to him. Before predicting the consequences of these various options, let's list them in order:

(1) Run more tests; if the same results appear, urge a recall.
(2) If option one fails, go along with management's decision.
(3) If option one fails, still press for a reversal of the policy.
(4) If option three fails, try whistleblowing.

In seeking reasons for choosing one option over the others, John Doe likely considers the *consequences* of each course of action. Do you think he is in a tight corner where any choice he makes will mean the loss of something significant to him? What *predictions* can you make about the outcomes of each of the four options? Will his running more tests and urging a recall meet his professional obligations to consumers? Will going along with management's decision prove his loyalty to the firm, confirm his reputation as a good team player, preserve friendships in the workplace and protect his family's financial security?

How reliable are these predictions? As you know, this question is really about the correctness of the accumulated understanding that grounds predictions and can be formulated as *theories*. John Doe is relying on his accumulated understanding in interpreting his test results and in estimating the fire danger. Less clear is how likely he is to harm his job security if he presses for a reversal of management's decision. An answer to this question depends on his familiarity with various personalities and the "atmosphere" in his workplace. Does the corporate climate allow room for dissenters? Is there encouragement of independent judgment or is there a culture of "yes-men"? Such questions revive the diagnosis problem since the theories may be known but which one of them applies to a specific situation has to be determined. Can you identify the theories John Doe must take into account? For example, in a culture of "yes-men," what tends to happen to anyone whose loyalty is suspect? More dramatically, what tends to happen to whistleblowers? Are they likely to return, not to their old jobs, but to any job in their chosen profession? What are the precedents John Doe and you might cite? On the other hand, are there precedents for whistleblowers succeeding in exposing corporate and governmental malfeasance? Consumers and taxpayers have benefited, but, again, what tends to happen to whistleblowers?

Suppose the following: in keeping with the professional code, John Doe chooses the first option but is ignored; since he is convinced of the fire danger, he still presses the case (option three), but he is told to drop the subject. Now his choice appears to be between silence and whistleblowing. Which option should he choose and why? One of the "operations" here is a *ranking of goods,* and the "instrument" is a *priority.* Review the competing goods and claims: professional integrity, the safety of anonymous consumers, loyalty to others in the workplace, the well-being of his family. In what order would you place these goods?

While you may expect elected officials to put the public good above their private (family) good, should you expect the same of the private citizen, John Doe? If you assume all the parties in this case are due equal consideration, you may expect John Doe to be impartial in judging between the interests of his family and those of anonymous consumers. Is this a fair expectation? Recall the remarks in Chapter Eleven about the good of order. All persons are due consideration as moral equals but not necessarily due equal consideration. Why not? Is John Doe's first duty to care for the well-being of his dependents? Ordinarily his family's welfare would take precedence over his obligations to employer and consumers. In other words, if he has to choose between options three and four, he should choose the former and not put his career and family in jeopardy. Do you agree?

Will it matter what you think the risks to consumers and the risks to John Doe's family are? If you estimate them to pose approximately the same level of harm, you probably will put the good of family first. But if you estimate the dangers to be far greater for consumers than for John Doe's family, then you may decide he should blow the whistle. Why? Does the risk of death outweigh the risk of financial insecurity and thereby offset the claim of dependents to preferential consideration? Can you formulate a *priority statement* that expresses your understanding of why anyone should choose option four?[2]

In the next case, you have an instance of a decision already formulated as a proposal. Here the question is whether you agree with what the writer proposes be done and the reasons for doing it. As opposed to the first case, in which John Doe had not yet made a decision, in this second case you will need to duplicate some of the steps in the procedure. After identifying the writer's diagnosis of the situation, the chosen purpose and selected means, your efforts to envision objections may lead you to a different diagnosis of the problem and a different choice of means and ends. Doing so becomes a test of creative intelligence and imagination, but also of research and background understanding of the situation.

CASE TWO

In some countries bribery of government officials to win contracts is a common practice and is treated as an ordinary business expense. If our corporations are to do business in these countries, they must adapt to local conditions, and that means paying bribes to win construction contracts for highways, airports, telecommunications systems, harbors. Now some of our citizens decry the practice and call for legal penalties against any of our corporations that pay such bribes. But if we adopt such sanctions, we can be sure our German, British and Japanese competitors will not. Then we will have succeeded in putting our international trade at a competitive disadvantage. We may not like the practice but it is how things have been done for centuries in some places. Let's not try to reform other countries; after all, we have enough problems of our own. Or have we forgotten that political campaign contributions are an accepted business expense here?

What is the *problem?* Competition among trade rivals occurs in cultures where bribery is a routine way of doing business, but many citizens criticize the practice and wish to penalize any of their corporations that pay bribes. Why does the writer think this issue is *significant?* If the practice is made illegal for domestic firms and penalties are enforced, they will be put at a competitive disadvantage. The writer's formulated *purpose* is to avoid economic harm to domestic firms engaged in international trade. The recommended action is to accept bribery as customary and not to impose penalties for engaging in it.

The writer's main *prediction* is that, if there are no penalties, domestic traders will be able to compete on the same level as their rivals. What is the implicit *theory* here? Is it some version of the deterrence theory of punishment? How reliable is it?

The writer's *ranking of goods* should become more detectable if you play the devil's advocate and invent objections to this proposal. You may already be familiar with one of the standard criticisms: accepting the practice of bribe-giving does nothing to change the "facts." While a realist may believe bribery is an inevitable evil, critics believe customs can change for the better.[3] If a leading nation in international trade were to ban the practice and to enforce the law for its own corporations, this would set an example for other nations. In time more nations might agree to adopt similar laws. But why make the effort? What is so wrong with the practice? Some critics condemn it as morally dishonest, and, if they are deontologists, they need to say no more about whether the practice is acceptable.[4] Other critics, if they are consequentialists, may predict that tolerating the practice abroad will encourage corruption at home.

You might think the reasoning expressed in this proposal is an easy target for criticism. Is the author saying that, because the practice is widespread and apparently approved of, it must be right? But, as an argument, how is this any better than the five-year-old's "Everyone else does it"?[5] In addition, the writer ends by noting that domestic practices are not above reproach. But does this mean criticism of one morally corrupt practice is invalid because the critics tolerate a similarly corrupt practice?[6]

Despite these objections, you may be sympathetic to the proposal or at least wonder whether, in international trade, any nation or its corporations are ever obligated to sacrifice their self-interest to avoid harming non-citizens? This question may bring to mind earlier sections on group bias and the problem of borders. How confident are you in handling these issues? What may help is some research into the consequences of routine bribery in international trade.

You may have noticed that the diagnosis contains no mention of the effects of bribery on parties other than corporations and government officials. Can you think of others who may be affected? How do those who pay the bribes recoup this expense? One way is to inflate the costs in contracts; another is to use substandard materials in doing the job. Shoddy work may result because contracts are let not on the basis of competence but on the basis of ability to pay bribes to key officials. But this means governmental agencies are spending tax dollars or foreign loans on projects lucrative for officials and not necessarily on projects serving the welfare of the general public. An old maxim is, "The money is in the cement." What this means is that large construction projects (e.g. airports, highways and large government office complexes) provide opportunities for enormous bribes. It is not unusual in impoverished countries to see six-lane highways ending a few miles outside the capitals or to land at very modern airports and then to drive past shantytowns on the sides of such superhighways.

So what harm is done and to whom? Are funds routinely lacking for schools and hospitals, for rural roads and pumps able to supply clean water to rural populations? Are governmental loans available to set up village cooperatives or to fund local irrigation systems? Do the police and health-care workers receive adequate pay or do they stoop to bribe-taking as a way of feeding their own families?

You may suspect the original diagnosis was far too narrow. The waste of tax dollars and foreign loans, the inefficient economic decisions of governments, the mounting debts and public distrust of government, the squandered lives and the recurrent neglect of public needs – these are part of the problem of systemic bribery. And the list of ills can go on. To foreign investors, a country where bribery is systemic will appear riddled with corruption at the highest public levels; its economy will be precarious and its political future insecure. But then any investment there would be quite risky. So how will such a country attract capital investment or find the funds to pay its foreign debts? At a minimum, investment dollars will only flow if the interest rates are high enough to offset the risks to investors. But this solution just adds to the debt burden and means even less money is available for pressing domestic needs. You might guess that there is a vicious cycle at work in this case. Some of the same international corporations that accepted bribery as a customary practice may, in investing at higher interest rates, benefit from the practice and, by continuing it, earn even higher rates because of increasing instability. Of course many will blame the citizens in those unstable countries for not demanding domestic reforms. Even without this rationalization, some investors will feel comfortable knowing that their own governments have already guaranteed the risky investments they have been making.

Has your diagnosis of the problem changed? Do you bring an expanded understanding back to the earlier question of whether one nation is ever morally obligated to put its economic self-interest second to the interests of non-citizens?

So what alternatives can you offer in place of the original proposal? Perhaps it is enough to point out the flaws in the original decision and its supporting reasons. If you were to compose your own account of what you think should be done about bribery as part of international commerce, what *ranking of goods* would you employ? Because this step in the procedure causes some people difficulty, the following brief cases focus just on it.

CASE THREE

A close friend confides in you, and, since the information she shares is potentially embarrassing to her, you promise to keep it confidential. Later she asks you if you had told a mutual acquaintance what you had promised to keep confidential. As a matter of fact, you had carelessly shared the information with the third party. Now you are wondering whether to admit that you had been thoughtless and to apologize or to deny that you were at fault. What should you decide and why?

Limiting yourself to these two options, what are the likely consequences of each? In a real case you would be able to predict how your friend would react to the truth. How angry will she be? Will the friendship be over? Will a sincere apology and other gestures restore trust between you? In a hypothetical case, you can estimate how you will feel if you lie, but in a real case will there be competing desires?

Can you identify the different rankings of goods presupposed by either choice? Admitting your careless mistake would show you think honesty with this friend, even if it may hurt the relationship, is better than dishonesty. If you bother to formulate the priority statement, it could read: "Prefer basing genuine friendships on truthfulness over maintaining them through deception." On the other hand, denying that you had broken your pledge would indicate you believe trying to preserve this friend's good opinion of you is more important than risking its loss by taking responsibility for your action. How might a priority statement read in this case?

Here are two more cases, each containing a proposal at odds with the other. Again, the focus is on detecting the implicit ranking of goods in each.

CASE FOUR

Studies have shown cigarette smoking is dangerous to one's health. A legitimate function of government is to provide for public safety. This function includes measures to protect the health of citizens. Therefore, the government should ban the sale and manufacture of cigarettes.

What *purposes* has the writer decided to pursue? What means has the writer recommended? Again, the means will be an answer to the question of what people should do; the purpose will be an answer to why they should do it. What generalized understanding does the writer rely on in linking the means to the purposes? Try to formulate the implicit *theory* here. Is there any evidence for its reliability? What ranking of goods has the writer adopted? "Public safety" and the "health of citizens" are mentioned, but what goods are being subordinated to them? A contrasting proposal will offer some clues.

CASE FIVE

It would be better if individuals did not acquire or continue in the harmful habit of smoking cigarettes. However, a total ban on the sale and use of cigarettes would not work. Did we learn anything from Prohibition in the 1920's? Besides, if competent adults choose to endanger their own health, that is their business. Government should intervene only if their choices harm others.

What are some differences between these two proposals? Clearly they differ in regard to means. The second writer rejects any attempt at a total ban on cigarette sales and use. You can surmise that the reference to Prohibition is an attempt to undermine the prediction and its implicit theory in the first proposal. Is this sufficient evidence that a total ban would prove to be ineffective?

The key differences are in regard to purposes. Both writers consider health something good, but they disagree on its importance in relation to other human goods. Why does the second writer mention "competent adults"? Apparently they should enjoy discretion in how they act and be free from governmental interference. The conventional label "liberty" refers to this belief. Notice that the writer must rank it above health since adults who endanger their own health are said to have the liberty to do so. However, is there some other good ranked higher than liberty? A clue lies in the remark that adults' liberties could be restricted "if their choices harm others." This may remind you of J.S. Mill's principle of non-interference. But why this exception? What do you have to assume about persons before you believe that the choices of any one of them can justifiably be limited to prevent harm to any other person? Why is liberty limited? Perhaps you have heard some version of the maxim, "Your freedom to swing your fist stops at my nose." Why should it? Pragmatic arguments may come to mind, e.g. how else maintain a civil society unless the freedom of each is respected? But why show each person respect and restraint, especially since not every person is able to retaliate against you or against a far more powerful group? Can you fill in the missing term in the sequence that includes "health" and "liberty"?

A CHECKLIST OF LEADING QUESTIONS

Before turning to further exercises with the analytical procedure, you may find it useful to have a checklist of leading questions as a guide to more careful reflection on decision-making. By now you are quite familiar with the sequence of the four main questions. You also recognize their ordering as a reflection of the basic pattern to your own wondering and intelligent caring. Does making all this explicit mark an improvement over how you were operating prior to opening this text?

I. *What Is the Situation/Problem?*
   a. What evidence is there of a problem?
   b. How do you diagnose the situation?

II. *Why Is It a Significant Problem?*
   a. Who are the parties affected?
   b. What are their interests, preferred outcomes and obligations?
   c. How have you checked for the presence of bias?
   d. What ends or purposes are worth pursuing?

III. *What Can Be Done?*
   a. What options are there for achieving the purposes?
   b. What consequences do you predict for each of them?
   c. What theories are you relying on for these predictions?
   d. How reliable are these theories?

IV. *What Should Be Done?*
   a. What option do you recommend?
   b. Why do you choose it?
   c. Why do you reject the alternatives?

To this checklist you could add further questions that specifically check your own performance in retrospect. As an additional way of being careful in decision-making, consider the following:

1. How did you check for competing obligations had by persons who belong to different communities, i.e., different forms of the good of order?

2. How much effort did you make to imagine creative alternatives to the more commonly recognized options?

3. What questions did you ask about the reliability of the theories presupposed by your recommendation?

4. What use of role-taking did you make in evaluating the various options?

5. Why did you think the ranking of goods "behind" your decision was best?

EXERCISES

1. As a thought experiment, imagine that you are one of the speakers at a town hall meeting called to discuss a recent drug bust at the local high school. Two previous speakers have already proposed that all of the town's high-school students be liable to random drug-testing whenever they are on campus. First, compose a summary of what you imagine their statements had in common. Second, present arguments opposing their proposal and offering an alternative. Third, explain why one of the two positions is more defensible than the other.

2. Return to the hypothetical town hall meeting in the preceding exercise. This time your task is to build consensus among those present on what the school policy should be. You need to anticipate the diverse concerns and rankings of goods of those in the audience. First, identify the diverse concerns, the different goods and how they can be ranked. Second, describe how a proposal for deterring drug use among the local high-school students could satisfy most, if not all, of those concerns.

3. In so-called "hard cases," very basic notions of what is good are present, and decisions tend to sacrifice what at least some will consider an inviolable good. Read the following scenario and, then, imagine you are one of the Supreme Court Justices hearing the case. What are the fundamental goods involved? How might they be incompatible in this case? What do you decide and why?

The Supreme Court agrees to hear a case brought against private elementary and secondary schools established after mandatory desegregation of the public schools in a particular state. The defendants in the original lawsuit were divided into two groups: (1) operators of private schools run as businesses and not supported by tax monies, and (2) operators of established private schools that were affiliated with local churches and also not receiving any tax monies. The question before the Court is whether it should uphold a lower court's ruling that required both classes of defendants to observe the laws and court rulings banning all racial discrimination in admissions policies at public schools.

The plaintiffs argue that amendments to the Constitution and more recent legislation guarantee the right of all citizens to treatment as equals; to exclude some from private schools on the basis of race is just as illegal as excluding them from privately owned motels, restaurants and workplaces.

The first group of defendants claims the schools they run are similar to private social clubs which the high court has already exempted from anti-discrimination legislation, in effect allowing their owners complete discretion over whom to admit and whom to exclude.

The second group of defendants argues that, since their schools are church sponsored, they are exempt from governmental control over admissions policies. A fundamental tenet of the Constitution forbids such meddling by the state in Church activities.

EPILOGUE

One goal of liberal education is to enable you to explain why you say what you say, do what you do and believe what you believe. Has this text contributed to that aim for you? Its stated aim was to indicate how you might test and improve your own performance in decision-making. There were two general means to this end: understanding the *operations* that occur in making decisions and learning to ask *critical questions* about those operations and their products. The first step toward understanding the operations was to introduce puzzles that might draw your attention to your own mental acts. Are you now better able to say what you are doing when you carefully reflect on how to provide someone with a better time? The route toward identifying critical questions began with a focus on the instruments commonly used in formulating decisions. Have you grown more confident in how to go about evaluating your own choices and other people's proposals? Are some questions becoming "second nature"?

You perhaps found it easier to learn about the instruments, including the procedure with its list of critical questions. Doing so was much like learning other skills you have acquired through years of schooling. Learning about your own operations may have been more difficult and may still appear less productive and less practical. However, you have noticed some "practical" benefits in being more familiar with how you make decisions. For example, once you differentiate the various contexts of operation, you are less likely to believe that any set of policies, laws or institutions will be immune to abuse and betrayal. Furthermore, if you understand that the question for deliberation is a reaching for possibilities and an invitation to creative thinking, you are more likely to detect the recurrent oversight in general bias and political realism. Have the political and economic "facts" of the last century been immune to change? Is the nonsense inherited by this century beyond all hope of reversal?

An actual historical situation results from decisions people have made. Those decisions may have followed upon careful efforts to be intelligent and responsible, but they may also have sprung from failures to be intelligent and responsible. Thus, you may face complex situations today that are the consequences of bias, stupidity and moral fault. No surprise perhaps since, besides development, there is also decline. But, if the effects of decline are apparent in the nonsense of what political realists may call "facts," there still is the possibility of development.

Chapter Two offered some preliminary remarks about moral development. Later chapters expanded upon them. A look back at those comments can point you toward future possibilities. Suppose that development is of two kinds. Imagine two vertical arrows, one pointing up, the other down. The first image suggests how your development can be from *below upwards*. Have you sometimes creatively puzzled about your experience, arrived at understanding, formed sound judgments and made responsible decisions? Did doing so change you for the better? The second arrow represents how you can understand changes in your life that progressed from *above downwards*. The easiest examples occur when others give you the gift of their prior learning. They hand down to you what they know but which you affirm as a matter of belief. Recall how much of what anyone claims to know is in fact taken on faith. But this type of development also occurs as a result of love. How so?

Chapter Seven identified the presence or absence of moral conversion as one of the sources of moral diversity. That chapter only cited examples of morally converted persons. But what might "moral conversion" mean? In terms of the three uses of "good," could it mean the shift from a concern for individual satisfaction to a concern for providing others with a better time, where by "others" you could mean an expanding number of persons? Initially love of family can lead you to sacrifice for family members and to take responsibility for your decisions affecting them. Eventually love of community and respect for persons as persons may be directing how you respond to your own desires and how you decide to live. Love of others in these cases becomes a guiding form of caring that can lead you to root out your own biases, to dismiss feelings of resentment and to resist calls for retaliation. As a result, you may avoid adding to and may even diminish some of the accumulated nonsense in your society; your own development may play a role in reversing the effects of social decline.

In Chapter Seven there was also mention of religious conversion. Again, only examples were offered. What might this type of conversion involve? How could it result in development from above downwards? Suppose religious conversion is being in love with God. How might this "gift" make a basic difference in your thinking and doing? As intelligent and responsible decision-makers, persons create the worlds in which they live; but, as sources of nonsense, they also infect those worlds with cycles of violence and malice. Insights can accumulate and produce progress; the effects of unintelligent and irresponsible choices can accumulate and produce bitter memories of betrayal and injustice. So in living with one another, persons need intelligently creative ways of "healing" the effects of past and current evils. But, in contrast to indifference and despair, the healing efforts require both caring and hoping. Does recognizing and returning God's love provide a "higher" perspective on such challenges, one that can transform anger and despair into forgiveness and hope? Can religious conversion liberate your intelligence from the discouraging "facts" accepted by the political realist and orientate you toward providing a better time for others?

This line of questioning may bring to mind references to dialectic in Chapter Three. There the two terms of the dialectic were your capacity for "whatting" and your opinions inherited as part of socialization. The question was what allows you to detect and to escape inherited nonsense. The brief remarks on religious conversion suggest a third term for this dialectic. In actual, historical situations suppose there are three basic elements: *creative intelligence* intent on understanding the situation and finding ways to improve it; *biased intelligence* intent on defending some nonsense against the needed insights and decisions; *intelligence hopeful* that persons can live up to their own inner demands for being intelligent and responsible. The creative element is the spontaneous caring about understanding and about others with which this text began. The biased element is the misdirection and underdevelopment of that caring, so that evils endure and accumulate. The healing element is the first term, creative intelligence, given hope in the face of those evils.

Can you locate these terms in your own experience? If not, you might think of some earlier examples of religiously converted persons. What evils did they find creative ways of resisting? Were they hopeful despite the odds? And the odds are not good:

> We do not know ourselves very well; we cannot chart the future; we cannot control our environment completely or the influences that work on us; we cannot explore our unconscious and preconscious mechanisms. Our course is in the night; our control is only rough and approximate: we have to believe and trust; to risk and dare.[1]

Trusting and risking are acts that do not occur when there is no hope of success. Even addicted gamblers have their fantasies. So what reasons do you have for believing and daring? Given some hints in earlier chapters, you may have tracked your own experience with moral development. You may have recalled experiences of having a guilty conscience when your actions were at odds with your better judgment. You may also have remembered feeling good when you knew that you had done the right thing. What you felt in both types of experiences you probably assume is present in other people's lives. At least in the lives of those honored as heroes or reviled as villains, you have found examples of both moral progress and moral decline. Both are possibilities for persons who can make meaning or nonsense of their lives. What determines which possibility will become the truth about your life? Is it no surprise that the answer is "Yes"? But now in saying "yes," are you affirming more than the first term in the dialectic?

APPENDIX ONE: MAKING DECISIONS

CASE ONE

Suppose you work for the city-owned utility company. During the winter your supervisor sends you out to a house to turn off the gas because the people living there have not paid their bills for six months. When you arrive, you find a single-parent household with two small children. The mother says she has been ill and out of work; what little savings she had went toward medical expenses. While you feel sympathy for the family, you know that what the supervisor is expecting you to do is legal. Furthermore, if you leave the gas on, the supervisor will be mad and will send you or someone else right back to do the job. You can hear his angry words already: "If you let every deadbeat or family having a rough time get free service, why should you expect anyone to pay?"

What should you do and why?

CASE TWO

Imagine a high-school friend you have not seen for several years shows up one day and tells you the following:

> I am living in a three-bedroom house with seven other people, most of whom are selling narcotics and all of whom are addicted to methamphetamine and cocaine. I have been living like this for nearly two years. Our days consist mostly of sleeping until the afternoon and then proceeding to indulge in various substances and not stopping till dawn the next day. I know that I am wasting both time and money participating in this lifestyle. I feel trapped in this house, but I don't have anywhere else to go. Still, I know that I cannot continue living like this. But, when you are an addict, it is hard to

201

make a break from something that so dominates your life and the lives of those around you.

What should you do and why?

CASE THREE

Suppose your sixteen-year old brother brags to you about all the CDs he has been able to shoplift from the music store at the mall over the past three months. You know that he has enough spending money to pay for most of them, so you ask why he stole them and ran the risk of getting caught. He replies that the thrill of the experience is what he was after. You admit that might be true, but you feel you need to persuade him to change his mind and behavior.

How do you go about doing this and why?

APPENDIX TWO: EVALUATING PROPOSALS

CASE ONE

"Modern medical technologies are extremely expensive in many cases. Organ transplants and cancer therapies are available but not to everyone because the demand often outstrips the supply. If patients who cannot afford the high medical costs are allowed access, who pays their bills? It is fine to talk about equality in access to health care, but, if hospitals are forced to treat the uninsured no matter the costs, how long will those medical facilities stay in business? Keeping hospitals on a profitable basis will allow them to serve future patients. Profits from paying customers provide any business with the resources to expand its services to a broader population in the future. Distributing expensive medical treatment on the basis of ability to pay will eventually benefit the greatest number of people."

CASE TWO

"Most consumers in the West were surprised a few years back to learn that many of the imported products they buy are produced by child labor. As reports of child labor practices abroad began to show up in the popular media, legislators proposed new laws to block imports originating from labor practices the West outlawed just eighty-some years ago. But one result of this proposed legislation may actually be to harm the children who are producing the soon-to-be-banned goods. Most of us may assume that, if the market for their products dries up, the children will leave the sweatshops, enroll in school and do all the other things we in the West associate with childhood. The real outcome may be far different. By western standards the salaries these children earn are meager, but the alternative for them and their families may be an even lower standard of living. In many cases the alternative to child labor is not school but starvation.

What is the humane course of action? We recommend a *laissez-faire* stance, i.e. one that avoids moral judgments as largely irrelevant to economic behavior and that rejects efforts to ban common economic practices as usually counter-productive. We will have to wait for history to abolish child labor just as it did in the West. Enough time and enough economic development will relieve any population of the need to rely on child labor for their economic survival. If we try to coerce an early end to the practice, the result will condemn the very children we meant to save to a loss of their meager wages that often are the only alternative to starvation."

CASE THREE

"Everyone complains about big government, but few suggest what to do to control its size. Finally, however, we have the means to act on these complaints; specifically, I am referring to sunset legislation. This legislation will eliminate government programs that duplicate one another, waste tax dollars, and add unnecessarily to the federal deficit. This legislation will get results. Every five years each federal program will be subject to legislative review. Any program not deemed worthy will be discontinued. Duplication of services, excessive costs or inefficiency will be grounds for discontinuing programs or at least for reducing their budgets. Every five years each program will have to justify renewal of its funding; no program will automatically have its previous budget renewed. In time sunset legislation will weed out waste in the federal bureaucracy and restore public confidence in government."

NOTES

NOTES TO THE INTRODUCTION

1. Franz Kafka diagnosed this process of mis-education and missed understanding: "Probably all education is but two things, first, parrying of the ignorant children's impetuous assault on the truth and, second, gentle, imperceptible, step-by-step initiation of the humiliated children into the lie." Quoted in Ernest G. Schachtel, *Metamorphosis: On the Development of Affect, Perception, Attention, and Memory* (New York: Basic Books, 1959), 293.
2. Gaston Bachelard identified such reflective reading with genuine reading. *The Poetics of Space* (Boston: Beacon Press, 1970), 14.
3. Here and in the remainder of this text the authors are evading the endless debates over the "naturalistic fallacy." The pivotal issue that sustains the debates is whether reasoning is a deductive process. Subsequent exercises in self-attention may convince you reasoning is not to be identified with formal deduction. An alternative to joining the debates is to draw your attention to how your caring about understanding and about others is a spontaneous part of your living and to ask how it develops both in individuals and in the history of social orders.

NOTES TO CHAPTER ONE

1. Among the contending voices about "ethics" are some claiming that it is the application of universal principles to cases; others assert that it is a descriptive study of human emotive responses to situations; still others say that it is a study of how human evolution has favored certain beliefs and practices over others. Rather than enter these debates and perhaps add one more voice to the babble, this text takes a different road, one less traveled. The focus is on the performance of the reader as an empirical basis or "specimen" of moral decision-making. Self-study by the specimen can provide an empirical basis for assessing some of the contending claims about ethics. But where should the self-study begin?
2. Have you met persons who objected to the treatment of animals and trees as mere resources for satisfying human needs? Should they also object to calling people "resources"?

3. Helen Keller, *The Story of My Life* (Scarborough, Ontario: New American Library, 1988), 8.
4. Ibid., 13.
5. Ibid., 18.
6. Linguistic meaning is not the whole story about making sense of our experiences. We communicate in many ways besides with words. Helen, like the rest of us, expressed meanings before her discovery of linguistic meaning. She was able to express her love, her needs, her frustrations and even a sense of humor before that remarkable day at the well. If you reflect on your routine experiences, you will notice the importance of gestures and symbols. How many times do you use them to communicate to others what you have in mind? Likewise, how often do you read the body language, tone of voice and smiles of others? These are important ways of making sense of the world you live in. Notice that the various arts – music, painting and dance – express meanings that do not require words. The sense to be expressed and understood is mediated by the pattern of sound or movement or color. How do you read the dancing of your partner on the dance floor? How do you read the sound of the guitar or voice at a concert or the arrangement of color in the painting on the wall? These are all avenues by which we express our meanings.
7. While the checklist or mapping device hardly merits the label "method," it does share some characteristics. If we assume that a method "is a normative pattern of recurrent and related operations yielding cumulative and progressive results" [Bernard Lonergan, *Method in Theology* (New York: Herder and Herder, 1972), 4], then a checklist composed of leading questions may yield progressive and cumulative results. We ask questions before we understand; once we answer the questions, those answers can be the basis for a further round of questions that we may in time answer. Gradually we may come to some expertise in a certain area of inquiry; hence, the meaning of "cumulative and progressive results." The ordering and asking of questions do not guarantee reaching successful results, but the odds of doing so improve.
8. Customary practices precede theoretical reflection on them. People first solve the problems of living together and only later have the leisure time to reflect on more than the pressing needs of the day. People boiled water before knowing why it boiled. Ideally ethics as "theory" would be as remote from the common-sense, practical understanding of morality as aerodynamics is from buying an airplane ticket. The current reality is something less than ideal. Ethics is more a field of inquiry than a formal discipline. An indication of its relatively undeveloped status is that most of the major writers in the field are easily accessible for an audience employing its common sense.

NOTES TO CHAPTER TWO

1. Lonergan. *Method in Theology*, 235-236.
2. Chapter Seven will offer further comments on this shift or "conversion" to theoretical understanding.
3. A common-sense maxim suggests that many people already have some understanding of this third use of "good" – "What is sauce for the goose is sauce for the gander."
4. To follow up these clues, you may want to puzzle over the following. "If we ask further how the good is defined, we can say only that it is whatever is in so far as it is the object of complacency. We have not here a vicious circle, but the simultaneous definition of two terms by one relation. On the side of the object the relation is not real, nothing is added to being over and above its being to make it good, and so the notion of the good derives from the subject's relation to it in willing; the order is: being, knowledge of being, love of being, the notion of being as good." Frederick E. Crowe, "Complacency and Concern in the Thought of St. Thomas," in *Theological Studies* (20) September 1959, 346.
5. These remarks on "being careful" in moral decision-making have focused on changes in the lives of individuals. There are further questions about broader developments occurring in cultures. Then the focus is on the history of morality. "History" here can have multiple meanings. For example, besides one's personal growth in caring, which, if understood and formulated, would yield an autobiographical record, there is the history of one's culture and the potential for tracing changes in its beliefs and practices. Think of the slow emergence of an understanding of the equality of persons. In addition, there are questions about the broader context in which entire civilizations come into being and pass away. "History" then refers to a horizon of understanding inclusive of all biographies and cultures. What might it be like to think of caring from this third perspective on human history? At least this question may suggest a view of ethics as ongoing historical reflection, sometimes careless, sometimes careful, but not guaranteed to be either since it is dependent on persons as the puzzling participants in an unfinished experiment called "human history."
6. A remark attributed to James Joyce captures the motivating strategy of this chapter. He supposedly said, "Hell is the obvious." Is it possible to be oblivious to being in hell?
7. The example is borrowed from Philip McShane, *Wealth of Self and Wealth of Nations* (Hicksville, N.Y.: Exposition Press, 1975), 17. He goes on to write: "There is no denying the native wonder of man. Years of faulty education and discouragement can undoubtedly quell that wonder. Pressure toward feats of memory, toward information rather than formation, can rush the adolescent past the effort genuinely to understand. A superficially sophisticated society can condition its young members into concentration on eloquence and a cloaking

of any suspicion of radical nescience. A culture which should know better can leave unquestioned the illusion that, while man does not understand everything, still he has a jolly good idea."

8. A brief description of the experiment is available in Edmund Blair Bolles. A *Second Way of Knowing: The Riddle of Human Perception* (Prentice Hall, 1991), 79-80.

9. This puzzle is adapted from McShane, 40-42.

10. "To See and Not See," in *An Anthropologist on Mars* (New York: Vintage Books, 1995), 108-152.

NOTES TO CHAPTER THREE

1. In Chapter Eight this new complexity will appear in remarks about "prospective judgments."

2. Tennessee Williams captured the puzzle in these words: "We are all condemned to solitary confinement within our own skins." Quoted in McShane, 42.

3. One important source for this position is the writings of the thirteenth-century philosopher-theologian Thomas Aquinas. See his account of the relationship between will and intellect in *Summa Theologiae* I-II, qq. 6-17. Another source, of course, is the relationship of will and intellect occurring in your own deliberations and decisions.

4. The notion that an evil results from a failure to meet the standards for careful deliberating and deciding has a long history going back to Augustine's view of evil as privation. See, for example, Chapter 12 of *The City of God*. This position is further developed by Aquinas in *Summa Theologiae* I, qq. 48-49. The question of moral fault will reappear in Chapter Six in the section entitled "Limitations on Effective Freedom."

5. McShane, 56-57.

6. A standard approach to ethics is to study various normative theories, their general principles and the arguments supporting them. Then one is expected to apply the principles to cases as rules for deducing what should be done in those cases. The inductive approach in this text is a more accurate reflection of how we make moral choices.

7. Another reason for formulating the reasons for a decision is that, if you act according to those reasons and the results are disappointing, it may be too late to take back the decision, but what you can change is the rationale that guided it. Learning from mistakes is not a matter of eliminating the mistakes but of changing the understanding upon which they were based. Thus, a clear formulation of that understanding can provide a focus for later reflection and improvement.

8. Chapters Five through Eight will explore how differences among persons are sources of diversity in moral judgments.

9. The classic study of this social dialectic is Peter L. Berger and Thomas Luckmann, *The Social Construction of Reality* (New York: Doubleday, 1967).

10. You might return to the comments on the distinction between belief and knowledge to puzzle about what is properly termed "knowledge." Is an opinion just a guess? Is the guess an answer to an is-question or a what-question? Are the unquestioned opinions of some group in the same incomplete condition as private opinions?

11. The common-sense insights here were formulated by Aristotle: "Understand similar cases similarly." By simple extension one should also treat similar cases similarly. Of course, the practical question is: Are the cases similar? This raises the question of diagnosis.

12. To apply the puzzle regarding Newton's invention and discovery of gravity to the origins of methods: persons invent methods, but, in doing so, are they discovering something about their own capacity for operating well? Is this part of the drama of human history? Might it take us the lifetime of the species to discover who we can become?

NOTES TO CHAPTER FOUR

1. This difference in degree of awareness is an experiential basis for the distinction between sensation and perception appearing later in this section.

2. How are these distinct types of data related? Answering this question is beyond the scope of this chapter and indeed beyond the scope of ethics. The fields of cognitive psychology and epistemology are the appropriate disciplines for pursuing this question.

3. Advertizers implicitly make this distinction between sensitive flows and perception. They use their ingenuity to disrupt an audience's expectations by incongruous and surprising sights and sounds that draw attention to a product. Jerome Bruner wrote of the role of surprise in revealing and disrupting what we have been taking for granted. See "Possible Castles," in *Actual Minds, Possible Worlds* (Cambridge: Harvard University Press, 1986), 46-47.

4. This issue of "fit" will reappear in Chapter Eight with its discussion of objectivity.

5. "Freely the subject makes himself what he is; never in this life is the making finished; always it is still in process, always it is a precarious achievement that can slip and fall and shatter. Concern with subjectivity, then, is concern with the ultimate reality of man. It is concern not with the universal truths that hold whether a man is asleep or awake, not with the interplay of natural factors and determinants, but with the perpetual novelty of self-constitution, of free choic-

es making the chooser what he is." Bernard Lonergan, "Cognitional Structure" in *Collection* (New York: Herder and Herder, 1967), 238.

6. Ibid., 222-223.

7. "If one does not attain, on the level of one's age, an understanding of the religious realities in which one believes, one will be simply at the mercy of the psychologists, the sociologists, the philosophers, [who] will not hesitate to tell believers what it really is in which they believe.... But to communicate one must understand what one has to communicate. No repetition of formulas can take the place of understanding. For it is understanding alone that can say what it grasps in any of the manners demanded by the almost endless series of different audiences." Lonergan. *Method in Theology*, 351.

8. For a general notion of "method," you might review endnote 7 in Chapter One.

NOTES TO CHAPTER FIVE

1. Lonergan, *Method in Theology*, 31.

2. The distinction between nonintentional and intentional responses is not parallel to the distinction between motivations and orientations. Both types of responses are data of consciousness that persons can choose to resist or to encourage depending on their orientations toward what they judge to be good. For example, have you deliberately tried to shake off a gloomy mood when friends arrived? Or have you ever caught yourself laughing at someone else's expense, seen the hurt in her eyes and changed your response?

3. Examples of this operation of ranking goods are part of Chapter Eleven's presentation of the instrument called a "priority statement."

4. Defenders of ethical egoism and some utilitarians emphasize individual satisfaction or cumulative satisfaction as the measures of what is right. In doing so they generate controversies about a ranking of terminal goods. Consider the contrast with a Christian ethics that holds self-sacrificing love to be the highest good. A Quaker who endorses pacifism presumably believes that there are some things worth dying for and others that are not. For example, preserving one's own security is something good, but it is not worth the price of taking a human life. Can you make sense of this stance?

NOTES TO CHAPTER SIX

1. Lawrence Kohlberg. *The Psychology of Moral Development* (San Francisco: Harper and Row, 1984).

2. Bernard Lonergan. *Insight: A Study of Human Understanding*, in *Collected Works*, Vol. 3 (Toronto: University of Toronto Press, 1992), 643-647.

3. "The Hollow Men" in *The Complete Poems and Plays: 1909-1950* (New York: Harcourt, Brace and World, 1971), 58. The gap between aspiration and performance is apparent in the well known studies by Stanley Milgram showing the ease with which persons submit their own judgment to authority and invent rationalizations to mask their own feelings of uneasiness. The classic account of his research is *Obedience to Authority* (New York: Harper and Row, 1974).

4. Jerry Z. Muller, *Adam Smith in His Time and Ours* (New York: Routledge, 1996), 2-4.

5. This section is heavily indebted to Lonergan, *Insight*, Chapter VII, 218-232.

6. This view has a long history. One example is Charles DeGaulle's retort to the Prime Minister of Israel who said he thought the two countries were friends but then complained that France was not siding with Israel in one of its conflicts. DeGaulle supposedly replied: "Nations do not have friends; they have interests."

7. Lonergan, *Method in Theology*, 55.

8. A classic statement of this realist position is found in Machiavelli's *The Prince*. "Since there is so great a discrepancy between how one lives and how one ought to live, whoever forsakes what is done for what ought to be done is learning self-destruction, not self-preservation. For a man who wants to practice goodness in all situations is inevitably destroyed, among so many men who are not good." Chapter 15, lines 7-20. James B. Atkinson, translator (Indianapolis: Bobbs-Merrill, 1976), 255-257.

NOTES TO CHAPTER SEVEN

1. Rainer Maria Rilke's poem "Archaic Bust of Apollo" ends with the line, "You must change your life." (p.61) In "Requiem for a Friend," he identifies how much resistance any resolve to change may face:

We can so easily
slip back from what we have struggled to attain,
abruptly, into a life we never wanted;
can find that we are trapped, as in a dream,
and die there, without ever waking up.
This can occur. Anyone who has lifted
his blood into a years-long work may find
that he can't sustain it, the force of gravity
is irresistible, and it falls back, worthless.
For somewhere there is an ancient enmity
between our daily life and the great work.

The Selected Poetry of Rainer Maria Rilke. Stephen Mitchell, editor and translator (New York: Random House, 1982), 85-87.

2. The corresponding terms in Machiavelli's text are *Fortuna and virtù*.
3. Comments in the next section on intellectual and religious conversions will suggest more details about such developments. That significant shifts or differentiations in understanding can occur is evidenced by the contrast between a contemporary physicist's talk of unimaginable subatomic particles defined by wave functions and an undifferentiated understanding of such particles that imagines them as floating about like dust particles caught in the sunlight streaming through the window. A not uncommon puzzle captures the basic issue here. If the universe is expanding, what is it expanding into? Undifferentiated common sense is likely to respond with: "It's expanding into space." What is your understanding of "space"?
4. Puzzle awhile, if you like, about how you might square this assumption with the earlier remarks about there being no reason for a failure to do what you know you can and should do.
5. What was said earlier about moral development applies here: religious feeling and understanding can be developed. A transcendent mystery is the goal of religious intending, and various practices can be concrete means of moving toward that goal, e.g. religious rituals, meditation, charitable works, theological studies.
6. An old saying captures the dialectical relation between individuals and institutions here: "If you ever find a perfect institution, don't join it – you'd ruin it."

NOTES TO CHAPTER EIGHT

1. Note the use of the word "reliable" instead of the word "certain." Certainty as a standard in knowing was an ideal of classical thought. More contemporary accounts of knowing will usually favor talk of probability or suggest that certainty is a matter of degrees. Rehearsing the various debates and arguments about these terms belongs to a different type of text providing a historical study of theories of truth.
2. Among the contending candidates for the decisive role as the measure of truth are standards of logical validity, coherence among ideas, correspondence between understanding and what is real, durability of belief, utility and so on.
3. The assumption here is that for the foreseeable future the state of Texas will continue to execute prisoners at a higher rate than any other state in the U.S.
4. Of course it is possible to stay "at rest," to hold securely to familiar patterns of thinking and acting and so avoid changing. But then you will have to stay on guard against conversations that disturb your resting place. Entrenchment in a defensive position and avoidance of venturing out into the open tend to follow. The defensive attitude will require vigilance since conversations tend to take unpredictable turns. Much of the chatter that passes for conversation obeys rules of engagement: some topics shall not be mentioned; some questions shall not be asked.

5. J.S. Mill's belief in freedom of the press and the avoidance of censorship rested on the assumption that the free circulation of ideas, even faulty ones, offered the best chance of the participants arriving at the truth.

6. Recall the remarks on religious leaders and institutions in the preceding chapter.

7. Notice that "conversation" is a familiar word that anyone can use without more than a nominal understanding of what it means. What makes a conversation what it is? If someone suggests that it involves communication between the interior states of the participants, does this seem at odds with the picture of two persons chatting face to face? Can you "picture" interior states? This is a puzzle that reinforces the theme of differences among the participants in moral controversies. Some will remain at the level of "picture thinking" and so think that conversation as a source of transformation just involves hearing new information or better arguments. What more goes on in serious talk? Can you recall a serious conversation with someone? What was happening?

8. You might find a negative experience makes the point more clearly. Have you met some persons who have botched their lives? Would you seek them out as sources of good counsel? Perhaps – if you thought they could tell you what *not* to do with your life. However, you probably assumed their own flawed subjectivity was a likely barrier to objectively sound advice and so went elsewhere.

9. Karl Jung's remark about intellectuals making the worst patients applies here. Human intelligence may serve many ends. Its capacity to generate rationalizations and to prolong arguments can be developed into very refined skills that allow one to put off assenting to troubling insights and so dodging the question of decision.

10. A memorable example of such questioning occurred at a conference when a speaker shocked an audience by claiming that the railway system of Nazi-occupied Europe was a good of order even though it delivered millions of persons to death camps. Note the further questions: a system may deliver services on time and so function properly, but is its function consistent with the best understanding of morally developed persons? Is its purpose consistent with the cultural ideals of the society? Do its results promote personal relationships of trust and respect without which social order either decays or survives through threats and fear?

11. The absence of informed consent in this experiment and concern for the possible harm to the naive test subjects in it prompted controversy and eventually the development of professional guidelines for future experiments in social psychology – guidelines that prohibit a repetition of Milgram's fascinating and alarming study of our liabilities to subordinate our feelings and better judgment to authority figures and to dismiss our resulting doubts with rationalizations.

12. Here is a possible class assignment far more significant than the usual fare: go through these rationalizations and dissect them as "bad reasons for bad behavior." Why bother? They may be the types of excuses you hear (are tempted to give?) years from now.

13. Note the rationalization this encouraged: "I'm not hurting anyone; it's someone else who pulls the lever." Does your understanding of social order as a web of interdependent agents and activities make this excuse less plausible?

14. This section is indebted to the analysis of the structure of the good by Lonergan in *Method in Theology*, 47-52.

15. You could consult the end of this section where the results of this mapping are presented in schematic form. The categories of the schema are not linked by the usual arrows of a "flow chart," but putting them in may be a helpful way of expanding your understanding of the complex relations among human capacities, operations and their products.

16. "Terminal values are the values that are chosen; true instances of the particular good, a true good of order, a true scale of preferences regarding values and satisfactions. Correlative to terminal values are the originating values that do the choosing: they are authentic persons achieving self-transcendence by their good choices. Since man can know and choose authenticity and self-transcendence, originating and terminal values can coincide." Lonergan, *op. cit*, 51.

17. Quoted in Eric Voegelin, "Eternal Being in Time," in *Anamnesis* (Columbia: University of Missouri Press, 1990), 140.

18. See the first endnote of Chapter Seven.

19. The "map" is adapted, with one minor change, from the schema found in Lonergan's *Method*, 48.

NOTES TO CHAPTER NINE

1. Talk of a "new perspective" and of a new way of doing ethics presupposes an emerging understanding of the complex performance that precedes and gives rise to articulated stances in moral controversies. It may not be helpful to refer to this alternate approach as a new type of pragmatism since this label is already subject to a variety of different usages. Still, there is a need for some label for this focus on performative conditions to moral decision-making. "Transcendental method" is one candidate, but it is both obscure and easily misread as referring to Kantian projects. "Self-attentive inquiry" will suffice *faute de mieux*.

2. The usual way of handling the issues is "conceptualist," i.e. one begins by pretending to clarify the terms "objectivity" and "liberty" in the expectation that, once the concepts are clear, one will be able to deduce answers to questions about specific cases. The usual way of doing ethics follows the same conceptualist strategy. First one constructs a "theory" that justifies a range of concepts or

normative principles; then one applies them to cases and argues for consistency between the theory and the individual applications. The earlier remarks on the diagnosis problem indicated one of the flaws in the conceptualist approach. Have you detected others? Does the following remark attributed to Julius Paulus offer a clue? "What is right is not derived from the rule, but the rule arises from our knowledge of what is right."

NOTES TO CHAPTER TEN

1. The analytical procedure outlined in these final chapters is an adaptation of the work of Eugene J. Meehan on methods in policy analysis. See his *The Thinking Game* (Chatham, New Jersey: Chatham House, 1988).

2. These comments are indebted to Heidegger's famous study of everyday ways of "being in the world" and of how we use common objects or "equipment" as objects "ready-to-hand." See *Being and Time.* Translated by John Macquarrie and Edward Robinson. (New York: Harper and Row, 1962), 96-99.

3. Be aware that, while all theories are generalizations, not all generalizations are theories. Classifications, correlations, or forecasts, and generalized priorities are among the other types of generalizations.

4. "Ideal" because accounts of decisions often leave implicit one or more of the key components, i.e. purpose, means, prediction, theory. In the "ideal case" the formulated choice would contain the explicitly identified purpose and means, a clear prediction linking the two, the theory supporting the prediction and mention of past cases when the theory worked as expected. In contrast, stated proposals often omit some of these components, e.g. "We need to get tough on drug dealers by imposing mandatory sentences on anyone convicted of trafficking in illegal drugs." Can you fill in the missing components?

5. Can you rephrase this talk of "evidence" in terms of "fulfilling conditions"? Recall the remarks in Chapter Eight on objectivity in judging.

6. Do you anticipate differences between an ideal frequency and a real frequency, i.e. between an expected rate of occurrence and an actual rate? Think, again, of the concrete example of car accidents along a stretch of highway. Why might accident rates vary from a well-established pattern or ideal frequency?

7. Such were the origins of a variety of programs in the United States, e.g. federally subsidized school lunches, Headstart, urban recycling, school vouchers, magnet schools.

8. You may be familiar with examples of so-called political horsetrading and pork barrel legislation. Actions and programs funded by tax dollars may be known to be ineffective; their underlying theories may be nonsensical, and yet they remain in place. You are already alert to the mistake of trying to make sense of nonsense. In these cases, do you have to look beyond their stated purposes for

an understanding of the aims of such programs and actions, e.g. keeping political constituencies employed and so happy? In your own experience have you operated with an unreliable theory while your real objective might have been unstated? Think of persons who pound on vending machines to extract products they have already paid for. Are they really confident this will work or is their purpose to vent frustration and to derive at least some satisfaction from the failed transaction?

NOTES TO CHAPTER ELEVEN

1. Recall how "ought" presupposes "can." You are obligated to do something only if it is possible for you to do it. So answering a question for decision presupposes some prior answer to a question for deliberation.
2. Notice that you may have had no problem thinking of this objection. Do risks to younger employees show up more readily on your "radar screen"? What of the preceding objection in terms of harm to stockholders? Is this a population you are less likely to consider? Just a reminder that bias need not show up only in regard to differences in race, gender, or nationality.
3. Why even try to form such an estimate? If an economy is a vast range of interrelated patterns of activities, estimating how a policy might affect those patterns is a way of showing consideration for others, even if nearly all of them are anonymous individuals. Again, an "adequate" horizon for moral decision-making requires development in intelligence and care.
4. Have you heard anyone claim that critics should provide their own better alternative before attacking any proposal? Should this be a requirement for criticism?
5. The usual fare begins with a version of ethical relativism or egoism, moves on to one or more versions of utilitarianism, reserves space for a deontological theory (usually Kant's), and ends with some account of virtue ethics. Recent textbooks have begun to include divine command theories. If you recall the problem of multiplicity, is this approach to the teaching of ethics a remedy or a symptom?
6. In this imaginary case, a choice will depend on your estimates of how well you can handle anger, how self-confident you are in standing before an appeals board, how likely the instructor is to retaliate, how best to word your appeal, etc. These are questions that underline the significant role of the "diagnosis problem" in making decisions.
7. Think of how many of Milgram's test subjects might have acted differently if someone had stated their unvoiced priority: "Prefer obeying authority over risking an ugly confrontation, even if obeying means you will kill an innocent and helpless individual."

8. The fact that theories of ethical egoism are usually the first entries in traditional ethics texts is a sign that the writers assume such positions are the easiest to cover and to criticize. Could the temporal priority of the good of satisfaction in human living be a reason for this?

9. Recall Kohlberg's early stages of moral reasoning described in Chapter Six.

10. Of course, much simpler cases may have occurred in high school. Did anyone ever argue that you should prove your loyalty to one group by betraying the trust of some other group?

11. Recall the use of equity courts mentioned in the preceding chapter. To what type of problem are they an intelligent solution?

12. Some of the details of this thought-experiment are borrowed from John Rawls and his invention called "the original position." See *A Theory of Justice* (Cambridge: Harvard University Press, 1971). Missing in this adaptation is the fiction of the veil of ignorance. Comments about the good of order and the legitimacy of preferential treatment of "insiders" over "outsiders" suggest that complete impartiality is not obligatory in every moral choice.

13. These steps in assessing options will reappear in the next chapter as part of the analytical procedure. Case studies and practice exercises there are intended to help you become more familiar with them.

14. Even if this is not part of your understanding of human history, are you at all curious about this long running drama of human history? For example, have you ever wondered what someone meant by human "progress"?

NOTES TO CHAPTER TWELVE

1. If you think in terms of the "good of order," is it plausible to include on the list all consumers of manufactured goods in a particular society? Consider how ongoing commercial transactions presuppose repeated acts of promising and trusting. If there is a breakdown in trust, how will such exchanges continue? What if the maxim "Buyer beware" becomes the common expectation of both buyers and sellers? Far short of that, firms that lose the trust of the buying public tend to go out of business unless they make extraordinary efforts to regain that trust. A first step is usually replacing the old managers. Do any cases come to mind?

2. One possible version: "Prefer avoiding irreparable harm to strangers over exposing one's family to some remediable harm." What is the alternative? "One's family comes first in all things, and let others take care of themselves"?

3. Recall the comments in Chapter Six on political realism. Did the case study there make you suspicious of claims that some "facts" about human behavior are beyond improvement?

4. You might refer to the previous chapter and its brief presentation on non-comparative principles, e.g. "Never tell a lie."
5. Are you familiar with the traditional label of the *ad populum* fallacy? Just because people believe something is true or good, does that make it so?
6. Again, there is a traditional name for this complaint: the *tu quoque* fallacy. If physicians advise patients to give up smoking but continue to smoke themselves, is their advice no longer sound? Hypocrisy or inconsistency between knowing and doing could be charged against the physicians, but their advice should be weighed on its own merits. Confusing the question of who is making a proposal with the question of the merits of that proposal shows up under another traditional heading: the "genetic fallacy."

NOTE TO THE EPILOGUE

1. Bernard Lonergan. "*Existenz* and *Aggiornamento*," in *Collection*, 242.